Human Rights and Peace

Human Rights in International Perspective
Volume 1

SERIES EDITOR

David P. Forsythe
University of Nebraska–Lincoln

ADVISORY EDITORIAL BOARD

Peter Baehr
University of Utrecht

Kevin Boyle
University of Essex

Jack Donnelly
University of Denver

Virginia Leary
State University of New York–Buffalo

Ivan Savicky
European Centre for Human Rights Education

Laurie Wiseberg
University of Ottawa

Human Rights and Peace

International and National Dimensions

David P. Forsythe

University of Nebraska Press • Lincoln and London

An earlier version of the argument presented in
chapter 2 appeared in the *Journal of Peace Research*
29, no. 4 (November 1992). © *Journal of Peace
Research*, 1992.

Library of Congress Cataloging-in-Publication Data

Forsythe, David P., 1941–
Human rights and peace: international and
national dimensions /
David P. Forsythe.
p.   cm.—(Human rights in international
perspective)
Includes bibliographical references and index.
ISBN 0-8032-1989-X (cl).—ISBN 0-8032-6880-7 (pa)
1. Human rights. 2. Peace. I. Title. II. Series.
K3240.4.F677   1993
341.4'81—dc20
93-9848
CIP

Contents

Preface

Human rights and peace compose an interesting but complex relationship that has been much talked about but not so often carefully studied. This book seeks to at least make a start toward a more careful study.

One part of this relationship has finally attracted much serious work from social scientists. My first chapter focuses on the now proven pattern that major and long-standing democracies, which implement civil and political human rights to a great extent, do not engage in overt international war with each other. In reviewing this pattern, I add some attention to social and economic human rights, suggesting that their acceptance and practice probably reinforces international peace among democracies.

Following the pioneering reflections of John Mueller, I also suggest that developmentalism—namely, a certain standard of material welfare—probably reinforces international peace as well. This is an important idea, difficult to prove to be sure. It suggests that the authoritarian Soviet Union, having experienced major wars and having achieved a "developed" status, was as anxious to avoid major war as the democratic West in the post-1945 period, despite its lack of real commitment to most internationally recognized human rights.

Thus three factors may be reducing the probability of overt international war among the major states: attention to civil and political rights, attention to economic and social rights, and modern (post-1945) development.

Perhaps the most intriguing subject matter in the following pages concerns the comparison between international peace among especially elected governments in developed states and the U.S. covert overthrow of a series of elected "developing" governments during the cold war. While there was, after 1945 (as before), international peace among developed elected governments, there was a covert "war" carried out by the United States against some developing elected governments. Contemporary American students may be unaware of the genuine elections, whether parliamentary or popular, that led to the exercise of power by Mossadeq in Iran, Arbenz in Guatemala, and Allende in Chile, among others. These three, and other genuinely elected leaders, were overthrown at the insistence of the United States, through actual or suggested force.

In explaining why there was international peace among major democratic states but a covert "war" between the democratic United States and certain elected governments, I use three types of analyses. I note the U.S. fear of expanded Soviet influence from the late 1940s through the 1980s. Borrowing from Michael Hunt, I next use the idea of an American informal ideology that led to a persistent opposition to nonwhite and revolutionary regimes, as a component of an American self-image of greatness. And then, relying on Michael Doyle and the neo-Kantian literature about general principles of democratic foreign policy, I note that only some democratic states qualify for membership in the community of peaceful states. Only "mature" democracies qualify, not "barely participatory" states.

All three types of analyses help to explain why the United States considers overt war with, say, France, unthinkable, despite numerous differences and political conflicts, but has actually carried out the threat or use of force against some developing elected governments. A central paradox remains. The broad practice of civil and political rights inoculates against overt international war among those practitioners. But practicing political rights through genuine elections did not always inoculate against covert "war," especially when U.S. foreign policy during the cold war was at issue. Thus in the first part of this book we see that there is a relationship between human rights and international peace, but the exact nexus is more complex than often presented.

In the second part of this book I focus on human rights and national peace. The causes of domestic "war," particularly revolution and civil war, have been much discussed, albeit without the emergence of a widely accepted theory. Focusing on the central idea of political legitimacy, or perceived correctness of rule, I argue that the notion and language of human rights can add to our understanding of this phenomenon. Without trying to develop a full theory or model, I present a typology of sources of governmental legitimacy, some international and some national. Endorsement and practice of human rights can in some situations contribute to national legitimacy—and peace, whether we are speaking of national or international politics.

Against the background of this typology, I then use the case studies of major domestic unrest in Sri Lanka, Liberia, and Romania to discuss whether human rights violations contributed to the lack of national peace in significant ways. The choice of cases proved fortuitous, because in both Sri Lanka and Liberia the domestic unrest continued (unfortunately) through the time of production of this book. Further major unrest cannot be ruled out in Romania.

My basic conclusion about human rights and national peace is that a focus on rights does indeed aid our understanding of the disintegration of, and projected restoration of, national peace, but in different ways in different nations. Without suggesting that other approaches lack insights of their own, I show that in Sri Lanka, rights pertaining to minorities, language, education, and work affected the Tamil armed struggle against the Sinhalese majority. In Liberia I show that rights pertaining to participation and a range of civil rights were important in the absence of legitimacy for several actual or would-be governments. In Romania I show that the inconclusiveness of the 1989 revolution stemmed in part from the lack of clear commitment to internationally recognized rights on the part of those who made the revolution.

Equally important, in all three cases I show that the legitimacy of national governing arrangements is affected by much more than the presence or absence of a human rights tradition. Governmental performance, positively in doing good things for its citizens or negatively through effective repression, can produce at least public deference if not a sense of legitimacy. Either may contribute to peace, although sometimes it is a peace without much social justice. Likewise in international politics, "correct" political alignment may produce foreign support and thus effective grants of legitimacy in some eyes, even though there may be gross violations of human rights. Above all I show that an understanding of perceptions about human rights and legitimacy needs to be combined with an understanding of power.

Human rights may be important to national peace; but they are only one element in a complex equation, and they may be superseded in significance by other sources of governmental legitimacy. We still lack, and perhaps always will, a theory that explains the importance of rights practice for national peace across different nations. But we can be sensitive to issues of human rights that, when combined with the ability to exercise power, can sometimes affect the legitimacy and stability of governing arrangements.

This study was made possible primarily because of a research grant from the United States Institute of Peace, and I am grateful to the Institute for its interest in the subject matter. The grant was administered by the University of Nebraska–Lincoln (UNL), whose Political Science Department made the necessary adjustments in my teaching schedule to allow me to pursue my research interests.

An early version of some of my thinking was presented at the annual meeting of the International Studies Association held in Vancouver during the spring of 1991, and I am indebted to those who provided commentary through that channel. I should like to thank especially the following for their extended and written comments: Richard Claude, of the University of Maryland; Jack Donnelly, now of the University of Denver; Rhoda Howard, of McMaster University; Dane Kennedy, of UNL; Robert Oberst, of Nebraska Wesleyan University; David Rapkin, of UNL; and Raphael Zariski, of UNL.

My research assistants—Helen Lanham, Kelly Pease, and David Taylor, graduate students at UNL—were very helpful. Ms. Lanham was especially helpful concerning the chapter on Romania.

I am particularly grateful to Peter R. Baehr, of Leiden University in the Netherlands, and Claude E. Welch, Jr., of SUNY–Buffalo, who read and commented on the entire manuscript.

Jan Edwards worked tirelessly on the production of the final manuscript.

Faculty and student commentators alike will be relieved to know I am following conventional procedure by accepting responsibility for what follows.

Introduction:
An Inquiry into Human Rights and Peace

Two of the most important questions in political inquiry concern the causes of what we can initially if simply call international war and internal war. These perennial questions, whose very durability suggests elusive answers, have been compounded by new perspectives. Since 1945, and especially since about 1970, we have witnessed not only an explosion in rhetoric about universal human rights but also repeated assertions that human rights are linked to peace—internationally and internally. This study inquires into that asserted linkage.

The 1948 Universal Declaration of Human Rights states in the first paragraph of its preamble, "Recognition of the inherent dignity and of the equal and inalienable rights of all members of the human family is the foundation of . . . peace in the world." So universal human rights are seen as the foundation for international peace. The declaration then goes on to say, in the third preambular paragraph, "It is essential, if man is not to be compelled to have recourse, as a last resort, to rebellion against tyranny and oppression, that human rights should be protected by the rule of law." So universal human rights are also seen as the basis of domestic peace.[1]

Two general questions logically stem from these assertions, although they lead to several specific inquiries along the way. First, what is the relationship between a state's human rights performance at home and international violence, both overt and covert? For democratic states, namely those that implement civil and political rights to relatively great extent, does this domestic political condition imply that they will manifest peaceful foreign policies? Does democracy at home imply that there will be fewer wars abroad, or at least fewer wars with other democracies? And does democracy at home imply that covert violence abroad will be reduced in general, or at least reduced toward other democracies?

There is also the view that states of advanced economic status, most of which recognize socioeconomic rights at home, have an added reason to avoid international war. For the advanced industrialized states, war among them may be perceived as too costly in material terms. In its usual form, this is not an argument about human rights per se but is rather an argument about states' economic status and their proclivity to avoid major war among themselves (but probably not against perceived weaker adversaries). Yet we should at least note that these advanced, or "developed," states recognize socioeconomic as well as civil-political rights, with the leading exception of the United States. The subject is complicated still further by the fact that most of the industrialized advanced states are also democracies. What, then, supposedly produces international peace: implementation of civil-political rights at home, implementation of socioeconomic rights, or advanced economic status? In any event, our first topic of concern is the relationship between internationally recognized human rights within a state and that state's use of violence in overt and covert foreign policy.

Second, what is the relationship between human rights violations and domestic violence? Ever since there have been governments, there have been revolutions against them. Are democracies less prone to revolutions than other forms of government? Are democracies that also respect social and economic rights less prone to revolution? In the twentieth century, increasingly an era of internationally recognized—or universal—human rights, do authoritarian governments that deny various types of human rights run an increased risk of revolution? Do only certain types of authoritarian governments, such as "developing" ones, manifest a high risk of internal war, whereas other types, such as advanced police states like China, show resilience despite their systematic and gross violations of human rights? Or is national political revolution mostly affected by factors not associated with human rights? Despite a state's commitment to various types of human rights, does sheer inefficiency in problem solving produce revolution? In sum, what is the place of human rights conditions (or performance) in what can be called domestic peace?

One of the principal "side questions" links the two primary concerns. Is there a pattern of foreign intervention in the context of domestic revolution perhaps brought about by human rights violations? Are domestic peace and international peace linked in this way? That is, to what extent do we find that violations of human rights within states contribute to domestic political revolution, which then leads in some way to international war? How do we first explain the dynamics of a situation like the northern Persian Gulf in 1979–80, in which the political revolution in Iran seemed to lead to Iraq's armed attack on Iran? And how prevalent in international relations is this type of sequence? In other words, can human rights violations trigger both domestic *and* international violence? If so, how often does this transpire?

The separate subjects of human rights and peace do not constitute virgin territory, which is both a blessing and a curse. There certainly have been many studies of international as well as internal war. Equally numerous are studies of political revolution, by whatever name—rebellion, revolt, insurrection, instability, etc. I attempt to draw on many of these studies. But there have not been so many inquiries into the linkage between human rights and wars—whether international or domestic. (By *domestic war*, I refer to both internal armed conflict and violent political revolution involving mass mobilization.)

And there have been precious few studies using the international conception of human rights as a prominent variable. As specialists on these matters know, the international bill of rights contains not only civil and political rights but also economic, social, and cultural rights. Thus the international definition of human rights is quite broad, and the analyst must be careful to specify which right or type of right is being linked to violence.

It should be mentioned at the outset that the omission in the following pages of any attention to the asserted third generation of solidarity rights is intentional. I concentrate primarily on the first generation of civil and political rights and secondarily on the second generation of social, economic, and cultural rights. Thus I am not inclined to give attention to an asserted human right to peace as one of the third-generation solidarity rights (the other claimed rights in this category are the rights to development, common heritage, and healthy environment).

It is true that Article 28 of the 1948 Universal Declaration of Human Rights proclaims, "Everyone is entitled to a social and international order in which the rights and freedoms set forth in this Declaration can be fully realized." And it is equally a fact that in 1984 the United Nations General Assembly adopted a resolution articulating a right to peace. This "Right of Peoples to Peace" proclaimed "that the peoples of our planet have a sacred right to peace," declared "that the preservation of the right of peoples to peace and the promotion of its implementation constitute a fundamental obligation of each State," and emphasized "that the policies of States be directed towards . . . the renunciation of the use of force in international relations and the settlement of international disputes by peaceful means." (A/RES/39/11, 12 November, 1984).

I discount this diplomatic rhetoric, for two basic reasons. The first, and minor, reason is that these claimed rights of the third generation have never been formalized into legal principles, much less specific legal rules. They remain fully in the realm of political rhetoric and have never reached the stage of constituting legal obligations for states. We have treaties on the other two generations of rights but not on the third. Thus third-generation rights are not on a par with the other two, having never been legally endorsed by the international community.

This is not a compelling reason. The Helsinki Accord of 1975 is also not treaty law, but it does merit attention. This is so because it has independent meaning, we can know specific obligations under the document, and it has generated considerable influence in the behavior of states, private organizations, and individuals.

Thus the second, and more important, reason for my opposition to a right to peace, as well as to its companions such as a right to development or to safe environment, is that these claimed rights, either as originally formulated or as subsequently addressed, have no independent and specific meaning. Consequently, they have failed to generate much, if any, influence in world politics—and will probably remain without much influence in the future.

Consider, at least briefly, the right to peace. Those who address the subject immediately find themselves in the realm of the traditional international law of security having to do with the prohibition of force except in self-defense.[2] In essence, the meaning of the right to peace is that we should pay more attention to international security law, particularly *jus ad bellum* concerning the rules for recourse to force. *Jus ad bellum* already contains concepts like anticipatory self-defense, intervention, armed attack, individual and collective self-defense, and expanded self-defense encompassing reprisals. Focusing on the right to peace therefore leads to a rehash of another well-established body of international law. There is nothing new and independent in the right to peace not already covered in the rules pertaining to security law.

Likewise, for purposes of illustration, a scholarly definition of the right to a safe environment is a composite of other rights already identified and formalized, mostly in the category of first-generation rights. Thus most of the specifics in the right to a safe environment are in reality civil and political rights already recognized in the first generation.[3]

Again for purposes of comparison, the proclaimed right to development turns out to be, even after years of scholarly and diplomatic debate, the sum total of all other internationally recognized human rights. According to a United Nations publication in 1991, which reflects an international conference of governmental and nongovernmental participants, "The right to development is the right of individuals, groups, and peoples to participate in, contribute to, and enjoy continuous economic, social, cultural and political development, in which all human rights and fundamental freedoms can be fully realized."[4] This is mumbo jumbo par excellence. The key word *development* remains amorphous. Moreover, the new right to development means the sum total of all other rights.

There is no independent meaning to the right to development, or to safe environment, or to peace. At best, they are synthetic or composite rights, drawn from other recognized rights and used to emphasize or educate or socialize. As such, there is nothing wrong with them as political devices. They could be useful in a political sense to draw special attention to major problems. But for these rights to be useful in this way, we need to know what we are obligated to do under them. Alas, we do not and probably cannot.

Consider the right to peace. Are we obligated to disarm? The experience of Belgium in 1914 would seem to indicate otherwise, since Belgium did not participate in the arms races of its time yet was victimized by war. Indeed, the failure of the Western democracies to push an armaments program in the 1930s in order to deter aggression by the Fascists is said to be one of the background or general causes of World War II. Are we then obligated to arm as a deterrent to war? The experience of Germany in 1914 would seem to indicate otherwise, since German armament, specifically the contesting of British naval power, was one of the general or background causes of World War I. Would the world be safer if all states possessed nuclear arms, since no nuclear weapon has been fired in anger since 1945 and certainly none ever between two states capable of mutually assured destruction? Why, then, is it the policy of numerous states not to seek nuclear weapons? If we are sometimes to arm and sometimes not to arm, or arm in different ways at different times, in pursuit of peace, what is our specific duty under the right to peace? We are enjoined to renounce threat of force, but did not the prospect of massive destruction help produce the "long peace" among the great powers from 1945 on?

In summary, not only do the claimed rights of the third generation have no independent meaning, but we have no idea of our specific duties under those rights. How are we supposed to bring about international peace, aside from following at least some of the rules of international security law?

Precisely because third-generation rights provide no independent and specific meanings and obligations, they have had virtually no influence in world politics. If they are not intellectually compelling, they stand little chance of becoming politically compelling. Given repeated—and unsuccessful—efforts to breathe specific content into, in particular, the right to peace and development, I remain unconvinced that these solidarity rights can provide important influences in the future.

I am sympathetic to internationally recognized human rights in principle, but they must have independent meaning and indicate specific behavior that is permissible and impermissible. The civil and political rights of the first generation meet this twofold test on balance—and rights and duties are being made more specific with each passing year.[5] In relative historical terms, these first-generation rights are more important than in the past. The socioeconomic rights of the second generation are not as specific as the first, but again an international process is under way that is making more specific state obligation under the treaty law.[6] There is some prospect that these second-generation rights may have influence in the future. But the third generation of rights remains uncodified and amorphous, or perhaps they are uncodified because they remain amorphous. There is no evidence that convinces me these solidarity rights will ever be either independent or specified. Debates to date convince me of the impossibility of giving them specific meaning. They are likely to remain unimportant in international relations.

I do not pursue what is posited by some scholars, namely that the concept of "peace" equates with psychic satisfaction or social justice. In this study I consider peace in the traditional if narrow sense of absence of violence. Thus I do not find terribly useful that school of thought that seems to hold that violations of human rights *ipso facto* mean denial of peace because those violations produce some type of psychic anguish. There is a commonsense meaning to the phrase "mental peace" or "the mind at peace." But this phraseology should not be allowed to confuse inquiries into the causes of direct violence.

Also, in this work I do not emphasize structural or indirect violence.[7] Thus I do not equate peace with social justice, and I do not equate violence with threat of state coercion in behalf of injustice. It is a valid point to note that states supposedly monopolize legitimate coercion and that the law of the territorial state is backed by ample threat and sometimes actual use of force. I consider it important to analyze whether or not state law denies social justice, relying on state coercion to enforce that law. In discussing human rights and domestic war, I delve into the question of repression and brutality, as well as the central idea of legitimacy of rule.

But there is a risk here of confusing the traditional notion of peace, meaning absence of direct violence, with ideas like social justice and law enforcement. It is more confusing than helpful to lump all these ideas under the one concept of peace. I do not find it analytically helpful to refer to forceful law enforcement as violating the peace by creating structural or indirect violence. Thus I prefer the traditional terminology that equates peace with the absence of direct violence. An exploitative state can be at peace even though it enforces an unjust legal order.

To set the stage, it is advisable to review briefly at the outset some of the traditional views about human rights and peace. At the international level some policymakers as well as scholars have argued that implementation of human rights is necessary for international peace. From Immanuel Kant through Woodrow Wilson to Ronald Reagan, the argument has been articulated that a world of democracies would be a peaceful world, since democracies are inherently peace-loving. The United Nations Charter asserted, in Article 55, that human rights are "necessary" for "peaceful and friendly relations among nations." This proposition may sound nice to the democrat's ear, but there is more to this matter than first meets the eye.

For one thing, international attention to a state's human rights situation may create considerable conflict—including violent conflict. If official explanations can be taken at face value, which we do here only for purposes of discussion, the democratic United States invaded both Grenada and Panama in the 1980s for reasons of human rights, at least in part. Washington also forcefully intervened in Nicaraguan affairs during the 1980s. If the public statements of U.S. officials can be believed, one of the main U.S. reasons for organizing and supporting the contras was to remove a government in Managua violative of human rights. Indeed certain Americans, some of whom were governmental officials, made an expansive interpretation of the United Nations Charter, arguing that state unilateral use of armed force supposedly to protect human rights was permissible under contemporary international law.[8] Thus, at least in theory, a concern to correct human rights violations may lead to international violence.

Indeed, at least in legal theory, the United Nations Charter would seem to endorse violence to correct human rights violations—under some conditions. The Charter has been interpreted to mean that given a threat to or breach of the peace, not just an act of aggression involving presumably imminent or actual armed attack, the Security Council can authorize legally binding enforcement action. On two occasions, in Rhodesia starting in the mid-1960s and in South Africa starting in 1977, the Council authorized binding economic sanctions (but not violent action) in response to, at least partially, human rights violations in those polities. More to the point, in 1991 the Council declared that Iraq's repression of its population, especially the Kurds, constituted a threat to the peace. Citing this resolution, a number of states forcefully entered Iraqi territory, that is, without that state's consent, to create a humanitarian enclave for the Iraqi Kurds.[9] Later in 1992, several states used force in the south of Iraq purportedly to defend the human rights of Shi'ite Iraqis, claiming implied authorization from this same Security Council resolution (S/RES/688).

The cases of Rhodesia, South Africa, and Iraq provide the background for the Security Council decision, in the summer of 1992, authorizing "all necessary means," a euphemism for force, to ensure the delivery of humanitarian relief in Bosnia. (There is the precedent of the Council's authorizing the British navy to intercept oil shipments off Portuguese Mozambique destined for Rhodesia.) Thus, rather than ensuring international peace, a concern for human rights may encourage violence, individually or collectively, at least in the short or intermediate run. It is not an unreasonable proposition to suggest that given gross violations of human rights within a state, forcible termination may be preferable to continuation of those violations. This was clearly U.S. rhetoric regarding Iraqi nationals in 1991 and 1992.

Second, democracies may commit aggression, popular mythology to the contrary notwithstanding. The democratic United States—

whatever the legal judgment about its use of force in Grenada, Panama, and Nicaragua—was certainly responsible for the Spanish-American War despite the pacific efforts of imperial Spain. And three democracies (France, Israel, and the United Kingdom) initiated armed attack against the one-party state of Egypt in 1956, an action regarded by most of the international community as aggression. Even if we set aside very complex issues, such as naming the aggressor in the war between Argentina and the United Kingdom over the islands in the South Atlantic (the Falklands or the Malvinas), it would seem that implementing civil and political rights at home can give rise to, or fail to contain, a bellicose nationalism.

The other side of this coin merits noting as well. Any number of states have grossly violated human rights, however defined, at home; yet they have maintained a relatively peaceful foreign policy. Fascist Spain, for example, remained neutral during World War II and attacked no one thereafter. Indeed, when Poland, speaking for the Soviet coalition, sought United Nations sanctions against Fascist Spain in the 1950s, it had to admit that Spain had carried out no aggression against another state. Poland argued that violations of human rights constituted a threat to the peace and merited international action. Although Poland's logic did not prevail at the United Nations in the 1950s, as shown above that same logic did prevail in later cases: Rhodesia, South Africa, and Iraq. (The Council resolution concerning Bosnia in 1992 was somewhat different, in that it did not cite violations of human rights as the trigger for authorizing possible force to secure relief.)

Communist Romania and Albania, for a considerable time two of the more repressive and oppressive of modern European states, never carried out armed attack or formal aggression against any of their neighbors, much less against any state farther away. During the first several decades after independence, most states in sub-Sahara Africa were authoritarian. Yet the number of international armed conflicts among black governments was relatively small. In Latin America over almost a century, despite the prevalence of authoritarian governments until the late 1980s, only two international armed conflicts were fought among neo-Iberian governments.

These opening remarks should indicate that the relationship between civil and political rights, on the one hand, and international violence, on the other hand, is not as simple as Immanuel Kant may have thought. Peace, understood as the absence of international armed conflict, may be broken by democracies. Peace may also be maintained among a considerable number of authoritarian states for a considerable length of time. A concern for human rights may require the breaking of the peace to correct human rights violations.

Increasingly, scholarship is making it clear that although there is a grain of truth in the hoary attitude that implementing civil and political rights is positively linked to peace, the point can be overstated. The present study will review the literature on this first subject of human rights and overt international war, making refinements along the way. Then, in a subsequent chapter, there will be a rather striking comparison with the subject of human rights and covert international "war," showing that even though democracies do not overtly war on each other, they may covertly do so in certain situations. It would seem that very few scholars have thought to inquire into whether democracies covertly overthrow other democracies through violent or quasi-violent policies. On the surface, this may seem an absurd proposition to investigate, just as some would question the need to study the possibility of war between or among democracies. There have been, in fact, several studies of war among democracies or, more precisely, of why there is a lack of such wars most of the time. There have not been studies focusing on the central question of democratic overthrow of other democracies or, closely related, the question of democratic covert intervention, with force, against foreign democratic policies.

This latter type of inquiry can produce some surprising and thought-provoking results. After all, the U.S. overthrow of the Iranian government of Prime Minister Mossadeq in 1953, with British cooperation, occurred in a polity that was at least partially democratic. The same characterization of partial democracy fit equally well in President Arbenz's Guatemala in 1954, also overthrown by the democratic United States, with democratic Britain expressing more concern than support this time around. Thus we need to pay closer attention to the intriguing question of covert war by democracies against democracies—or perhaps against quasi-democracies.

If we look at national rather than international affairs, a line of thought suggests that implementing human rights contributes to domestic peace and stability. It has often been remarked that the stability of the United States has stemmed from the implementation of the Bill of Rights, concerned with individual freedom, as well as from the implementation of tax and welfare policies presumably concerned with "fairness," or if one prefers, with socioeconomic justice (but not, in the United States, socioeconomic rights). More generally, the governments in Western Europe, which not only acknowledged but also actively implemented both civil-political and socioeconomic rights, seemed mostly immune to domestic revolution or internal war. (One cannot generalize from the historically unique situations in Northern Ireland and Basque Spain.) Once again, however, matters turn out to be more complex than a simple glance would indicate.

Some nations manifest relatively long periods of stability despite political repression and/or socioeconomic injustice. Saudi Arabia, for example, has always been an authoritarian state with severe restrictions on most civil and political rights. It has never known either democratic government or equal civil rights regarding gender or religion. Furthermore, it does not officially recognize socioeconomic *rights*, and its distribution of socioeconomic *benefits* is highly skewed. Yet its modern domestic history has been mostly peaceful, with only minor violent protest—some of which was of foreign and not domestic origin. (Some Iranian pilgrims to Mecca were involved in violent clashes in the 1980s.)

To take another example from contemporary times, one can note that Stalinist Czechoslovakia was clearly a repressive political system from 1948 to 1989. Yet it was only in 1989 that the Czechs and Slovaks roused themselves to get rid of their Communist oppressors. Admittedly, the Prague spring of 1968 was a brief departure from this authoritarian pattern, but when Soviet tanks arrived, the Czechs and Slovaks did not resist, just as they had not resisted when the Nazis took control in 1938. From 1969, a consumer-oriented "social contract" was frequently cited to partially explain peace in Czechoslovakia. The regime provided readily available consumer goods and an easy life, which was supposedly sufficient to ensure the status quo. The denial of civil and political rights and the conditioning of socioeconomic rights on political conformity did not lead to widely supported challenges to this system for several decades (the dissident movement Charter 77 was not widely supported, at least not overtly, until 1989). At a minimum, the case of Czechoslovakia raises the question of what triggers a domestic revolution (in this case mostly nonviolent, since there was no internal war) when denial of human rights has been ongoing for a considerable time. It is clear that in both domestic peace and domestic revolution or war, something more complex than denial of human rights is at work.

At both the international and the national levels, even a few (albeit carefully chosen) examples make it clear that the relationship between human rights and peace is complex. The nexus between human rights on the one hand and international and domestic peace on the other invites further inquiry.

PART ONE

1

Human Rights and Overt International War

The study of international relations has centered on war, its control and elimination. It is widely accepted that in international relations, an anarchical society lacks a formal central government with a monopoly on force but manifests other institutions (meaning patterns of behavior) that at least sometimes manage war to some extent. Two major points of view have arisen concerning the nature and management of war in this anarchical environment.

"Realism" focuses on competitive states and their calculations of power, regarding war not only as a problem but also as a traditional means of instituting some order in international relations. Those states that win the major wars "govern" international relations or a sizable part thereof.[1] "Liberalism" emphasizes international cooperation through shared moral values, legal rights, and formal organizations, regarding war basically as a problem that can be managed by diplomacy and the rules of the game. Liberals would substitute diplomatic and legal peaceful change for the systemic or hegemonic war that leads to a dominant "governing" coalition.[2]

There are many aspects of both realism and liberalism that I will not pursue in this chapter. I primarily want to compare realist and liberal views on human rights and war. I argue that each point of view both comprehends and ignores aspects of reality. Specifically, realists should pay more attention to human rights; liberals should recognize the importance of power. I will then argue that other factors beyond those emphasized by realism and liberalism merit attention when analyzing international war. Specifically, the notion of "development," when added to the subject of power and democratic states (which practice civil and political rights), stimulates our thinking about war.

REALISM

I do not wish to write an extended critique of realism, comparing its subdivisions. This school of thought is usually associated with such names as Hans Morgenthau, Robert Gilpin, and Kenneth Waltz in academic circles and with the likes of George Kennan and Henry Kissinger in both academic and diplomatic circles. It is well known that Morgenthau's realism stemmed from a view of the individual (fundamentally evil and lusting for power), whereas Waltz's realism stemmed from a view of the international political system (fundamentally anarchical and thus requiring power calculations without regard to "the nature of man").[3]

All realists share a primary and central concern with power, and all regard morality, law, and organization as distinctly minor factors in a rational foreign policy that is properly adjusted to the conflictual realities of world politics. Realists, whether focusing on the individual, as does Morgenthau, or on the overall international system, as does Waltz, do not put much emphasis on the state—namely, whether it is democratic or authoritarian. A democratic state, by definition, is one in which there is relatively great attention to the practice of civil and political rights.

My first point in this chapter is to show the extent to which realists mostly omit human rights considerations from their analysis of war. This is part of their downplaying of cultural, moral, legal, and organizational factors in general. I will eventually show that this is a profound error. The primary foil for my analytical thrusting is Geoffrey Blainey, a realist whose major book has won wide acclaim and has been assigned in many classrooms. Blainey is thus spreading a major error of analysis. Some other contemporary realists have partially, but not entirely, corrected his basic mistake.

Geoffrey Blainey's *The Causes of War* is now in its third edition. He and his work are representative of modern realists. His survey of international wars since 1700 leads to the central judgment that "a clear preponderance of power tended to promote peace."[4] To Blainey, war is certainly not a phenomenon stemming from the authoritarian nature of government. Rather, he states, "War is a dispute about the measurement of power."[5]

That Blainey's thesis about the causes of international war concerns perceived power relationships can be seen in his own summation of his book:

> One may suggest that nations, in assessing their relative strength, were influenced by seven main factors: military strength and the ability to apply that strength efficiently in the chosen zone of war; predictions of how outside nations would behave in the event of war; perceptions of internal unity or discord of the enemy; memory or forgetfulness of the realities and sufferings of war; perceptions of prosperity and of ability to sustain, economically, the kind of war envisaged; nationalism and ideology; and the personality and mental qualities of the leaders who weighed the evidence and decided for peace or war.[6]

Blainey's book is mostly about perception of power. He mentions "nationalism and ideology," but he neither defines those concepts nor gives them much attention. They do not figure prominently in his analysis. Arguably, democracy and human rights could be considered ideological subjects. Blainey pays them no attention. "Human rights" is not in his index, and "democracy" is mentioned on one page, in reference only to Anglo-Saxons.

His core view is that states that have a self-defined preponderance of power and that are dissatisfied with the status quo tend to be the first to carry out armed attack, since their anticipated costs are relatively low. States viewed by others as powerful will not be attacked, since the costs to the attackers will be high. War is mostly a matter of rational calculation of power, although subjective factors intervene to complicate the calculus of power relationships. War tends to occur when power relationships are either unclear or mistaken.

In this same tradition of rational power calculation, one could place Melvin Small and J. David Singer, who argue, "The decision to initiate hostilities is related, in [large] part, to the expectation of victory."[7] Likewise Seyom Brown stresses attempts at calculations of power rather than emotive, ideological, or cultural factors. "The final decision to use military force is typically surrounded by an elaborate process of deliberations among high officials, involving assessments of the advantages or disadvantages of alternative courses of action."[8] John Stoessinger, who uses a framework of analysis entailing four concepts (self-image, and image of the adversary's character, intention, and power), finally concludes that the fourth factor of power relationships is the key to explaining whether or not states engage in international war.[9] Others too, like Jack Levy, stress the costs and benefits involved in power calculations. For Levy, what is important is the correlation between the high costs of war and its declining frequency among industrialized nations.[10] In most of these and other analyses making up the realist school of thought about the cause of international war, there is not extensive treatment of factors such as the nature of government (democratic or authoritarian). This latter distinction, of course, hinges on civil and political rights. (During the cold war between the United States and the Soviet Union, especially toward the latter phase of that "long peace," it became fashionable in the United States to emphasize the concept of totalitarianism as a key idea in explaining foreign policy. Totalitarianism is but a type, usually in practice, of authoritarianism, and it probably makes no special contribution to explaining war.)

One should note, however, that several realist analyses of the cause of international war, while concentrating on perceptions of power, nevertheless make some room for "national and ideological" factors. Small, for example, cites several wars in which a state decided to fight when the prospect of victory was either remote or nonexistent.[11] Spain in 1898, Finland in 1939, and Holland in 1940 could have peacefully yielded to the demands of clearly more powerful adversaries, but some conception of national honor compelled them to undertake armed resistance. On the other hand, both Denmark and Czechoslovakia during World War II chose largely peaceful submission rather than large-scale violence, even if national honor and a way of life were sacrificed.

Thus some realist authors modify the tradition that emphasizes power calculation in order to mention, in particular, national honor. It takes two states to have international war, and although it is not so clear that a state will be the first in armed attack because of national honor, an invaded state may choose defeat in war rather than peaceful submission in the name of national honor. This awareness of the role of culture, or political morality, or nationalism as a type of ideology, in contributing secondarily to some international wars has little to do with democracy and human rights. It also apparently has little to do with aggression in the sense of the first armed attack.[12]

Every generalization has its exception, and it is possible to find a handful of examples in which a putatively weaker state was the first in armed attack—for example, Japan in 1904 and Japan in 1941. Thus there may be a few historical aberrations in the sense that superior putative power by a status quo state did not prove a deterrence to first attack.[13] Here one must be careful to distinguish between the attacking state's perception of weakness, yet a decision to attack anyway, and the attacking state's misperception of strength, which turns out to be weakness in the test of battle.

Realism and its heavy emphasis on power became the dominant prism for viewing international relations in the industrialized democracies from roughly the 1940s until today. In reaction to the rise of Fascist and Communist power, realism emphasized the importance of countervailing power. A survey published in 1991 of some of the leading international relations textbooks used in North America showed the continuing intellectual hegemony of realism.[14] Human rights, political morality, and international law and organizations were given scant treatment. In some of these texts, human rights were barely mentioned. The subject of human rights was not examined and then said to be of little importance; authors simply assumed that the subject had no relation to power and war. Brief chapters on international law almost always started with a question that indicated profound ignorance: "Is international law really law?" As I will show in the next section, realism's disdain for liberalism led to major gaps in understanding.

LIBERALISM

As mentioned briefly in the preceding chapter, the United Nations Charter, in its linkage of human rights and international peace, reflects a central tenet of liberalism. From at least the time of Immanuel Kant through Woodrow Wilson to Ronald Reagan, democracy (that is, government based on civil and political rights) has been linked to peaceful foreign policy. (Figures like Ronald Reagan, although called conservative, are classically liberal in two respects: they articulate a commitment in principle to civil and political rights, and they manifest a general belief in the value of private markets.) Wilson popularized the Kantian notion that democratic foreign policy should strive to make the world safe for democracy by establishing democracies throughout the world. Democracies, being inherently peace-loving, do not cause war; authoritarians do. Thus if one implemented the civil and political rights necessary for democracy, one would also achieve international peace. In the words of Ronald Reagan: "We've learned from history that the cause of peace and human freedom is indivisible. Respect for human rights is essential to true peace on earth. Governments that must answer to their peoples do not launch wars of aggression."[15]

Although, as noted above, realists have mostly ignored the impact of the nature of the state (democratic or authoritarian) on international war, there is now a growing awareness of a clear pattern: democracies—namely those polities that respect civil and political rights to a relatively high degree—do not war on other democracies.[16] Over a very long period of time, one cannot find many, or perhaps any, clear-cut cases of democratic armed attack against another democracy. The evidence is becoming so overwhelming on this point that Nils Petter Gleditsch, in the fall 1992 issue of the *Journal of Peace Research*, suggested that academics call off their "war" on this subject and admit that the evidence is clear.[17]

As usual, one can find some gray or borderline cases, or perhaps a few exceptions that tend to prove the general rule. One might cite the Athenian attack on the Melians, but some would say the Athenians had ceased to be a genuine democracy.[18] Some might note the war of 1812 between Britain and the United States, but others would say Britain had an authoritarian monarch with considerable power and did not become genuinely democratic until the 1830s. Some might say that for those who recognized the Confederacy as an independent state in 1861, there followed a war with each side having an elected president.

If the behavioral pattern is reasonably clear that at least stable and industrialized democracies, with policy differences and power superiority over other democracies, do not resolve those differences by force, academics continue to "war" over the reason(s) why. Democracies certainly have conflicts inter se. One line of explanation is that an ideological or cultural or normative predisposition rules out force in these conflict situations.

It is quite possible, although not proven, that the following logic prevails as predisposition: even if another policy conflicts with mine, if it is democratically established, it remains legitimate and must not be overturned by force; disputes must be resolved peacefully under the law. Ideological or cultural affinity may make irrelevant at least those power disparities based on military force. Michael Doyle, citing Kant, argues that mature democratic states accept the liberal notion that similar states should be free from outside intervention,[19] which includes forceful intervention through war.

Bruce Russett, of Yale University, speculated in a similar vein:

> Democratically governed people have a self-image as people who are able to resolve and limit their conflicts through peaceful political processes, without resorting to violence or the threat of violence. Since they have this image of themselves, they tend to apply it where similar institutions, processes, and expectations obtain, and to give other democracies the benefit of doubt regarding their commitment to peaceful conflict resolution. If we as democrats are substantially in control of our own destinies, not controlled by an aggressive oligarchy, this must be true of people in other democracies.[20]

Further research by Russett in 1992 confirmed the importance of this normative influence on stable democratic foreign policy toward other stable democracies.[21]

It is possible, in other words, that self-identification as part of a larger community of stable, or mature, or industrialized, democrats helps mitigate an important part of the "we-they" distinction that can contribute to war. We Americans are able to make war relatively easily against Vietnamese or Iraqis because they are not part of a community of democrats. "They," being they, can more easily become dinks, slopes, camel jockeys, barbarians—devoid of humanity, worthy of being killed and maimed. It has often been noted that one of the first objectives of a military establishment engaged in war is to dehumanize the enemy. During World War I, French-German fraternizing during Christmas truces was stopped precisely because such contact made it more difficult for each side to kill the other. Each side was being reminded of the humanity of the other.

It is also true that the French and Germans and Japanese remain "they," and aggravatingly so at times from some American viewpoints. Particularly if they have a different skin color, it may still be relatively easy to put them in a category of "they-ness." But insofar as they are also democrats, there is a "we-ness" undermining, to a considerable extent, their "they-ness." All foreigners are they and not we, but some are more they than others. It is remarkable that when Russians were labeled "authoritarian Marxists," it was easy to think of them as commies and reds, terms used to dehumanize. When they became something approximating democrats, it was easier to think of them as typically human—albeit cursed with poor government and a terrible economy.

We may be dealing here with a matter of "deep culture" that is not capable of being defined or measured precisely, despite its importance.[22] (I will return to these cultural factors toward the end of the next chapter.) One manifestation of this deep normative affinity among mature democracies is that constitutional democracies are more likely than other types of states to submit disputes to the International Court of Justice (ICJ).[23] Recourse to the ICJ in the 1980s by the United States and Canada, and the United States and Italy, were but examples of this larger pattern.

This point should not obscure the fact that sometimes democracies find themselves on the wrong side of disagreements with the ICJ as the United States did during and after *Nicaragua v. the United States* or as Iceland did regarding the interim judgment in *United Kingdom v. Iceland*.[24] Indeed, the United States walked out of the ICJ in the mid-1980s over the Nicaraguan case, refused to argue the substantive phase, and refused to implement the judgment in favor of Nicaragua. A slight propensity among democrats to use international adjudication should not be confused with the proposition that democratic states are frequently willing to go to the World Court or that they always abide by the court's judgment. In fact, in the "cod war" between Iceland and the United Kingdom, not only did the former refuse to abide by the ICJ's interim judgment, but also warning shots were fired by one or both navies in the dispute. Here we had two democracies engaged in very limited overt violence, although the phrase "cod war" was mostly hyperbolic.

A second line of explanation for the absence of international war among at least some democracies stresses not ideological or normative factors but rather structural or institutional reasons. Although not completely separate from the first line of argument, this second attempt at explanation stresses not attitudes but the legal and institutional restraints on democratic decision makers. Presumably, decisions for war are taken in public, under constitutional provisions, and frequently in a process of shared authority between the executive and legislature. Such legal and institutional restraints may produce slow, careful, calculated decisions on both sides of the democratic dyad. Furthermore, public participation, through the legislature, may be a restraining factor in war decisions. Voters who also turn out to be soldiers or draftees, or perhaps just the relatives of combatants, may not be eager for international war.

It is clear that these democratic structural provisions do not always restrain war when the other party is authoritarian. The American public and Congress were gripped by war fever in 1898 and pushed the Spanish-American War on a reluctant President William McKinley. Democratic state structures did not impede the United Kingdom in going to war over the Falkland Islands, with the public and Parliament being as enthusiastic as was the prime minister to fight the Argentines.

Whether democratic structures count for all that much in explaining the absence of overt war among democracies remains debatable, and some research shows this line of thinking to be less powerful in explanation than that stressing normative factors.[25] Nevertheless, even if the "why" remains worthy of examination, the "what" remains clear. At least some democracies—whether called mature, advanced, stable, or industrialized—do not use force *inter se* in their policy disputes. The United States and Japan obviously have conflicts over trade and other issues, but the probability of a forcible resolution of these disputes is zero.

Whereas mature democracies almost always settle their differences inter se short of armed conflict, there is considerable evidence that some democracies are war-prone. One study shows that whether one measures international war in terms of severity (measured in battle deaths), duration (measured in war months), or frequency, democracies rank near the top of the list of war-prone nations.[26] In a study covering 1816–1980, France ranked number one in frequency, Britain was tied for second, Italy was fifth, and the United States tied for eighth. (During some of this time frame, these states may not have been democratic.) We find not only that democracies are engaged in war on a frequent and intense basis but also that they actually initiate hostility in a rather large number of incidents. Thus even though democracies do not, in general, war among themselves, they do make war on others, and they engage in war as often as or more than nondemocratic states. Democracies are prone to the "power temptation" in dealing with authoritarians: if one has power superiority, there is a temptation to use it.

Contemporary uses of overt force fit with the broader pattern of violence in international relations analyzed here. There is nothing in the events of recent years that contradicts what we think we know about democracies and overt war. The democratic United States has initiated overt force against several authoritarian parties—for example, in Grenada, Libya, and Panama. Democratic Israel also has initiated overt force against authoritarian adversaries—for example, in Iraq in 1981. There is no contemporary example of international war among stable democracies.

When democracies anticipate or actually engage in war with authoritarians, power calculations come into play, as they do in authoritarian interactions. Thus realists like Blainey have something important to say about those situations. On the other hand, realists should be paying much more attention to liberalism's correct projection that democracies do not engage in overt international war among themselves. The promotion and protection of human rights may be considered a liberal program, but it is also realist in its clear impact on the exercise of power in certain situations. That is a very profound finding about war and international relations. It is also interesting that social science cannot yet scientifically prove why this is so. International relations involve two types of "games." The game among democracies is governed by liberal rules; the game otherwise is frequently governed by realist rules.

THE LIMITS OF LIBERALISM

It is worth noting that when democracies war with authoritarians, implementing civil and political rights at home does little to block the war process. The U.S. invasion of Grenada, a case of democratic wrongful use of force, as evidenced both by a vote of condemnation in the United Nations General Assembly and by the views of our European allies, was sustained by domestic support. A tolerant if not bellicose nationalism accepted the strained presidential rationales.[27] As long as the use of force appeared relatively successful, brief, and without heavy casualties, legislative and popular opinion proved supportive. It is typical that real and extensive practice of civil-political rights at home did little to restrain democratic impermissible force abroad, at least against authoritarians. This same permissive attitude was present in other U.S. uses of force that some considered wrongful uses of force—for example, the invasion of Panama in 1989 and the initial stages of the use of force in Lebanon.

Democratic political currents play themselves out in similar ways in other democracies. The democratic tripartite invasion of Egypt in 1956, judged to be a violation of international law by the Eisenhower administration, did not initially have to overcome great opposition from popular and legislative opinion in the attacking states.

Should the democratic use of force prove costly and controversial, then implementing civil and political rights at home may lead to effective opposition to the controversial, or perhaps illegal, policy of force and may lead to curtailment of violence abroad. The example of the United States and the Vietnam War comes to mind. The case of the United States in Lebanon in the 1980s was beginning to show the same pattern at the time that U.S. military forces were withdrawn. Congress was becoming restless, which reflected unease in American public opinion.

Therefore, the exact impact of civil and political rights at home on forceful policies abroad *against authoritarians* varies with the situation. One has only to compare American public opinion and related congressional action in Vietnam after 1968 with Grenada in 1983. The basic political rule of thumb seems to be that public and legislative opinion will automatically support executive use of force for a short time, at least until protracted struggle and therefore higher costs transpire. Such is the continued strength of nationalism and the "rally 'round the flag" effect. The British population rallied behind an unpopular Thatcher government and its use of force in the South Atlantic in 1982, so much so that not without reason can the Argentine military be credited with the reelection of Margaret Thatcher. Thus the practice of civil-political rights at home does not necessarily block wrongful or other use of force abroad (the question of recourse to force) against authoritarians.

Might not the implementation of civil and political rights at home generate restraints on the process of war through greater attention to the law of war, a large part of which concerns itself with human rights in armed conflict? This question leads to an interesting but probably inconclusive discussion. Although democratic states like to present an image of full commitment to humanitarian law (which is the same as the law of human rights in armed conflict) when fighting authoritarians, the record is certainly mixed.

First, some authoritarians have largely complied with the laws of war, or their behavior has not been grossly incorrect or inferior to that of democrats. The principle of reciprocity, which largely undergirds the laws of war, works for authoritarians as well as democrats. Argentina had an excellent overall record when dealing with prisoners of war in the fighting over the islands in the South Atlantic in 1982. Even Nazi treatment of Western prisoners of war was largely correct during World War II (but not of Soviet prisoners of war, who were not protected by mutually agreed-upon treaties).

Second, democrats have engaged in grave breaches of the laws of war on occasion, for example the Americans at My Lai or the Israelis in both planning and failing to stop the massacres in Lebanon in 1982 at the Sabra and Shatilla refugee camps or in the beating and/or torture of Palestinian prisoners.[28] The answer to the question of whether democrats, even while making war on authoritarians, might exercise more restraint in the process, depends of course not on incidents but on patterns. A detailed examination of patterns lies beyond the scope of the present work.

I would hypothesize, however, that democrats, being by definition constitutional democrats and therefore used to the principle of public authority under law, would initially be inclined to pay more attention to the laws of war than would authoritarians. Moreover, constitutional democrats permit more domestic criticism of their policies as evaluated by law-of-war standards, which is not to say that democratic military establishments welcome or easily permit criticism. But that criticism, in principle, could theoretically lead to more restraints on the executive in war.

Few authoritarians are genuinely constitutional, meaning that few give serious attention to restraining rules of law. But I have already mentioned authoritarian interest in reciprocity. And some authoritarians might respect the laws of war as part of military honor. It is not clear that the record of authoritarian Pakistan under the laws of war is very different from democratic India.

Also, it seems reasonably clear that even constitutional democrats, under the pressure of war, are capable of great violations of human rights in armed conflict. I think of British and American terror-bombing of German cities in World War II, of Lt. William Calley's becoming a national hero for killing women, children, and even infants at My Lai, and of Israeli toleration of torture and murder of detainees in its long struggle with the Palestinians (who themselves engage in mostly terror, meaning attacks against civilians). The passions of war, frequently linked to deep feelings of insecurity and frustration, are difficult to restrain even in states commendable for their serious attention to a variety of human rights for *their* citizens during times of *peace*.

DEVELOPMENTALISM?

Whereas realism approaches the question of international overt war from the prism of competitive power, and liberalism from the prism of cooperative rules, there have been many other interpretations of the basic causes of war.[29] I do not wish to write an extended essay on the differences between Marxists stressing bellicose imperialism, Angellians stressing the pacifying effects of trade and international commerce, neo-Eisenhowerians focusing on the push toward war by the domestic military-industrial complex, or any other traditional school of thought. I do wish to draw attention, however, to a provocative thesis by John Mueller, in *Retreat from Doomsday*, and to his implicit argument that realism and liberalism are insufficient for understanding international war.[30]

Mueller's central argument has two parts. The first is that modern war among industrialized states is definitely destructive to material prosperity and that this has been accurately perceived by all developed states. Part of Mueller's interpretation is that the pursuit of material prosperity is a dominant value in the industrialized world. This type of analysis goes beyond realism, even with the latter's attention to an amorphous "national interest." Whereas realists argue that states must pay great attention to the strategy and tactics of both deterrence and war fighting, Mueller argues that such attention is largely unnecessary. Since industrialized states include the pursuit of prosperity in their conception of national interest, and since war among industrialized states would be terribly destructive, as shown by the two world wars of this century, for Mueller this provides the first step toward the renunciation of war for them.

Thus Mueller argues that since World World I, developed states have sought to avoid war. He believes that World War II can be explained only by the machinations of Hitler and that most belligerent states entered that war reluctantly, knowing the terrible destruction that was to come. He also believes that the strategy and tactics of security policy, including especially those pertaining to nuclear weapons, were mostly irrelevant to international peace after 1945. His basic argument is that all developed states know that even a conventional major war would not be in their interests.

But as Mueller goes on to note, international wars for a long time have been terribly destructive in material terms, relatively speaking, yet wars have persisted. Unlike Norman Angell, Mueller does not believe that material cost alone is sufficient to block major wars among the great powers. He believes that awareness of physical destruction must be combined with a moral rejection of war as a debasing process. He points out that wars can be fought for things like national (or sub-national) honor in an irrational process involving great material destruction. (Were the wars in the Balkans, Lebanon, Somalia, and Liberia rational from the standpoint of beneficial expenditure of scarce resources or with an eye to long-term economic gain?) Finally, he notes that outside the developed world, some wars might actually still be materially profitable. Mueller would have been proven correct had Iraq's rapid seizure of Kuwait, its oil, and its harbors gone unchecked.

The second part of Mueller's overall argument is that at work among developed states, whether democratic or authoritarian, is a moral revulsion against war, not just a rational or calculating opposition on economic grounds. Mueller raises the interesting example of the American Civil War. He argues that despite the terrible human and physical cost of that war, war remained a romantic notion, especially in the area of the Confederacy. (Nevertheless, he notes that the southern area has not tried secession again.)

Mueller argues that a broad historical learning process has been at work for centuries, a process in which war has lost its romantic appeal, now replaced by "revulsion" at the "psychic costs" of war—at least in the developed world. For him it is not democracy and legal rights that are important to peace, as liberalism suggests, but a broader morality in opposition to war. In his view, authoritarian Russians and Ukrainians, having experienced World War II, were just as opposed to war as any democrat in France or the United Kingdom.

It is worth adding, in passing, that if there is growing moral repugnance to war, the Pentagon's extensive censorship during the Persian Gulf War of 1991 probably had the long-term effect of making a repetition of war more likely, since that censorship left unchecked the romantic notion among American citizens that a major conventional war could be fought without much pain or suffering. For Americans, "Desert Storm" was largely bloodless. Journalists were not allowed to report on either coalition or enemy suffering to any significant extent. U.S. governmental efforts to suppress reports of relatively large numbers of civilian deaths in its use of armed force in Panama may have had the same effect. By comparison, assertive American journalism about the Vietnam War, though it surely made U.S. prosecution of the war more difficult at the time, may have had a salutary effect on restraining the war impulse more generally.

The jury may still be out regarding Mueller's accuracy on his second point, concerning revulsion at the human destruction in war. In the 1991 Persian Gulf War, President George Bush and his allies moved ahead with the decision to undertake armed conflict despite Pentagon reports anticipating very high American and allied casualties. Fortunately the Iraqi military establishment largely collapsed, despite having held fast during eight years of a nasty war with Iran. The fact remains that in the key decision taken by President Bush in early 1991, the prospect of relatively large numbers of killed and wounded in a short period of time did not make recourse to war repulsive. Of course, Mueller wrote mainly of war among industrialized states, and Iraq, at best, was semi-industrialized. Also, the human toll anticipated in the 1991 Persian Gulf War was far less than what could have been expected in even a nonnuclear war between the United States and the old USSR.

The jury may also be out on Mueller's argument that key players in industrialized states have also tired of civil war, in addition to international war. The violence in the Balkans during the early 1990s and events in parts of the former Soviet Union during the same period did not give complete assurance that destructive civil wars in the industrialized Northern Hemisphere were a thing of the past. (Was the fighting in the Balkans a civil war stemming from the former Yugoslavia or a civil war in Bosnia with outside participation?)

Nevertheless, Mueller argues that these two trends, recognition of material cost and psychic horrors, mean that major war—whether international or internal—"has lost the romantic appeal it once had, and it has been discredited as a method for obtaining desirable goals."[31] At least on the part of developed states, there has been an incremental revolution in thinking leading to "retreat from doomsday." Thus Mueller believes that international relations are no longer characterized as centering on war, at least for international relations among developed states.

It is true that both international and civil wars have been increasingly rare among and within highly industrialized and technocratic states. The violence that occurred in the Balkans and the former Soviet Union during the 1990s occurred in and between states that were far less economically developed than those in Western Europe. Whatever the stage of economic development in those areas, moral opposition to overt war, whether international or internal, seemed weak.

If Mueller is correct that an important part of the world has been "Hollandized," in the sense of viewing major war as "obnoxious," then realism and liberalism are partially correct but also insufficient for understanding war. That is to say, Mueller finds several states "Hollandized" in the sense that Holland and Sweden and others went through a period in which war was seen in the realist view—as a permissible and useful instrument of statecraft. But for Mueller, because of economic and moral development, states like Holland and Sweden have essentially and profoundly changed their view toward war.

There is a link between realism and what Mueller argues. Realism stresses state power, and it is the destruction wrought by industrialized power that may account for developed states' renunciation of war—as long as that destructiveness is accurately perceived. Some realists, however, believe that one can tolerate the destruction of a limited nuclear war and that winning such a war would make the destruction tolerable.

There are two links between liberalism and what Mueller argues. Most of the industrialized states are democratic, and as noted, democratic solidarity blocks overt international war within that community of states. So there is a large overlap between Mueller's emphasis on development and liberalism's emphasis on democracy (civil and political rights). Also, through an emphasis on morality, law, and personal rights, liberal values feed into a view that the human destruction from war is intolerable. There is a large overlap between Mueller's emphasis on morality and liberalism's emphasis on individual human rights as a means to personal dignity. But for Mueller, in the last analysis, it is not the liberal focus on democratic rights that is important but rather a broader moral opposition to war.

Perhaps Mueller's argument adds up to a new "ism," in the sense that William Ebenstein wrote of *Today's Isms*.[32] In addition to realism and liberalism, perhaps we should speak of a "developmentalism" containing a material and a moral component. Mueller is not a realist, for he believes that power alone, without moral developments, cannot explain the demise of war among developed states. Mueller is not a liberal, for he does not emphasize democracy and civil-political rights alone; he believes that an authoritarian can come to disavow war as much as a democrat. He believes that the communist USSR wanted to avoid major war as much as the democratic United States.

If Mueller proves correct, namely that material and moral development eradicates war, what could prove more peaceful than a global community of democratic, industrialized-technocratic states that have experienced war and thus know its horrors? And is this not what we find in a large and significant part of international relations in the 1990s?

At this point I would like to supplement both Mueller's thesis and traditional liberalism to comment on how socioeconomic rights may play a role in peace among major states. It may be that there is an economic dimension to our subject matter beyond the economic development stressed by Mueller. In addition to what has already been said in this chapter about civil-political rights, socioeconomic rights may make an *indirect* contribution to peace. Such individual or personal rights certainly enhance the value of human dignity in society. By focusing on the value of people in socioeconomic terms, this second generation of internationally recognized human rights probably contributes to the view that the killing of large numbers of people through war is, in Mueller's terms, morally "debasing." In this way, socioeconomic rights may contribute to the idea of war as "subrationally unthinkable" in important parts of the world—similar, according to Mueller, to dueling, cockfighting, and slave trading.[33]

All recognized human rights enhance the value of the person and implicitly argue against human destruction in war. Of course, this theoretical linkage between rights and peace has not been strong enough to prevent democracies from being war-prone or even from initiating some wars. Nevertheless, at least abstractly, socioeconomic rights reinforce civil and political ones in emphasizing human dignity, which should be at least some barrier to large-scale killing. Moreover, the second generation of socioeconomic rights might even contribute to peace in another way. If strongly accepted and taken seriously, socioeconomic rights might aid the process in which military budgets are reduced in favor of socioeconomic goods and services.

In sum, whereas realism stresses competitive power, and liberalism stresses transnational cooperation and legal rights, there may be reason to emphasize economic development and a general moral opprobrium. As usual, the lines of demarcation among these four ideas are not crystal clear.

CONCLUSION

Overt international war is definitely affected by the implementation of civil and political rights at home. Stable democrats do not war with similar democrats, for reasons we cannot yet fully explain. When war involves authoritarians, in whole or part, supposedly rational power calculations dominate, affected by nonrational factors such as subjectivity and emotionalism. Civil and political rights may not exercise much consistent impact on this type of purely "we-they" international conflict.

The practice of civil and political rights may at times encourage rather than restrain a bellicose nationalism against authoritarians. There would have been no Spanish American War if the United States had also been authoritarian. The implementation of those same democratic rights may tolerate major violations of the laws on human rights in armed conflict, even though the laws were designed to restrain the process of war regardless of the earlier decision to have recourse to war. Lt. Calley may have been a hero to many in the American democracy, but he was an embarrassment to many professional officers in the authoritarian U.S. military. Socioeconomic rights may make some indirect contribution to peace, by further emphasizing the innate worth of the individual and thus enhancing moral opposition to war as debasing of human dignity.

But it may be the case that a broad rejection of overt international war is occurring because of its high costs and psychic disapproval, among developed authoritarians as well as among developed democratic states. It would be logical for authoritarians, having experienced major war, to want to avoid its repetition, even if they despise the notion of individual human rights. I think it is a correct interpretation of much thinking in the old Soviet Union to say that although invading Afghanistan was somewhat tolerable, invading NATO territory would never have been. The material and psychic costs would have been too great.

It may be that four trends all point in the same direction—toward less international war—in an intertwined or overlapping process: growing attention to civil-political rights; growing attention to socioeconomic rights; increased industrial-technocratic development; increased moral development or interdependence. It seems evident that all four trends are relatively weak in the Southern Hemisphere of developing countries. But in the south, as in the north, to advance human rights on the moral-legal plane, and economic development on the material plane, may be to accelerate the eventual reduction of overt international war. Whether the process is realist, liberal, or developmental becomes a matter of academic semantics.

2

Human Rights and Covert International War

Given what is increasingly obvious, namely that stable democracies do not engage in overt international war with each other, few scholars have probed the question of whether democracies might engage in covert forceful intervention against each other. It is this question that I pursue in this chapter, referring to such intervention as covert international "war." I want to know if a democratic foreign policy has ever used force covertly against the existence or policies of other elected governments.

If implementing human rights in the form of civil and political rights seems to inoculate, most of the time, against military attack among democracies, implementing these same rights at home does not inoculate against *covert* undermining of those rights abroad, as we shall see in this chapter. At least on occasion, democratic governments have led or supported covert violence against other governments that are, clearly in some cases and arguably in some cases, democracies. U.S. foreign policy during the cold war showed that considerable implementation of civil and political rights in a foreign polity did not always prevent covert violence in or against that polity. Sometimes it makes practical sense to speak of a "war" between democracies, although regular military units are not engaged in overt combat.

I will explore three possible ways of explaining this intriguing and largely ignored pattern. The simplest explanation stems from U.S. definitions of its national interest during the cold war. A deeper explanation focuses on an American cultural predisposition affecting the definition of national interest. A general explanation suggests that only some democracies avoid violence among themselves, whereas other democracies engage in at least covert violence.

FOCUS ON THE UNITED STATES

Covert interventions, by their very nature, are difficult to pinpoint in time and place. When carried out by the United States, however, they usually become public knowledge eventually. Steven Van Evera has asserted that on about a dozen occasions since 1945, the United States has covertly intervened against what he terms democratic governments.[1] Six of these twelve claimed interventions involved violence or its direct threat, whereas others were "peaceful" in the sense that force was not clearly used or directly threatened. Some of these interventions may have sought some goal short of the overthrow, violent or otherwise, of the targeted government. Intervention consists of dictatorial interference in domestic affairs, mainly by forcible action; it covers attempts to dictate a policy as well as to dictate a government.[2]

As will be shown, it can be substantiated that the United States organized or aided six covert interventions involving violence against elected governments between 1947 and 1991, not counting clearly bogus elections as in the Soviet alliance. These covert actions, against governments that had been elected in reasonably free and fair elections and that otherwise implemented civil and political rights to a considerable degree, involved Iran (1953), Guatemala (1954), Indonesia (1957), Brazil (from 1961), Chile (1973), and Nicaragua (from 1984).

There were other U.S. covert interventions against the policies, if not the existence, of democratic governments, involving British Guyana (from 1953), Costa Rica (from 1955), and Ecuador (from 1960). In these three cases, rather than leading or supporting actual or threatened military activities, the United States acted via propaganda, political influence, and economics in an effort at dictatorial determination of governments or governmental policies.

There are still other cases in which assertions of CIA involvement against democracies, or perhaps against policies *in* democracies, or perhaps against democratic elements in mixed political systems, have not been clearly substantiated. These cases involved, at a minimum, the United Kingdom (1959), the Dominican Republic (1965), Greece (1967), Jamaica (from 1976), and India (at various times).

In should also be noted that the CIA was instructed to intervene on *behalf* of democratic governments on occasion, particularly in Western Europe during the early days of the cold war, as in Italy and France. The United States has also sought to overthrow authoritarian governments, as in Albania during the Truman administration. But our focus here remains democratic forceful intervention against elected governments.

In reviewing configurative material, we want not only to confirm the use of force but also to say something about the extent of civil and political rights practiced in the target state.

TWO WELL-KNOWN CASES

The first two violent U.S. covert interventions against elected governments can be considered together. In 1953 and 1954, when the classic cold war characterized Soviet-American relations, the United States covertly intervened to topple the governments in both Iran and Guatemala.[3] Washington's proclivity to see these governments as troublesome did not alter the fact that the Mossadeq government in Iran and the Arbenz government in Guatemala had been elected. Mohammad Mossadeq had been chosen by a clear majority in parliament and Jacobo Arbenz Guzmán by a clear majority of the popular vote.

Neither political system was fully democratic. The Iranian parliament had to share power with the monarch, and it proved a contentious question whether the shah could dismiss a prime minister who had majority support in parliament. Elections in Guatemala were restricted by the army in alliance with conservative economic interests. Fraud and intimidation existed. Yet both Mossadeq and Arbenz would probably have won completely fair and free elections.[4] Both reflected widespread populist movements. Policies of land reform, redistribution of wealth, and even expropriation of foreign-owned property did not alter, indeed were consistent with, democratic government. An active Communist movement in both countries did not mean that key leaders necessarily held Marxist-Leninist or other authoritarian views.

This last point is crucial and raises difficult questions of analysis. It is reasonably clear that Mossadeq in Iran was neither a Marxist nor a Leninist, since he opposed the Iranian Communist parties on any number of issues and principles. He did tactically cooperate with some of them when political calculations demanded, but on other occasions he suppressed them brutally.[5] Whether he harbored authoritarian tendencies is more difficult to establish, in the same sense that it would be difficult to prove that Abraham Lincoln or Franklin Roosevelt or Winston Churchill never considered authoritarian moves when faced with national difficulties. The fact remains that Mossadeq was a genuinely if indirectly elected leader at the time the United States engineered a coup.

The case of Arbenz in Guatemala is perhaps more complex, but in the last analysis Guatemala was basically democratic in 1954. Behind U.S. policy were the same suspicions that were to arise about Salvador Allende in Chile in the 1970s—namely, that commitment to democratic processes and values might *lead to* the eventual implementation of Communist values and policies. An exhaustive study of Arbenz by Piero Gleijeses shows the complexity of clear judgment. Gleijeses concluded:

> Granted, Arbenz could have had communists as allies and not been one of them. The evidence, however, indicates that the communists were his closest personal and political friends and that, at least by 1952, he felt like one of them, even though he did not join the party until 1957.
>
> Nearly forty years after his overthrow, Jacobo Arbenz remains an elusive, enigmatic figure. . . . The complexities of Arbenz's personality and of his position are distilled in his relationship with the army, a relationship that embodied the strain, the distance he had traveled in his own life. He was a respected officer, and, increasingly, he was a communist.[6]

This last judgment is still, despite the research, based on an interpretation not free from controversy. Officially Arbenz was not a Communist in 1954. Moreover, in both theory and practice, it is possible to combine Marxism, as well as something close to it that lacks a clear label (e.g., left-of-center reform movement without pretensions to scientific certitude), with democracy and national independence. Concerning Marxism, one can recall Josip Tito's Yugoslavia and Nicolae Ceausescu's Romania. Concerning non-Marxist reform movements in places like Zimbabwe, there are Marxist officials who respect the rule of law, the outcome of elections, and a wide range of human rights.

Moreover, in many places there are democrats who believe in full or partial socialism.

For every piece of evidence that seems to show sympathy by Arbenz for communism, such as his declaring public mourning for Joseph Stalin's death, there is a contradictory piece of evidence or line of interpretation (e.g., the silence for Stalin was simply a political gesture deemed necessary in political calculations). Consider the much-cited arms deal between Arbenz and Czechoslovakia. The deal did not change the fact that politically, Arbenz was not closely tied to the Soviet Union, with whom his government had no formal relations. Also, the Czechoslovak arms were dated and mostly useless to Guatemala; the arms deal represented more a swindling of Guatemala than an example of socialist brotherhood.[7] Given the U.S.-led arms embargo on Guatemala, Arbenz's search for arms from Eastern Europe could be highly pragmatic.

Some facts are agreed on: Guatemalan Communists held a very small position in Arbenz's governing coalition, in the executive branch, and in the country at large; Communists were influential in the labor movement; Communists were the main allies of Arbenz in his efforts at socioeconomic reform.[8] But all of this proves nothing in a definitive sense about Arbenz's fundamental political views or about Guatemala's future under him.

Even if true, Gleisjeses' conclusion that Arbenz was, to use the language of the cold war, at least a Communist sympathizer in 1954 if not a full Communist does not negate the fact, as Gleisjeses admits, that in 1954 Guatemala had an elected, non-Communist government. He wrote: "U.S. officials were alarmed by the rising influence of communism in Guatemala. And yet they knew that the communists were not in control of Guatemala. Neither the CIA nor embassy officials nor the military attaches ever claimed that the Guatemalan army was infiltrated by communists—and the army, they noted, was Guatemala's key institution."[9] What the United States feared in 1954 was the future.

As the cliché has it, one thing is clear. U.S. policy toward Guatemala in 1954 was not very much interested even in civil and political rights, and certainly not in socioeconomic ones. The definitive proof of this is the type of government the United States installed by covert force: a repressive one. It was moderate only by comparison with the more brutal ones that followed, all with U.S. support until the 1980s.

The only remaining question is whether the United States understood that it was replacing a government with considerable claim to democratic credentials with a distinctly authoritarian one. It is clear that lower- and middle-level officials knew this. Whether President Dwight Eisenhower and Secretary of State John Foster Dulles believed their own public rhetoric about Arbenz's having fallen under Soviet control is more problematical to prove.[10]

My interpretation regarding both Iran in 1953 and Guatemala in 1954 is that a combination of concern for economic advantage and for perceived national security led the United States to engage in covert international "war" against regimes that were partially (Iran) and basically (Guatemala) democratic and certainly far more democratic than what followed. Western or U.S. economic advantage became intertwined with the cold war struggle of capitalism vs. Soviet-led socialism; in the minds of U.S. policymakers, the two became inseparable.

On this point Gleisjeses has it right. To use a phrase later well known, what the United States feared in Guatemala in 1954 was a Cuban-model state even before the Cuban revolution. That is, the United States feared a successful land-reform program involving expropriated American (and other) property, a program that would encourage similar developments in other hemispheric states. Gleisjeses wrote:

> Even without the hazy prospect of a communist takeover of Guatemala . . . Arbenz posed an intolerable challenge. In the heart of the American sphere of influence, in an upstart banana republic, there stood . . . a president [whose] agrarian reform was proceeding well, the [communist party] was gaining popular support, *and basic freedoms were being upheld.* It was an intolerable challenge to America's sense of self-respect.[11]

Certainly the Arbenz government constituted a clear and present danger to the profits and power of the United Fruit Company. But this was not the main issue for officials in the U.S. government in 1954, nor would American commercial interests be the main issue in Chile in 1973 for key officials like Henry Kissinger. In the minds of people like John and Allen Dulles, even without misrepresentation of events by officials of United Fruit, Arbenz's policies represented an attack on the American way of life as the epitome of what the United States was fighting for in the cold war. Economics was the minor issue intertwined with the major issue of national security defined as protection of a way of life.

Mossadeq's takeover of the Anglo-Iranian Oil Company was

viewed in the same light: as a challenge to Western economic interests and as a leftist move equated with sympathy for Soviet-style communism. It made no difference to Washington that the Iranian expropriation was overwhelmingly supported by the Iranian parliament or that Iran governed by the shah alone would be more authoritarian than had heretofore been the case. In Iran, as in Guatemala, U.S. fear of Communist inroads in the future, fear mixed with a drive for extensive political control and a sense of affront by upstart politicians who took American and Western property, negated concern for the considerable, if incomplete, practice of civil and political rights.

Given the elected nature of the target governments in question, and given some wider practice of civil and political rights beyond elections in both states, it is not clear that a U.S. policy of overt overthrow through military attack could have been justified to the American people. Both Iran and Guatemala were far more democratic than other states holding elections—for example, states in Eastern Europe. One might recall, however, that Senator Joseph McCarthy's hysterical maneuvers during that era made rational discussion of U.S. policy difficult, to say the least. Likewise, one might recall that a *New York Times* reporter cooperated with the CIA in providing key military intelligence useful in the overthrow of Mossadeq[12] and that the same paper proclaimed lack of U.S. involvement in the Guatemalan affair.[13] The domestic political climate in the United States might have led to acceptance of even more brazen administration rationales for use of force than were actually employed—and those already fit in the category of "the big lie."

Neither target government had carried out any armed attack on anyone, depriving the United States of any claim to collective self-defense under international law. The U.S. government had publicly, and correctly, stated that expropriation of foreign-owned property was a legal act under international law, as long as proper compensation was forthcoming. More important, a covert operation seemed more economical. The degree of democracy present in Iran and Guatemala—that is, the considerable implementation of civil and political rights—proved no barrier to U.S. preoccupation with perceived national interests, whether defined in terms of geopolitical security or economics or, most likely, some combination of the two tinged by other motivations. Moreover, the democratic United States was urged to overthrow the elected Mossadeq in Iran by the democratic United Kingdom.[14]

TWO MORE CASES

The Sukarno government was elected in Indonesia in 1955 in a relatively fair and free process.[15] Later Sukarno restricted a number of civil and political rights under his "guided democracy"; there is no doubt but that "guided democracy" became something quite different from parliamentary or presidential democracy as found in the West.[16] The CIA covertly intervened against the Indonesian government in 1957.

There does not appear to be any evidence suggesting that the quality of democracy in Indonesia had anything to do with U.S. support for a violent movement against Sukarno. On the contrary, at least some of the U.S. concern stemmed from Sukarno's implementation of proportional democracy. Since the Indonesian Communists received about 25 percent of the popular vote in 1955, Sukarno decided to give about 25 percent of cabinet posts to Communists. This, and Sukarno's normal relations with the People's Republic of China, plus some warming of relations with the Soviet Union, did not sit well with Washington in the mid-1950s. The result was Washington's decision to encourage, through direct military and other assistance, an armed revolt by a military faction. Authors differ as to whether the goal of U.S. covert intervention was the actual overthrow of Sukarno or just pressure against his policies.[17]

It remains a fact that the United States directly participated in violence against a government that was genuinely elected and that remained at least partially democratic. The shooting down and capture of an American pilot who was working for the CIA and supporting the armed rebellion put an end to the U.S. policy of armed intervention without a full resolution of differences with Sukarno. After some euphoria in Washington about the utility of covert military interventions, stemming of course from events in Iran and Guatemala, U.S. policymakers manifested growing doubts not about intervention against elected governments but about the wisdom of direct U.S. participation in military action. (In fact, the Guatemalan operation had been rife with mistakes and confusion, leading, among other things, to the sinking of a British ship carrying coffee and cotton. Not only the British government but other knowledgeable ones as well were less than happy over the tactics of the Guatemalan operation.)[18] Sukarno too changed at least tactics, if not basic policies. Thus the United States and Sukarno engaged in their version of peaceful coexistence for the rest of his tenure as president.

The fact that the United States tried to discredit Sukarno by at-

tempting to make a pornographic movie about his romantic pro-
clivities indicates the climate of the times.[19] A nonaligned regime
could become the target of U.S. covert intervention despite considerable political moderation and absence of close ties to the Soviet Union.
Under Eisenhower and Dulles, Washington developed a foreign policy
that equated Third World nonalignment with evil. The degree of respect for civil and political rights in Indonesia, which was considerable
relative to other regimes past and present but certainly not perfect,
failed to influence Washington policymakers prone to see the world
only in terms of two hostile camps, Communist and non-Communist.
During the 1950s almost any position by less-developed countries
short of full commitment to U.S. policy caused them to be viewed
with suspicion and concern; the fact that some of them implemented
political and civil rights to a considerable degree was almost irrelevant.

It is a fair question whether matters changed all that much in the
1960s. In Brazil in the first half of the 1960s, the CIA provided encouragement and support for threatened violence, which proved sufficient
to bring down at least one basically democratic government and perhaps two. In 1961 Jânio da Silva Quadros clearly won a basically fair and
free election, only to resign seven months later. The U.S. role at that
point remains cloudy. It is not clear whether the United States supported a Brazilian military threat to take over the government unless
Quadros resigned.[20]

João Goulart, as vice-president, assumed the presidency. Like his
predecessor, and like Arbenz in Guatemala, Goulart was a democratic,
nationalistic, nonaligned, and reformist leader who worried the Brazilian traditional elite as well as the United States. The Kennedy administration, more or less like that of Eisenhower and Dulles in 1954,
focused on an alleged tilt toward the Soviet Union and the unwise toleration of Communists in Brazil. Overt U.S. concern with private economic interests seemed to be less in Brazil, compared with in Iran and
Guatemala, although Goulart supported restrictions on repatriation of
profits by foreign corporations. (Those who support a purely economic
interpretation of U.S. foreign policy should note the absence of *major*
economic factors in propelling the U.S. intervention in Indonesia.)

At a minimum, in 1964 the CIA supported the Brazilian military
with money, weapons, and advice in order to assist the military's overthrow of President Goulart.[21] Although there was no overt violence
during this period and particularly during the 1964 bloodless coup, it
seems probable that U.S. support for a military revolt would have in-

cluded support for violence, had that occurred. Covert intervention leading to the threat of military force against an elected government is well within the ambit of our present focus. And there is no doubt that the United States fully supported, and may have actively encouraged, the overthrow of Goulart. It was U.S. policy to intervene in Brazilian politics in several ways, one of which was to either engineer or support a military takeover.[22]

CHILE, 1973

Events in Chile in the early 1970s were similar to those in Brazil in 1964 but produced both more violence and more controversy. A brief review can sort out major factors. Chile, especially in 1973, should be viewed against the pattern, noted above, of U.S. covert violence as well as against the pattern, noted below, of U.S. covert nonviolent intervention in hemispheric politics.

Chile had manifested a relatively long history of democracy. Increasing political difficulties led to the election in 1970 of a minority socialist president. Salvador Allende garnered 36.2 percent of a reasonably fair and free vote. Consistent with Chilean traditions, he was then elected by a majority of the parliament. He thus became a democratically elected socialist president in a nonsocialist political economy. In the congressional elections of 1973, his governing coalition got about 44 percent of the vote whereas the opposition parties got 55 percent; parliament remained under center-right control. A national leader with plurality but not majority support is not an unusual feature of democratic polities and is regularly seen in multiparty democracies like Israel, Belgium, the Netherlands, Denmark, and others. It is also not unusual, at least in Chile, for outside parties to participate financially in elections. If the Chilean Communist party received outside support, so did the Chilean Christian Democrats and others.[23]

The democratic nature of the 1969, 1970, and 1973 elections in Chile proved no barrier to U.S. attempts to get rid of the Allende government. Henry Kissinger wrote many pages in his memoirs trying to convince his readers that the United States was not involved in intervention, violent and nonviolent, toward that end.[24] But these protestations are not convincing, especially since Kissinger told his colleagues that he did not "see why we have to let a country go Marxist just because its people are irresponsible."[25] This was basically the same attitude that had contributed to U.S. intervention in Guatemala some two decades earlier; democracy would not be respected if it appeared irresponsible to U.S. security concerns broadly defined. Even in his memoirs, Kissinger spends much time explaining why Allende presented such a challenge to the United States.

It was precisely because of that political evaluation that the United States tried to bribe the Chilean Congress to block Allende's election and to fund truckers in their disruptive strikes, both of which Kissinger admits, and to encourage elements of the Chilean military to use force against Allende.[26] The United States took it upon itself to help correct the "mistake" made by a controlling plurality of Chileans, not to mention a majority of the legislature, in naming their own president. Once again, U.S. fears overrode respect for democratic procedures. Once again, since the United States was deprived of any plausible legal rationale for overt overthrow, and since covert action seemed more economical, Washington chose to act covertly.

Had Kissinger been convincing in his view that Allende was not really committed to democratic values, the United States would not have had to act so covertly. Allende was, in fact, a moderate leftist in the context of Chilean politics, however revolutionary that position may have appeared to Kissinger. Allende was consistently committed to political rights. There is no doubt that Allende intended to severely restrict property rights as a type of civil or economic right and that he and/or his supporters pushed other proposals that would have restricted other civil rights, such as access to an independent judiciary, had they not been blocked by the Chilean Congress. But in the final analysis, as Mark Falcoff, not one to lionize leftist politicians, has noted, Allende "had long been identified with the [socialist] party's 'electoral' wing."[27]

CIA agents like Kermit Roosevelt played a leading and direct role in the overthrow of Mossadeq; the leading U.S. role in the overthrow of Arbenz was only transparently shielded by Guatemalan dissidents; and the United States had an eventually obvious relationship with the Indonesian rebels. In Chile, the United States managed to keep a discreet distance from those acting to force out Allende, just as it had kept its distance in supporting a military takeover in Brazil. Chileans themselves finally acted against Allende in 1973, as Brazilians had against their president, but Richard Nixon and his team made it clear that anti-Allende violence had U.S. support and that a new military government would be quickly rewarded with diplomatic recognition and foreign assistance. Despite Kissinger's protestations of innocence, one cannot meet clandestinely with military officials, urge them to use force against an elected president,[28] and then disclaim any responsibility for the subsequent violent coup, even though it was carried out by others. Covert violent intervention to overthrow a government may assume a leading or supporting form. When it takes the latter, it is still intervention.

Once again, in the Chilean case as in the Iranian, Guatemalan, Indonesian, and Brazilian cases, we find the democratic United States at least supporting if not leading political violence against an elected leader. The Allende team's real attention to a wide range of human rights in Chile did not protect it from U.S. policies supportive of political violence against an elected government. Indeed, Allende's attention to economic and social rights, which implied great restrictions on private property rights, helped trigger active U.S. opposition. Nixon and Kissinger were able to convince themselves, if not all others, that Allende was not really a democratic Marxist whose vision of radical socioeconomic change was combined with considerable respect for political rights. The possibility of a democratic Marxist in the Western Hemisphere following a path of national independence was still as unacceptable to Washington in 1973 as it had been in 1954.

Whereas the Johnson administration had been able to support Alexander Dubček and "communism with a human face" in Czechoslovakia in 1968, the Nixon administration was unable to deal with a similar situation in Chile during 1970–73. Of course in Czechoslovakia in 1968, had Dubček been able to achieve considerable socialism with increased civil and perhaps eventually political rights, the Prague spring pointed in the direction of less Soviet influence; but in Chile in 1973, the Nixon administration was fearful of more Soviet influence. Also in Chile, American private economic interests were directly threatened by Allende's reforms. In the pursuit of national security, entailing protection of American economic interests, U.S. policy employed clandestine intervention involving support for, indeed encouragement of, political violence against the elected Allende.

NICARAGUA IN THE 1980S

This brings us to the case of U.S. violent intervention against the government of Daniel Ortega of Nicaragua in the 1980s, a case that became as overt as a covert policy can be. In the winter of 1981–82 when the Reagan administration began its policy of organizing covert military attacks against the Sandinista government, Nicaragua did not have democratic government. Whatever mechanisms existed for communication between the masses and the elite, such as Peoples Councils, fell short of meeting a minimum threshold for genuine democracy. Sandinista leaders were clear in their initial disdain for traditional Western elections, striving instead for other forms of popular participation.[29]

In 1984, in a Sandinista effort to improve international legitimacy, presidential and legislative elections were held throughout Nicaragua. Moderate-left opposition parties agreed to participate, gained further concessions from the Sandinistas, and were eventually free to conduct a critical campaign. They won about a third of the legislative seats. A number of respected human rights groups certified that the actual voting was reasonably fair and free. There were also reports, however, that the government and its supporters restricted and harassed opposition parties. The InterAmerican Commission on Human Rights, an independent body associated with the Organization of American States, concluded that the incumbents had used the power of the state to enhance their position in the campaign. The principal conservative opposition political party, headed by Arturo Cruz and linked to the United States in several ways, boycotted the elections. There were reports that the United States had pressured Cruz not to participate, in order to deprive the Sandinistas of political legitimacy from their expected electoral victory. The Sandinistas won 62 percent of the recorded vote.[30]

The 1984 elections resulted in an unclear situation as far as Nicaraguan democracy was concerned. Apparently an unfair campaign was combined with a technically fair vote in which about 38 percent of voters cast votes against the existing government. Certainly the Sandinistas continued to violate many civil rights during and after 1984.[31] For example, some political prisoners were kept away from visits by the International Committee of the Red Cross and were subjected to coercive interrogation. And certainly there were many violations of civil rights, and of the human rights law of armed conflict, by the rebel, or contra, forces that had been organized, trained, and supplied by the United States. The CIA had produced for the rebels a training manual that advocated "neutralizing" civilian officials and that condoned military attacks on civilians.[32] Neither the government nor the rebels seemed fully committed to democratic values.

Yet the Sandinista government was certainly not totalitarian, and under international pressure it had respected, albeit inconsistently and imperfectly, an increasing range of civil and political rights. Not to be overlooked is the undisputed fact that its record of attention to socioeconomic rights, particularly in the health and education areas, was exemplary, drawing praise from such independent agencies as the World Health Organization.[33]

The question of democracy in Nicaragua was a secondary issue for the Reagan administration. When, in 1981, Washington initially decided to start a military operation against the Sandinistas, there was neither public nor private emphasis on either human rights or collective self-defense. It was only later, when the U.S. role in the military operations became known, that Washington developed rationales mentioning either human rights violations by Managua or a request from El Salvador for collective self-defense. References to human rights and collective self-defense were essentially belated and secondary efforts to develop a public rationale for the real policy objective of eliminating a "Cuban-model state" in Nicaragua.[34]

What propelled the Reagan administration to the rollback of communism in Nicaragua, under the idea of the Reagan Doctrine, was a perceived security threat linked to international communism through Cuba and ultimately the Soviet Union. Above all, the administration did not want to face another Cuban missile crisis, in which a nearby state allowed the Soviets to place attack missiles on its territory. Whether the Nicaraguan government was basically authoritarian in 1981 or partially democratic by 1984 made very little difference to the Reagan team. That the Sandinistas had shown far more concern for real rights, including socioeconomic rights, than had the previous Somoza dynasty proved completely irrelevant to the Reagan administration.[35]

Reagan's policymakers were compelled to deal with the issue of human rights, which to them meant only civil and political rights, because of congressional and public opposition to the rollback policy, not because of an intrinsic interest in rights. The Reagan team eventually used the old argument that Managua violated human rights at home and was *therefore* aggressive against El Salvador abroad. Hence Washington had to focus on—that is, bring about by violence—change *within* Nicaragua in order to get at the question of Nicaraguan support for rebels in El Salvador.[36] This is, of course, a modern version of the old Wilsonian notion that authoritarian governments are the causes of international violence. In this view, there was continuing armed conflict in El Salvador not because of Salvadoran conditions but because of authoritarian Nicaragua next door (and authoritarian Cuba) and their support for the Salvadoran rebels. (Secretary of State Alexander Haig's memo to the president is relevant; Haig argued that U.S. policy should "go to the source" and coerce Castro's Cuba. The "source" of the problem was not internal to any Central American country but rather was the external meddling by Communist states.)

Although the degree of political and other rights in Nicaragua remained controversial until the 1990 elections leading to the replacement of the Ortega government, it should be noted that the increasing degree of democracy did not lead to a decreasing amount of violence orchestrated by the United States. That is because, as in other states, considerable attention to human rights within Nicaragua could not forestall U.S. covert attacks. Reagan policymakers, like others in Washington before them, had decided that a reformist and independent government constituted a threat to U.S. national interests. The issue of human rights in Nicaragua was mostly a smoke screen, useful to the administration in the tactical sense of trying to justify politically at home a policy of "covert" overthrow.

Just as the Reagan team tried to build domestic support for its policy in neighboring El Salvador by showing that the government there was democratic, so it tried to show that in Nicaragua the government was undemocratic and violative of all sorts of rights. Both policies led to great distortion of a complex set of facts. Washington was interested not in political and other rights but rather in the rhetoric of rights in the service of perceived national security concerns.[37] (For the same reasons, Reagan tried until the eleventh hour of the Filipino political revolution to explain away human rights violations by the Marcos government; the Reagan team was not genuinely concerned with rights but rather was interested primarily in stable anti-Communist allies.)

SOME NONVIOLENT INTERVENTIONS

It is relevant to recall other, nonviolent U.S. covert interventions in states with elected governments. Steven Van Evera claims that the CIA covertly intervened against democratic governments in British Guyana for over a decade, starting in 1953. He provides no supporting evidence.[38] A 1990 study by Charles D. Ameringer mentions the same situation but also provides no details.[39] Ralph McGehee, citing the report of a Washington private group, says the CIA destabilized an elected government in 1962 and 1963 through nonviolent methods.[40] According to John Ranelagh, free elections in British Guyana led both to a "Marxist" leader, Cheddi Jagan, and to CIA nonviolent interventions against him. Ranelagh alleges that after 1961, the CIA funded disruptive strikes and other impediments to the economy in order to discredit the elected government.[41]

Also in the mid-1950s, the CIA intervened through peaceful methods against the elected government of José Figuéres Ferrer in Costa Rica. Authors differ about whether the purpose of this action was overthrow or harassment and about how successful the policy was.[42] There are no claims that the United States supported or advocated violence, only that the United States sought to make trouble, through covert intervention in domestic affairs, for a democratic but moderately left-of-center leader in a clearly democratic polity.

In addition, according to several authors, the CIA covertly intervened against elected governments in Ecuador in the early 1960s. Apparently Washington's motive, at least in part, was these governments' normal relations with Castro's Cuba.[43]

It seems that these three cases of intervention were nonviolent. The fact that the targeted governments were elected appears not to have generated many moderating influences in policy-making circles in Washington. Whether similar interventions occurred in Greece around 1967 and Jamaica in the 1970s continues to be debated, as does the complex situation in the Dominican Republic in the mid-1960s. If, in 1959, the CIA funded Labour politicians who were opposed to nationalization in the United Kingdom, is this intervention?[44] If a Soviet source alleges CIA interventions at various times in democratic India, is this to be taken as proven?[45]

CONCLUSION

Controversies and gray areas should not distract us from a proven pattern. From the Iranian operation of 1953 to the Nicaraguan contras of the 1980s, considerable attention to civil and political rights in certain countries abroad did little to moderate an interventionist U.S. foreign policy driven by concerns that largely screened out substantive rights factors. Whereas U.S. support for civil and political rights in Western Europe is well documented (and the covert intervention there in *support* of democracy has been noted), the situation is not at all the same in the rest of the world.

The United States has repeatedly intervened covertly, sometimes with threat or use of force, against regimes that were not only elected but that could be accurately termed partially or basically democratic. In political terms, there were wars between the United States and these elected governments. In each case, the driving force behind U.S. policy was a fear that elected leaders either were Communists or would not be tough enough on Communists. As a result, Soviet interests would advance, and U.S. national security, including defense of property rights, would suffer. This is not an unreasonable concern. After all, Castro allowed attack missiles to be placed in Cuba in 1962, and although those missiles would not have changed the strategic balance between the United States and the USSR, a balance that was decidedly in U.S. favor at the time, those missiles could have reached U.S. territory.

In the cases reviewed above, the United States acted on a fear of future possibilities, even at the expense of considerable attention to civil and political rights, not to mention socioeconomic ones. An interesting question is, why did the United States adopt such a broad definition of its national security, so that the normal deference to other democratic policymakers was discarded? If democracies normally respect national self-determination inter se, what was so different in many of the cases above, leading the United States to choose covert threat or use of force? Why did the United States act on fears based on remote possibilities rather than on clear and present dangers?

The obvious and simplified answer is, as already suggested, fear of the Soviet Union and its political expansion during the prolonged cold war. But there are two other possible answers, more general and nuanced.

Michael Hunt has argued that an informal American ideology of greatness, racism, and anti-revolution has shaped U.S. foreign policy.[46] David Mayers has shown how George Kennan personified this racism by his disdain for human rights and democracy when he was writing of the less-developed nations.[47] It is striking how little civil and political rights mattered to U.S. covert policy, some of it violent, in the Third World. An informal ideology of American superiority, racism, and antirevolution seems to have informed more explicit concerns with security and economics.

When the democratic United States confronted an elected government that was non-European, weak, and reformist, or perhaps just
nonaligned, Washington at times acted to remove it—more than once
with threatened or applied violence. If such a government was in the
Western Hemisphere, it was especially likely to be targeted. There
were, of course, a number of governments in developing countries that
were reformist or nonaligned and that, as far as we know, were not the
targets of a covert "war" by the United States. Some of these were in
others' sphere of influence—for example, Algeria—and some just did
not matter to Washington—for example, Sri Lanka.

In general one can make a persuasive argument, drawing on Hunt,
that an American cultural predisposition encouraged but did not always cause U.S. covert action against certain regimes, including some
partially or basically democratic. At work seemed to be a combination
of disdain for non-European politicians, fear of social revolution, and
resentment that American leadership was rejected. All of this fed into
a greatly expanded conception of what was necessary in the name of
U.S. national security. And all of this Washington most keenly believed with regard to the Western Hemisphere. Of the governments in
Washington between 1947 and 1989, only the Carter administration
seems to have resisted this informal ideology.

But a theoretical explanation of U.S. covert action against elected
governments can also be persuasive. If we return to the literature cited
in the previous chapter about the lack of overt war among democracies, a close reading of some of that literature suggests that absence of
violence is to be expected among only *certain* democracies. Drawing
on Michael Doyle, who himself was relying on Immanuel Kant, one
can argue that the mature liberal or democratic state manifests three
fundamental characteristics: a representative government with separation of institutions, a political alliance with other democratic
states, and a commitment to essentially private commerce. It is *mature* democratic states, those with these characteristics, that do not
use force inter se, entering security communities where the probability of forcible interaction is zero.[48]

It would follow from this theoretical argument that the political
regimes targeted by U.S. covert action, especially forcible action, did
not meet the threshold conditions for a mature democracy. They may
have been, in Doyle's terminology, "barely participatory."[49] In some
cases they were not fully representational with functioning, separate
institutions of government. Their nonalignment ruled out a political

alliance with the United States and other industrialized democracies. Their reformism or socialism hedged commitment to the principle of extensive private commerce. In sum, the targets of U.S. covert action qualified, to quote Doyle, as "weak, non-liberal states,"[50] although they manifested *some* aspects of democracy (namely, some practice of civil and political rights).

There is a further theoretical point, hinging on institutions and procedures rather than democratic norms. According to some neo-Kantian thought, one reason democratic states do not make war inter se is that representational decision making is not apt to lead to a vote for a war likely to bring great destruction on the people. There is, supposedly, the phenomenon of "democratic caution."[51]

But when we come to covert forcible action, the decisions are not taken in the open, are not subject to the full range of checks and balances and popular participation. And in the cases reviewed here, there was no realistic prospect that U.S. covert forcible action would lead to large numbers of American casualties. Democratic assumptions about open decision making and popular desires to avoid the human and other costs of war do not affect secretive decisions entailing low-level violence carried out by mostly foreign personnel.

In sum, whether one relies on explanations stemming from (1) the cold war, (2) an American informal ideology, or (3) a theory of democratic foreign policy, there is considerable complexity involved in the U.S. record. In particular, there is room for debate over what constitutes a weak and reformist government and even over whether an elected government reflects commitment to democratic rights. Were the elected governments of Indonesia, Ecuador, and Costa Rica, discussed above, really reformist? Were Sukarno, Allende, and Ortega, all of whom were elected at one time or another, fully or genuinely committed to civil and political rights?

Yet one can still conclude that a considerable implementation of human rights, specifically civil and political rights, did not preclude the threat, use, or support of covert violence by the United States against certain elected governments. Foreign attention to socioeconomic rights certainly increased U.S. suspicions about communism during the cold war, feeding into a greatly expanded conception of what was necessary in the name of U.S. national security.

It is noteworthy that the Bush administration, by 1991–92, took a serious interest in civil and political rights in black Haiti—*and* had thrown its support to a Communist politician as a compromise choice in order to break a deadlock between a military government and the deposed leftist but non-Marxist elected president. This policy is certainly an aberration from the traditional pattern, noted above, of disregarding human rights, especially in the Western Hemisphere and especially in states with reformist governments. But by 1991–92, the cold war was over, and indeed the Soviet Union had disintegrated.

At this juncture, it is not clear what the record shows about other democracies and their covert foreign policy. In one well-publicized case in 1985, covert agents of democratic France used force against the environmentalist group Greenpeace in democratic New Zealand. But this violent intervention was not directed against New Zealand per se. Research has thus far failed to uncover other examples of democratic covert violence against elected governments, with the exception of the British support for the overthrow of Mossadeq.

Possibly democracies besides the United States have not seen themselves as putatively strong enough to undertake covert "war" against other democracies in contemporary times. During the cold war, democracies may have looked to the United States to take the lead on these issues. In an earlier era, by comparison, the British removed all sorts of elected councils in their colonies when such bodies proved troublesome. The elected nature of these bodies did not restrain superior British power. These councils, however, were not governments speaking for states, and thus the ideas of state sovereignty and national self-determination, much less a democratic community, did not apply.

In the final analysis, if we should pay more attention to the absence of war among mature democracies, we should also note that covert "war" has occurred with some regularity between a powerful democracy and some elected governments. Considerable practice of civil and political rights is not a barrier to international violence. This is true not just for relations between democracies and authoritarians but also for relations between powerful democracies and some genuinely elected governments.

PART TWO

3

Human Rights and Domestic War: A Framework

Thus far we have shown something about human rights and international peace. The implementation of civil and political rights is one, but only one, of several factors that have led to a reduction of overt international war among great powers (other factors being industrial development and moral opprobrium, the latter probably stemming partly from the experience of war itself). But the implementation of civil and political rights does not always prevent covert international "war" between democracies. The United States in particular has covertly intervened, more than once with force, in opposition to democratic governments and/or their policies. And serious attention to socioeconomic rights helped trigger such covert international "wars" by the United States during the cold war, as shown by events in Guatemala and Chile, for example. I now want to pose the question: can we say anything about human rights and domestic peace?

Does the implementation of civil and political rights forestall or encourage violent revolution? Or does the result of serious attention to these rights vary with the national political culture and/or a particular national situation in time? What is the effect of implementing, or ignoring, economic and social rights? In sum, can we say anything about internationally recognized human rights and relatively large-scale violence within states?

CLARIFYING BASIC IDEAS

This concern for the effect of human rights, or the lack of human rights, in relation to domestic peace leads us to a very large literature. Numerous observers have probed the subjects of revolution, internal war, civil violence, and related organizing concepts. As Thomas H. Greene has noted, we have many studies of "revolution, internal war, internal disturbance, civil war, anticolonial war, war of independence, guerrilla warfare, rebellion, revolt, insurrection, riot, coup d'etat, palace revolution, *jacquerie* or peasant revolt (peasant rebellion?), general strike, turmoil, uprising, mutiny, terrorism."[1] Robert Darnton remarked that there are differing conceptions of domestic revolution, "a phenomenon that historians and political scientists have given a going-over."[2]

To inquire into the role of human rights factors in domestic peace, I look at the other side of the coin. I focus on political revolutions, especially those of a violent nature. Some of these political revolutions reach the stage of internal armed conflict, with not only considerable mass mobilization but also relatively large-scale fighting and rebel holding of territory within a state. Thus my concept of "domestic war" includes both violent political revolution and the classic civil war. But just as there is some disagreement over what is an international war or armed conflict, and just as there is some disagreement over what is a democracy and what constitutes covert intervention against it, so there is ambiguity over precisely what is a domestic violent revolution.

A political revolution consists of rapid change in the governing arrangements of a state. I distinguish a coup from a political revolution on the basis of scope of change. A coup refers to a change in governing personnel without a change in the overall system of governing arrangements. Saddam Hussein overthrew Ahmed Hassan al-Bakr in 1978, but the Iraqi political system was not structurally (meaning fundamentally) altered. A coup may or may not lead to a political (and social) revolution. A political revolution may be effectuated by a larger or smaller number of participants. One type of interesting political revolution is that attempted by masses of people who have been deferential to authority and who become participants in an effort at rapid and extensive change. Political revolutions so defined can be peaceful or violent; I am primarily concerned with the latter but must pay some attention to the former to clarify analysis. The central concern remains:

when there is violent political revolution within a state, sometimes leading to internal armed conflict, can we generalize about the role of internationally recognized human rights in that situation?

My approach reflects a modification of the core conception of political revolution used by Samuel P. Huntington in his *Political Order in Changing Societies:* "A revolution is a rapid, fundamental, and violent domestic change in the dominant values and myths of a society, in its political institutions, social structure, leadership, and government activity and policies."[3] My conception encompasses less.

There can be a political revolution without a social revolution. Corazon Aquino replaced Ferdinand Marcos and made all sorts of institutional changes in the governing arrangements of the Filipino political system. Yet a social system of corruption, and of inequitable landholdings and income distribution, remains essentially unchanged. The Brazilian and Thai militaries engendered sweeping changes in political personnel and institutions. Yet after a considerable time, the social structures of these nations remain fundamentally the same. There can be a genuine political revolution, but the overall social structure of the national society can remain basically the same. Yet this is not to deny that on many occasions, political revolution does lead to social revolution, as in Cuba when Fidel Castro replaced Fulgencio Batista y Zaldívar or in Iran when Ayatollah Khomeini replaced the shah. Nevertheless, a political revolution is not the same as either a coup or a social revolution.

Political revolutions can be peaceful or violent; the central feature is rapid and extensive change of a governing system. There was minimal violence in Miloš Jakeš's Czechoslovakia and Marcos's Philippines, yet the old political system was swept away in both instances. Rapid changes in political institutions characterized both states. A genuine political revolution occurred despite the absence of general or concentrated violence. Huntington has overstated the role of violence, although it is present in many revolutions. In this study, I focus on violent revolutions, but that should not obscure the fact that peaceful political revolutions do, sometimes, occur.

I am not directly interested in whether a political revolution leads to a social revolution, but I am interested in social factors that contribute to political revolutions. Thus my primary concern is not to analyze whether a change of governing arrangements leads to a change in national mythology-ideology and a shuffling of class hierarchy. My primary concern is whether rapid and violent change in governmental institutions is stimulated by certain social situations.

Finally, there can be chronic violence, and hence no real peace, in a polity yet no real political (or social) revolution either. Some societies, particularly those characterized by several ethnic groups, may engage in protracted if intermittent violence without effecting a rapid or extensive change in governing arrangements. There is micro-instability within macro-stability. The political system continues to endure, learning to tolerate and contain inconclusive violent revolt. Thus there can be attempts at political (and social) revolution, without producing rapid and extensive change in governing arrangements. Northern Ireland, Turkey, and Myanmar, inter alia, might fit this description at various times.

IN SEARCH OF THEORY?

If we consider political revolutions in broad perspective, allowing for differing definitions, we do not lack for theoretical overviews.[4] There have been many studies of revolutionary change in a nation at large and what this means for the polity in question. One overview, no doubt nondefinitive, would find at least seven *types* of theories of revolution, broadly conceived: historical, Marxist, sociopsychological, systems, modernization, structural-social, and eclectic. Some of the prominent writers associated with each type are Crane Brinton (historical), Karl Marx (Marxist, logically enough), Ted Robert Gurr (first, socialpsychological; later, perhaps eclectic), Charles Tilly (systems), Huntington (modernization), Theda Skocpol (structural-social), and Jack A. Goldstone (eclectic).[5] The proliferation of studies of internal revolution has led Matthew S. Shugart to speak of *generations* of studies: first, descriptive; second, motivational; and last, social-structural.[6] But a 1991 study of recent revolutions would not seem to fit completely in any of those three categories.[7]

Had one of these approaches proven compelling, we would not confront so many alternative choices. In this part of social science, as in so many others, we would do well at the outset of inquiry to acknowledge the improbability of a rigorous theory acceptable to most. As Greene concluded in his 1990 study: "It is difficult to avoid the conclusion that what is at issue between the various 'theories' of revolution is *not fact* but *a point of view.* This in itself suggests that a *theory* of revolution, anchored as it must be in fact, is unlikely, improbable, beyond our reach."[8] Likewise James B. Rule, in his 1988 study of civil violence, concluded: "All [theories of civil violence] fall distinctly short of the rigorous requirements of accounting for variation in civil violence whenever and wherever it occurs. . . . The idea that there must exist underlying causes of civil violence *in general*—or invariant characteristics of its participants, organization, or settings—deserves much skepticism."[9] As Lucian W. Pye observed in 1966, "The character of any insurrection is largely determined by the peculiar social structure and pattern of political relationships of the society in which it takes place."[10] Darnton referred to the difficulty of obtaining agreement on the reasons for revolutionary change even in one nation. He wrote in 1990, apropos of changes in what was then East Germany, "The erosion of the power structure, a mysterious and invisible process, probably had begun long before 1989."[11]

This skepticism about general and precise theories of similar but disparate events is reinforced by reflection on contemporary events. The assassination of Benigno Aquino in the Philippines played a large role in the mostly peaceful political revolution leading to the downfall of Ferdinand Marcos. Police brutality against peaceful student protesters in Prague roused Czechoslovaks to throw off a Stalinist regime. Indiscriminate violence by the Nicaraguan National Guard under Somoza broadened the appeal of the then-small Sandinista revolutionaries. Different events in different countries greatly influenced contemporary political revolutions.

This is not to say that it will prove impossible to arrive at any generalizations about internal violence and political revolution. Indeed, the examples in the paragraph above suggest an inquiry into the possibly central role of repression in accelerating revolution. In this chapter I will develop an argument in behalf of a general understanding of violent political revolution. But that argument will be more of a typology of preconditions than a fully developed theory. The actual triggers and particular processes of revolutionary behavior vary from case to case. Ernst Haas has shown, with reference to international organization, that a typology of possible changes can stimulate thinking and help organize thought, even if the analysis does not add up to rigorous theory capable of prediction.[12]

In all extant studies of revolution, insurrection, civil violence, or revolt there is little emphasis on human rights as a separate and identifiable subject matter. Some of the works on revolution give passing attention to what are, in substance, rights issues, such as the severity of governmental repression. But by and large the myriad attempts to understand political revolution have not seen human rights as an important causal variable worthy of extended analysis. This is partially, or at times, incorrect, as I will show. Hence I add new perspectives to the subject of domestic peace (and war).

In the following discussion, I separate the sources of governmental stability into six domestic and three international sources of legitimacy. There is nothing magical about the categories, particularly those for domestic sources. One might want to combine several of them. But I believe it aids understanding to employ initially more rather than less categories, for the sake of clarity of exposition.

PRECONDITIONS: TWO LEVELS

In explaining revolutions, one needs to comprehend both national and international factors.[13] At both "levels of analysis,"[14] I submit, the central issue is the legitimacy of governing arrangements. By *legitimacy*, I mean the rightness or correctness of rule. This is the same meaning employed by Gurr when he wrote that legitimacy referred to "people's acceptance of rulers' right to make binding decisions."[15] When political revolution occurs, it does so because the established government undergoes a crisis of legitimacy.[16] The most important problem in understanding a legitimacy crisis is that different participants in the political process may hold differing views of legitimacy and may exercise varying influence. But even other authors who do not initially focus on political legitimacy return time and again to that key concept.[17]

Domestically, there are six sources of legitimacy. Human rights factors are involved in several of these. Internationally, there are three sources of legitimacy. One of these pertains to human rights. If the established government is successful in producing a widespread sense of legitimacy from one or more of these sources, its rule will be stable— that is, it will not face significant domestic revolution (although it could be attacked from abroad). Conversely, if those who would rebel can play on the absence or weakness of legitimacy from these sources, and can generate the expectation that the rebels' rule will fill the void(s), attempted revolution will probably not only occur but also succeed. Unfortunately for the quest for prediction, different governments combine different sources of legitimacy. Likewise, rebels are motivated by differing views on legitimacy.

A full-blown theory of political revolution, including the subsidiary concern for human rights and domestic peace, would be able to specify exactly what amount of legitimacy sprang from each source, for a given situation. Social science is not able to produce such a rigorous theory now—and possibly never will. It remains useful to have a preliminary typology, telling us what factors to look for, even if the interplay of factors varies from case to case.

Domestic Legitimacy

There are six sources of domestic legitimacy: legal, moral, historical, ideological, personal, and functional.

1. Governing arrangements are legitimate from the legal point of view if they are in keeping with the provisions of the national constitution. Insofar as ruling authorities conform to widespread expectations about proper legal procedure, they cultivate an important sense of legitimacy from legal sources. Max Weber referred to this process as one of rational legitimacy.[18]

It should be noted, however, that governments following legally approved procedures may become targets of revolutionary attempts if they fail to generate other sources of legitimacy. In particular, should they prove ineffective in solving the problems confronting society (a functional source of legitimacy), they may behave in perfectly acceptable procedural ways and yet still fail to generate the necessary support to continue governing. Certain democratic governments, particularly in South America but also elsewhere, have been overthrown not just by a military clique but by military forces operating with widespread, if sometimes passive, civilian support because of the failure of the democratic government to solve perceived problems. Nevertheless, adherence to national law is the proper starting point, if only that, for a discussion of legitimacy.

Rulers who violate their own national laws, as Manuel Noriega did in Panama or as the military leaders did in Myanmar, are widely seen as devoid of legal legitimacy. Rulers who rely on a continuous state of emergency to avoid "normal" constitutional provisions, as has been prevalent from Taiwan to South America, run the risk of the same fate. Some rulers, however, such as Muhammad Mubarak in Egypt, continue to rule by exceptional decree (a "state of emergency" legally existed in Egypt from 1981 until the time of writing) and violate national law, including laws on human rights (torture is a systematic practice in Egypt, according to Amnesty International). Such cases of governmental longevity despite violation of "normal" national law suggest that other sources of legitimacy are at play.

It should be noted that most national constitutions contain provisions on human rights. Much more will be said about this below; for now it suffices to observe that this situation reflects the extent to which moral judgments have been incorporated into fundamental laws.

2. Governing arrangements are legitimate from the moral point of view if they conform to widely held views on *national* political morality. This is an amorphous source of legitimacy, difficult to specify for time and place. The complexity of the subject may be represented by the fact that although most constitutions present a democratic facade, reflecting one view of political morality, actual rule may violate the civil and political rights enshrined in the fundamental law. This situation may go uncontested if large numbers of citizens regard authoritarian rule, and hence violation of many political and civil rights, as moral in context, regardless of what the constitution may imply about the primacy of democratic values. This was the situation in Taiwan, for example, from the 1950s to the 1980s.

Social scientists have not been very successful at specifying the political culture that engenders the political morality supportive of civil and political rights, although there has been much talk of a "civic culture" supportive of democracy. Part of the difficulty may be that a nation, or for that matter several nations within a state, may manifest different moral values; both the values themselves and the power ratio among citizens may be in a state of flux.[19] Thus a dominant notion of morality, and the underpinnings of dominance, may be difficult to specify.

The central point to be made in this part of our discussion is that regardless of laws, in some states persons revolt on the basis of indignation over moral injustice. The Filipino constitution, like most others, may legally permit exceptional rule of an authoritarian nature. At a certain point in time, a large number of people, or those uncommonly influential, may challenge that authoritarian rule, whether or not it is legally sanctified. It is well known that there is no necessary correlation between law and morality. It is also well known that most revolutions are justified by their supporters in terms of an appeal to a higher "law" of morality, since revolution, by definition, is illegal.

Despite all the difficulties involved in understanding national political morality, any understanding of revolution must try to account for differences between, say, Poles and Russians (by Russians, I refer to residents of the Russian Republic, the historical center of the defunct Soviet empire). Over considerable time, the Russians have been much more deferential to authoritarian rule; their sense of political morality insists less than some others on the implementation of civil and political rights. At the same time, one must be alert to the possibility that a people with a tradition of deference can become assertive; the examples of many Russians and many Algerians during 1991 are illustrative.

I develop the argument below that *international* sources of moral legitimacy, based on human rights standards, are becoming more important than in the past as a standardizing factor, across cultures, in evaluations of domestic political morality.

3. A dominant political culture entailing a view of political morality is usually affected by history. Governing arrangements may be widely viewed as legitimate (or not) because of history. Or history may strongly influence controlling views of morality. The Dalai Lama maintains a large following in Tibet not because of his winning a free and fair election but because of historical custom. Custom may become inextricably linked with political morality. The dominant view of political morality in Tibet is strongly affected by this custom. In other situations, at a given point in time the dominant view of political morality may be less historical, representing a break with tradition.

Being from the "right" social class or hierarchy, historically speaking, is an increasingly unstable source of legitimacy, given the rapidity of social change as well as the professed values in the interconnected world of the twentieth century. Hereditary or other traditional claim to rule is increasingly under attack in a twentieth century associated with ideas of equality and human rights. It is not clear, for example, whether reigning monarchs like Hassan of Morocco or Hussein of Jordan continue primarily because they are widely seen as the "rightful" hereditary ruler or because they effectively suppress challenges to their rule. (I discuss below situations of stability without legitimacy.) There are governing arrangements, especially in the non-Western world, whose legitimacy stems in important if partial ways from tradition. But these arrangements are increasingly unstable. The traditional political culture emphasizing authoritarian rule is increasingly challenged by contemporary values of political morality.

On the other hand, it bears recalling that even in polities like the United Kingdom that depend primarily on legal sources of legitimacy and that incorporate a widely accepted view of political morality—namely, democracy—historical sources of legitimacy play a role. There is not only the continuation of the monarchy, which lends added legitimacy, as does the emperor in Japan. There is also the phenomenon of blue-collar workers in Britain often voting Tory because they see the Tory party as associated with the "proper" governing class. For such voters, legitimacy comes in part from history. But that is not true for other British citizens.

The point to be stressed is that governing arrangements combining legal and moral sources of legitimacy that have been widely accepted historically are more durable than those lacking this tripartite combination. In most Western societies, adherence to the national constitution, with its component of human rights provisions, has become part of tradition. This can be contrasted with the modern constitutional authority in most non-Western states (and now in states newly liberated from the formal and informal Soviet empire), where modern state building, especially those efforts involving human rights, runs counter to the dominant tradition. This situation lays a foundation, or generates the potential, for political instability. And political instability can become violent revolution.

4. Closely linked to the moral and historical is the ideological source of legitimacy. Some governing arrangements endure for considerable time because they fit with a more or less formal set of ideas. Such ideas can be religious or secular. Again, the relationship with political morality and historical custom is very close.

For example, conformity to Islam, or to Catholicism in Latin America, can lend legitimacy to a ruler or government. Receiving the blessings of the priestly class, or at least avoiding its criticism, can affect legitimacy. This is understood by some secular leaders who face challenges from traditional religious circles. Anwar Sadat, for example, made sure he observed, and was seen to observe, Islamic religious rituals in public, even though he was a secular politician. Ruling elites in theocracies like Saudi Arabia and Iran, in particular, were heavily dependent for their legitimacy on the endorsement of the traditional ulemas. Especially for those states rejecting separation of church and state, state conformity to church principles is an important source of legitimacy. Where that separation is declared but not well established, the potential for political instability is high. In the 1990s, Algeria faced major difficulties in part because secular authorities failed to pacify Islamic fundamentalists and vice versa.

On the secular side, some version of Marxism served for a time as a major source of legitimacy for those rulers who claimed to know where the bus of history was headed and who therefore rejected any need for competitive electoral consultation with the proletariat (or any other class). Indeed, the party elite considered itself above state law, the latter being violated systematically. Marxism-Leninism called for the masses to submit to the avant-garde *party* dictatorship, which claimed "scientific" knowledge of how to achieve a classless society without exploitation. This constituted an important source of legitimacy, perhaps the principal source, as long as large or powerful sectors of society believed in the ideology. But reliance only on Marxism was a serious weakness in these regimes when large or important sectors of society no longer genuinely believed the dogma (as compared to formally professing "faith" for reasons of opportunism).

Nationalism too may be considered an ideology that confers legitimacy, although its workings, like social phenomena, vary with time and place. In the 1990s, appeals to nationalism generated legitimacy in much of the world, including in the United States, where many politicians tended to substitute flag waving for substantive debate. The most pervasive and enduring ideology for some three hundred years has been nationalism. Especially as a substitute for other sources of legitimacy, appeal to nationalism has been emphasized as a last resort of rulers seeking to engender support.

This was particularly true of Stalin during the crisis of World War II, when calls for defense of "Mother Russia" (a euphemism for the Russian empire) supplanted appeals to Marxism-Leninism. Similarly, appeals to "Islam" or "Pan-Arabism" may be facades for Iranian, Iraqi, or Egyptian nationalism. For Hussein, in Iraq, wrapping himself in the mantle of nationalism and its concomitant anti-imperialism was the dictator's main source of legitimacy, aside from attempts to build a personality cult (discussed below) and a calculated appeal to Islam despite the well-known secular nature of his regime. But in Western Europe, appeals to a strident and absolute nationalism were widely regarded as an anachronism, helping to delegitimize the rule of Margaret Thatcher in particular. (The situation was complex because British nationalism at the time of the war with Argentina over the Falkland Islands helped reelect Mrs. Thatcher. Later, however, her nationalism seemed out of step with public opinion, and she was replaced as head of the Conservative party by John Major.)

Nationalism, like other sources of legitimacy, can be elusive. Was there really a greater Soviet nationalism helping to legitimize the central government in Moscow, or were there only nationalisms on behalf of the several republics coexisting under the Soviet flag? Was there really a Yugoslav nationalism, helping to legitimize the central government in Belgrade, or only various nationalisms such as Serbian and Croatian? These are precisely some of the questions to raise in order to understand at least some of the preconditions for revolution in the Soviet Union and Yugoslavia in 1991. Similar questions were crucial for the future of a number of non-Western governments, especially in Africa but also in Lebanon. If there is weak or nonexistent nationalism on behalf of the central government, to which there might be an appeal for legitimacy, the probability of internal revolution increases. But other sources of legitimacy must be addressed.

Ideological sources of legitimacy, the historical ones, may have little to do with legal and human rights standards. Governmental conformity to Islam, Marxism, or nationalism may be used to bypass adherence to all sorts of laws, including individual human rights standards, because of an overriding concern for "piety," social revolution, or the national collective good.

In sum, correctness of governmental rule is affected, beyond legal factors, by a closely related series of moral, historical, and ideological factors difficult to fully separate. Perhaps this is why many political scientists prefer the composite notion of "political culture." Still, I find it useful to discuss these factors separately, even if they have to be combined in later analyses.

5. The personal, or charismatic, source of legitimacy is well known to various theorists. A Castro, a Tito, a Mao Tse-tung, or a Charles de Gaulle may engender a sense of correct rule because of personal standing in contemporary history. The idea of the "man on horseback" who saves the nation from some crisis is well known in traditional Hispanic political culture. Charisma can be a potent source of legitimacy when combined with other sources. The cult of personality orchestrated by Mao was combined with appeals to Marxism, as was true of Castro and some other Communist leaders. The cult of personality engendered by Kwame Nkrumah of Ghana was combined with both nationalism and history (that is, the tribal chief). Even in the industrialized democracies, which depend primarily on legal sources of legitimacy centering on constitutional procedures, the personal charisma of a de Gaulle or a Franklin Roosevelt may supplement legal legitimacy.

Despite assertions that many people long for strong and personalized leadership, possibly to compensate for mass insecurity, charismatic leadership can also be an unstable source of legitimacy, especially if other sources of legitimacy are largely absent.[20] National constitutions (and increasingly international law) usually mandate elections and other checks on personal power. Thus charismatic legitimacy, like authoritarian social custom, is increasingly in tension with legal developments of the twentieth century. Personalized leadership that fails to solve national problems is especially vulnerable to revolution, especially if repression fails to produce deference. Not only Mao and Nkrumah but also Ceausescu in Romania and Mobutu in Zaire (among others) saw their personal legitimacy erode over time.

6. Functional sources of legitimacy related to governmental performance are as important as they are difficult to analyze with precision.[21] In some situations, the ruling group's ability to solve problems generates a widespread sense that the rule is correct. Positive performance generates a de facto legitimacy, despite—in some cases—the absence of most legal sources of legitimacy. Functional sources can be combined with historical, ideological, and personal sources. The process can best be understood in the form of a null hypothesis.

Even if a government has legal legitimacy, if it cannot solve pressing problems it may yield to revolutionary forces. One can think of governments under the Weimar Republic of Germany in the interwar years, whose democratic constitution did not lead to management of major economic and social problems. One can also think of several elected governments in Nigeria or Turkey, whose democratic constitutions and procedures did not endure because of real or imagined failures in problem solving. In Mikhail Gorbachev's Soviet Union and Boris Yeltsin's Russia, some saw even Stalin's rule as more correct, because at least then there was bread in the stores.

In several Western Hemispheric countries, such as Chile and Uruguay, military revolution was supported by large segments of society, at least for a time, because of governmental success in controlling inflation and reducing unemployment, in addition to restoring order if not law. Even if the absence of a democratic constitution eventually proved a serious problem, for a number of years the relative success of authoritarian government, by comparison with the previous civilian government, in problem solving generated some legitimacy. In Augusto Pinochet's Chile, for example, some success in problem solving was combined with appeals to nationalism and the personal charisma

of the general himself. The result, at one point, was a national plebi-
scite endorsing his authoritarian rule. Temporary legitimacy was
achieved by that government, in the eyes of many Chileans, largely because of governmental performance.

One study argues very strongly that democracy, meaning the broad
implementation of civil and political rights, will prove stable only if
there is serious attention to economic and social rights, meaning the
pursuit of balanced development.[22] In this view, a democratic government that functions to achieve equity in socioeconomic terms clearly
has a better chance of avoiding "domestic war." Presumably, there are
differing national standards concerning what qualifies as equitable or
balanced development.

Governmental success in problem solving may produce deference
without generating real legitimacy. This may have been the case in
some of the European Communist systems from 1947 to 1989. In
Czechoslovakia and the German Democratic Republic, for example,
socioeconomic success (relative to other European Communist systems) no doubt made some contribution to the continuation of those
regimes. But the political revolutions of 1989 showed that for most citizens of those countries, the party-state apparatus had never achieved
a sense of correctness. It is possible that in nations like Czechoslovakia and East Germany, deference was produced not by the relatively
satisfactory socioeconomic rights (or benefits) but rather by the effective repression of dissidents.

One cannot scientifically determine which government has achieved
a sense of legitimacy, rather than just deference, from problem solving.
The Chilean case shows that the functional source of legitimacy, if
combined with other sources (historical, ideological, or personal) can
help produce stability—at least for a time. In addition, the combination of legal, cultural, and functional sources of legitimacy is a strong
foundation of stable government. There are few, if any, examples of
strictly internal revolution against a government that is law-abiding,
democratic, and effective at solving major problems.

One also should address in further detail the role of governmental
repression, particularly force and detention. As noted, repression can
produce at least deference, even if not positive support and legitimacy.
The effectiveness of repression can allow a government to bypass
questions of legitimacy, at least for a time. Communism in Eastern Europe endured without a sense of legitimacy from most citizens in part
because of effective repression by the Soviet Union and allied Eastern

European governments. Hussein in Iraq and Hafez al-Assad in Syria maintained rule for a considerable time largely through repression, although both made strong appeals to nationalism as an ideological source of legitimacy. (Hussein, essentially a secular leader, did *not* make appeals to Islam before the Kuwaiti crisis of 1990–91.)

On the other hand, ill-timed or indiscriminate governmental repression can facilitate a revolution. I have already cited the examples of the ill-timed assassination of Benigno Aquino in the Philippines and the indiscriminate use of force by Somoza's National Guard in Nicaragua. It may be true that reliance on repression is a weak reed on which to lean over time, since repression deals only with the symptoms and not the causes of discontent. Repression does nothing about the substantive social and economic problems that may give rise to dissent.[23]

There is no scientific way to be prescient about the effects of governmental force and detention against those who do, or might, revolt. Only after the fact, when one sees the effects of repression, can one analyze whether it contributed to the stability or destruction of a government. Obviously, certain repressive governing arrangements have lasted for decades despite the absence of some sources of legitimacy (but with the presence of at least some other sources). The Somoza dynasty ruled largely through repression unadorned by most sources of *domestic* legitimacy. (Important foreign sources are discussed below.) And in some cases, the effect of repression is mixed. The 1961 Sharpeville massacre in the Republic of South Africa had the short-term effect of reinforcing white minority rule; in the long term, it proved a rallying point for the growing strength of revolutionary forces. The 1989 massacre in Tiananmen Square in Beijing had the short-term effect of defusing student protests; in the long term, it further discredited Communist rule in China.

Effective governmental performance in suppressing opposition movements may contribute to stability without legitimacy, but only effective governmental performance in positively solving substantive problems leads to functional legitimacy. Governments ruling largely or significantly by repression, without major sources of legitimacy, run grave dangers when they fail to solve major problems. It should not have been surprising, therefore, that the Greek junta collapsed after the debacle of its Cyprus policy in 1974 or that the Argentine junta did the same after its defeat by Great Britain in the war of the South Atlantic in 1982. These military governments were largely lacking in domestic legal and moral legitimacy. When they suffered a major policy debacle and, in the process, forfeited claims to legitimacy by appeal to nationalism, they were immediately replaced.

It is in the interplay of these six sources of domestic legitimacy that one finds many of the preconditions for governmental stability and, conversely, revolutionary movements. The United States, for example, has combined mostly legal and functional sources of legitimacy, themselves related to perceptions of political morality. U.S. governments have, in general, followed constitutional procedures while coping adequately with various problems. Their adherence over time to concepts of "constitutionalism" and "freedom" reflects an American mainstream definition of morality, however much an outsider or dissident might dote on racism or material inequality. But regarding political stability, it is the dominant *perception* of morality that counts, not reality itself. In this sense, the prevalent myth of Americans as an exceptionally good people, with a government reflecting that goodness, does much to stabilize a society actually characterized by considerable discrimination and material inequality.

Since 1865, those few who have occasionally revolted have largely been those who have been left out of socioeconomic benefits and who feel that the constitutional system is impervious to their concerns. Legal, moral, historical, and functional sources of legitimacy explain, in general terms, the absence of revolution in the United States since the Civil War. The personal source of legitimacy has been highly marginal, and the ideological has been important only in the sense that American political morality can be said to connote an *informal* ideology.

On the other side of the coin, revolutionary situations entail the absence or weakness of one or more sources of domestic legitimacy. In Iran before 1979, the shah's authoritarian rule and gross violations of human rights such as freedom from torture delegitimized his rule in the eyes of some. Secular critics therefore denied his regime legal and moral legitimacy. Ideologues arrived at the same conclusion via a different path. The ulemas increasingly withheld their religious blessings from his secular government, whereas his close association with the United States undercut effective appeal to Iranian nationalism. Loss of historical legitimacy, linked to nationalism, stemmed from the fact, widely appreciated in Tehran, that the monarchy had been restored only through the machinations of the U.S. Central Intelligence Agency, cooperating with British imperialism, in 1953.

These lacunae were not filled with efforts to develop a personality cult around the somewhat reclusive, indecisive, and paranoid shah. And much of the wealth of the country, generated from oil, was not allowed to trickle down in great amounts to those frequenting the mosques and bazaars, where the anti-shah revolution was generated. Problem solving, or functional legitimacy, was not widely attributed to the shah's regime.

It was out of this situation that a successful revolutionary movement developed, with different challenges focusing on different aspects of legitimacy. The constitutionalists, such as Mehdi Bazargan, focused on law and human rights. The fundamentalists, such as Khomeini, focused on Islam. Both groups appealed to Iranian nationalism and anti-imperialism. Khomeini combined the elements of charismatic and religious leadership, both aspects lacking in the secular, moderate leaders, like Shapour Bakhtiar, who helped make the revolution.

In short, the Iranian revolutionaries captured most of the symbols of legitimacy, or they proved successful in generating legitimacy for their movement from varying sources—mostly moral and ideological (Islam and nationalism). The shah was vulnerable because of his lack of moral and ideological sources of legitimacy and because of his weakness in personal and functional sources. Ultimately, the prospect of effective repression melted away as the army fragmented. In this case, as in many others in contemporary times, important international factors were also at work.

International Legitimacy

There are three main sources of international legitimacy: legal, moral, and political. These interact with the domestic sources noted above in an untidy mix. Historically, the domestic have been more important than the international. This ratio seems to be undergoing some change, at least for some situations, because of the growing interdependence of states. Or in *relative* terms, international sources of legitimacy are increasing in importance, at least in some situations.

1. If elites who would rule are accepted by other established elites, a source of legitimacy is established. This international process is somewhat complicated, for it entails four distinct segments: unilateral recognition of states, unilateral recognition of governments, admission of states to intergovernmental organizations, and acceptance of governmental credentials within intergovernmental organizations.

When elites claiming to represent the state of Biafra during the Nigerian civil war of 1967–70 were recognized by only four established states and gained no admittance to intergovernmental organizations (IGOs), their claims to legitimacy as ruling authorities were undercut. Conversely, when Communist elites in China gained representation as the rightful governmental delegation in the United Nations in 1971 and were extended unilateral recognition by the United States in 1979, their legitimacy increased. Ambiguous situations exist. The state of Palestine was declared, with a government in exile, and was recognized by many governments (except for powerful Western ones), but it did not receive immediate membership in IGOs like the United Nations and the World Health Organization.

Political elites understand well the significance of this complicated international source of legal legitimacy, going to great lengths to either obtain international legal acceptance in its several forms or avoid losing the international legal acceptance already acquired. Israel struggled hard not to be barred from the United Nations General Assembly, as South Africa was. This was a question of governmental credentials within an intergovernmental organization. Rebel groups in civil wars have maneuvered to secure some sort of international legal acceptance, even if short of formal recognition and membership in IGOs. The Zimbabwean Patriotic Front, when fighting Ian Smith's government in British Rhodesia from the mid-1960s to the late 1970s, pledged adherence to the Geneva Conventions for victims of war in order to seek some sort of international legal acceptance by Switzerland, the depository state for the conventions. The "State of Palestine" did the same.

Although political elites are sensitive to international legal sources of legitimacy, it remains doubtful whether the masses in a given state pay much attention to this factor.

2. Increasingly, the implementation of internationally recognized human rights is a source of legitimacy. The reverse situation is also important. Ruling elites that do not implement internationally recognized human rights run a serious risk of losing legitimacy in the eyes of important political actors, even if they maintain other sources of legitimacy, domestic and international.

Elites that rule under authoritarian constitutions, that institutionalize "exceptional" authoritarian clauses, that torture, or that discriminate on grounds of race forfeit an increasingly important source of legitimacy. The traditional rulers of Kuwait, despite effective sources of domestic legitimacy, despite legal recognition by all other states, and despite membership in the United Nations and the Arab League, were challenged by certain members of Congress because of their authoritarian nature. Although the al-Sabah family failed to implement civil and political rights to any significant degree, that family was apparently still seen as legitimate by most Kuwaitis themselves. But when U.S. President George Bush spoke of restoring the legitimate government of Kuwait, more than one member of Congress questioned whether the previous authoritarian government was really legitimate. The implicit appeal by these dissenters was to universal standards on civil and political rights.

One of the major problems in granting or withholding international moral legitimacy is the decentralized and fragmented nature of decisions on this question. Different U.N. resolutions, passed by different bodies, emphasize different rights and different violators. Regional human rights bodies add to the static. Numerous private human rights groups, with different emphases and targets, contribute to the confusion. States make pronouncements on human rights while being greatly influenced by expediential interests.

Yet at certain times, for certain states, dealing with certain situations, the record of attention to internationally accepted human rights has been an important factor in governmental stability or in the existence and success of revolutionary movements. Increasingly, a common standard of international morality affects transnational politics. There has been an almost universal acceptance, increasing especially after the European political revolutions of 1985–89, of the 1948 Universal Declaration of Human Rights, listing thirty basic rights. This declaration has been incorporated into many state constitutions and statutes.

International standards of human rights and domestic perceptions of political morality may, in the future, be increasingly difficult to distinguish in an interdependent world. Normative legitimacy may be becoming an intermestic source—both domestic and international at the same time. Insofar as international human rights norms come to standardize considerations of domestic political morality, this would be an important development. In many places around the world this has yet to occur. It is still true, nevertheless, that international views on human rights affect political legitimacy, at least sometimes.

For example, the Carter administration worked hard to remove Anastasio Somoza Debayle from power in Nicaragua in large part because of his atrocious human rights record, and the dictator chose Miami over Managua in part because of a stinging report on his record by the InterAmerican Commission on Human Rights.[24] The lack of international moral legitimacy was a serious problem for Somoza, eventually impacting his domestic power.

3. Political legitimacy on an international scale is sometimes separate from international legal and moral sources. Important U.S. policymakers supported the shah of Iran until the very end of his rule, despite his authoritarianism and torture, because they saw him as playing a legitimate political role—whether as policeman of the Persian Gulf or as container of the Soviet bear. Likewise, U.S. policymakers did not question either authoritarianism or torture in Mubarak's Egypt because of Egypt's moderation in regional and global politics.

Thus, although private human rights groups, such as nongovernmental organizations (NGOs), may raise questions about the right to rule by those violating human rights, decision makers for states, acting on the basis of *raisons d'état*, may consider a government as legitimate because of its contributions to conceptions of the national interest. Different actors use different sources of legitimacy. In addition, the same actor may use different sources in different contexts (note Carter and Somoza, and Carter and the shah).

This last observation leads to a crucial point. The six domestic and three international sources of legitimacy play themselves out in different ways in different situations. This helps to explain the persistent difficulty in forecasting the stability of governments and the success of revolutionary movements. For example, there were substantive reasons that the CIA had such difficulty in forecasting revolution in Iran in 1979. Part of this difficulty stems from the fact that different actors are affected by different sources of legitimacy. Apparently most (but not all) Kuwaitis, as well as President Bush, did not question the legitimacy of the ruling family, whereas a few Kuwaitis and some members of Congress, looking at violations of universal human rights, did. Most attentive Americans did not question the legitimacy of the Mubarak government of Egypt, but some Islamic fundamentalist and secular human rights activists did—for different reasons based on different sources of legitimacy.

What needs to be known, beyond who holds what view of legitimacy, and what cannot always be known in advance, is the amount of power of those who are prone to revolution because of their view that the government is illegitimate. In some ways, observing revolutionary movements is like observing international war. Sometimes one has to fight the war to see who is more powerful. If one knew ahead of time which side was more powerful, there would be little need to fight the war. This is why Geoffrey Blainey argues that war is a dispute about power.[25]

Likewise, if one knew which domestic side was more powerful—the side that saw the established government as legitimate or the one that saw it as illegitimate—one would not need to undertake revolutions. If the government side is weaker, it should resign, since it will lose anyway. If the revolutionary side is weaker, it should not pursue a lost cause, unless it is driven by a martyr complex. This is precisely the point of much governmental repression as well as revolutionary violence: to make the other side's cause seem hopeless.

The combined sources of legitimacy, six domestic and three international, preconditions for both governmental stability and revolution, cannot be applied mechanistically to all situations. They must be analyzed state by state in a political study that considers not only which individual or group holds what view of governmental legitimacy but also which individual or group holds what power. These considerations can be only estimates, not precise and scientific calculations. All sorts of revolutionary movements have triumphed over great odds, from Vladimir Lenin's to Daniel Ortega's, because of mistaken estimates of power. But the starting point is to understand the sources of governmental legitimacy and to identify which actors are affected by which source.

It was only in the playing out of events in Iran in the late 1970s that one could determine the power of Zbigniew Brzezinski, who regarded the shah as legitimate because of his international political role as U.S. ally, and the power of Khomeini, who regarded the shah as illegitimate because of his non-Islamic and essentially non-Iranian nature (e.g., "stooge of the Great Satan"). One could not precisely predict such things as the cohesion of the Iranian army as an instrument of the shah's repression or the effectiveness of the mullahs in mobilizing traditional Islamic sectors. Neither could one scientifically predict whether the secular revolutionaries such as Bazargan and Bakhtiar could outmaneuver the religious revolutionaries such as Khomeini. One had to understand not only which political actor was affected by what view of legitimacy but also who exercised what power. Since actualized power depended on social and psychological phenomena difficult to know in advance, the process did not lend itself to precise prediction.

In the fall of 1990, Henry Kissinger testified in Congress that he feared for the stability of the Saudi government. One could not be scientifically precise about the prospects for domestic revolution in the Saudi kingdom, but one could raise the right questions about preconditions. On the one hand, the Saudi elite had combined mostly domestic historical, ideological, and functional sources of legitimacy to produce its stability, eschewing the legal and the personal. The Saudi government traced its lineage directly to a revered past, was endorsed by the high priests of Wahaba'ism, and was blessed with abundant oil and thus could solve economic problems. It had achieved international legal legitimacy, and much political legitimacy as well.

It remains to be seen whether the absence of much domestic legal legitimacy and, in particular, the almost total absence of international moral legitimacy will generate revolutionary forces. That there was no written constitution in the Saudi kingdom and no pretense of any type of equality seemed not to bother those committed to traditional Islamic values. Presumably Kissinger feared that the introduction of large numbers of Western soldiers into the kingdom, with their ideas of gender equality and other human rights, would lead to domestic unrest. In the fall of 1990, Amnesty International was reporting Saudi torture of expatriate Yemeni workers. Such reports have no effect on the Kissingers of the world, who continue to evaluate the situation in terms of the international political legitimacy of an ally. But the effect of such reports on other political actors might be open to question over time.

The example of Saudi Arabia demonstrates the analytical difficulty of separating ideological and moral factors. Because the traditional version of Islam practiced in the kingdom superseded commitment to civil-political rights—or socioeconomic ones, for that matter—there was not a domestic constituency of any power working in behalf of the political morality of democracy. Although it is difficult to categorize the situation in terms of moral or ideological factors, it is not difficult to understand dominant values. The difficulty was semantical rather than epistemological.

BEYOND PRECONDITIONS

Perhaps in the future it will prove possible to move beyond a typology of preconditions and to analyze with greater predictive ability how the sources of legitimacy from two levels affect probabilities of revolution. To say the least, it would be helpful to know what amount of legitimacy from each source is necessary to produce stabilizing support or acceptance for any given government. I have already indicated my doubts about the development of such a full-blown theory. But perhaps one could develop some insights of a middle-range nature, applying to many, but not all, situations. I certainly would not want to foreclose research on the subject.

One line of inquiry might fruitfully focus on domestic norms, in particular historical sources of legitimacy and what could be called national traditions. Some research seems to show that nations that have experienced violent revolutions in the past are more prone to revolutionary behavior.[26] The hypothesis is that a nation becomes accustomed to revolutionary attacks on established government. These attacks come to acquire a certain acceptability stemming from national history. Concomitantly, many citizens in such a nation manifest a low emphasis on adherence to domestic legal rules, particularly since such rules change frequently. To reduce the incidence of domestic revolutions in this type of situation, one is faced with the difficult task of breaking the cycle of expected and therefore "normal" revolutionary behavior.

Emphasizing domestic political culture and national history would seem to help explain the politics of revolution in many Latin American nations, as well as other nations such as Turkey or Nigeria. Military takeover of civilian governments seems institutionalized in some nations' histories. But this approach does not explain why some nations with a relatively long record of civilian governmental stability undergo, at a particular point in time, political revolution—for example, Chile in 1973. Nor does it explain why junior military officers decide to revolt against a relatively long pattern of military rule by their more senior colleagues—for example, El Salvador in 1979.

Several approaches to understanding revolution focus on what I have termed domestic functional legitimacy, which is linked to governmental performance. It is one thing to talk about the importance of governmental performance in general. It is another thing to specify how much is enough—for example, how much poor performance by a government there must be, or of what kind, or in what situation, for political instability to increase.

It has been asserted that a key factor in many revolutions is the existence of a socioeconomic class or group that has been advancing in society but that is then disappointed in some way.[27] When expectations about benefits, and hence governmental problem solving, suffer a setback, this class either becomes revolutionary or supports revolution by others. This scenario pertains to the J-curve of rising, then falling, expectations. It purports to explain why certain subnational groups become disenchanted with governmental performance, as well as why certain groups not doing well do *not* revolt—that is, they have never manifested rising expectations and do not become disappointed, perhaps believing that their poor condition is immutable.

As with other efforts to specify the probabilities of revolution, this approach would seem to explain the dynamics of some revolutionary situations but not others. In Czechoslovakia in 1989, no particular socioeconomic group had been advancing only to have its hopes unusually dashed. Conversely, some research seems to show that low personal income *is* associated with revolutionary behavior.[28] In this view, poverty itself proves fertile ground for attempted rapid change in governing arrangements, whether or not the element of rising expectations is present.

Still other research focuses on governmental performance in the sense of capacity for concerted and systematic repression.[29] As we have already noted, governmental success in repression can produce stability without legitimacy—at least for a time. Once again, however, specific propositions are difficult to validate.

Indeed, we find that scholars who thought they had presented a valid theory come to second-guess their own work and then suggest the need for still further research.[30] While this is a commendable process of scholarship, it still leaves us without an agreed-upon body of knowledge for understanding the *specific* "laws" of revolutionary political behavior across nations.

CONCLUSIONS

In this chapter I have outlined the argument for a typology of preconditions providing a framework of analysis for understanding political revolution and its converse, governmental stability. Governments that do not face a crisis of legitimacy will not face significant revolutionary challenges. But this may be only a truism unless we can explain why a crisis of legitimacy does or does not develop.

The central problem in understanding political revolution and governmental stability is the inescapable fact that there is no one source of legitimacy. Different actors rely on perhaps nine different sources of legitimacy, whose importance depends on those actors' values and experiences. Domestic sources can be dissected further, although trying to separate moral, historical, and ideological sources creates as many problems as it solves. And once one has identified, as clearly as possible, views toward legitimacy, the question of power remains.

Members of the American Communist party may view the U.S. government as illegitimate because it fails to measure up to the tenets of Marxism; however, the insignificant power of that group makes its views irrelevant to U.S. governmental stability. (For present purposes, it is not necessary to raise the issue of the commitment of the American Communist party to "bourgeois" legal procedures.) In other cases, the relative power of the government and its supporters on the one hand and of a revolutionary movement on the other is not so obvious. In the fall of 1979, it was not at all clear to observers, or to policymakers, whether the shah could outlast his challengers. In 1986, it was not at all clear whether Marcos could be removed as head of the government in the Philippines. In 1991, it was not at all clear whether the Yeltsin government or the Russian Federation, or the Commonwealth of Independent Nations, would endure or be overthrown.

Just as the United States had to fight the American phase of the Vietnam War to see whether Washington or Hanoi could impose its will on the other, so a country may have to experience revolutionary behavior to see whose view of legitimacy prevails domestically. Power is frequently such an elusive phenomenon that its rise and exercise cannot always be subject to precise analysis in advance.

Human rights factors, both nationally and internationally, can at times affect views of governmental legitimacy. Human rights standards are frequently part of national constitutional law and domestic conceptions of political morality. On a different level, human rights standards are now a part of international law and diplomacy, adherence to which is an international source of moral legitimacy. Governments that violate domestic or international standards on human rights run the risk of a crisis of legitimacy. But violative governments have other sources of legitimacy to which they can appeal—for example, domestic ideology such as nationalism, or international sources of legitimacy such as political alignment.

The idea of adherence to international human rights norms as an international source of legitimacy seems to be growing in importance.

Such norms are increasingly used by many actors to evaluate behavior under national constitutions; for instance, even if the national constitution permits "states of emergency" and other exceptional legal states, many actors believe such exceptional conditions should not allow violation of fundamental and universal human rights. The government that violates these norms is not always viewed as legitimate, although it is perhaps acting in conformity with at least some national law. One might recall that Indira Gandhi's national emergency of 1975, though perhaps procedurally correct, led to her repudiation by Indian voters as well as to her extensive criticism abroad. The violation of *universal* human rights standards is, in relative terms, increasingly subject to challenge, whatever national laws might say.

It should also be noted that revolutionary movements that *would* govern are increasingly expected, by some powerful actors, to implement universal human rights standards. The Nicaraguan contras, the Angolan rebels of UNITA and Jonas Savimbi, SWAPO rebels fighting white minority rule in Namibia, and the ANC fighting white minority rule in South Africa all came under some criticism for attacks on civilians and for killing or mistreating prisoners. To further the view that each of these insurgent parties had the right to rule—that is, was legitimate—each took steps to control for, or punish the violators of, human rights standards or at least addressed the subject rhetorically to create the image of doing something about violations. Questions about attacks on civilians split both the Irish Republican Army and various Palestinian organizations.

It must be stressed again that reference to international human rights, or any other source of legitimacy, varies with different actors. The Stalinist Soviet Union did not usually rely on attention to human rights in relation to either domestic or international sources of legitimacy. It sought its own legitimacy primarily in appeals to ideology— either Marxism-Leninism or nationalism. But occasionally it would stress universal human rights for opportunistic and expediential *raisons d'état*—for example, when it supported U.N. monitoring of the human rights situation in Pinochet's Chile. Likewise, although Saddam Hussein sought his own legitimacy mainly in appeals to nationalism and a personality cult, he did not hesitate to emphasize Israeli violations of human rights when that fit with his foreign-policy objectives.

And it must be stressed that understanding sources of legitimacy does not allow us to avoid the perennial problem of understanding power. The question of who has what view of legitimacy only directs us to a second question. For those who regard the government as illegitimate, what power do they have? But this is the proper sequence for understanding governmental stability and revolutionary potential, even if universal theorems still elude us. It is helpful to know that most of the international community and most Kuwaitis regarded the al-Sabah government as legitimate and that those actors held most of the power. Only a weak segment of Kuwaitis, and only a minority of members of the U.S. Congress, regarded that government as illegitimate because of its violations of civil and political rights. (Interjecting the views of Iraq into this equation changes the matter of what power was available to those who questioned the legitimacy of the al-Sabah government, although on the basis of a different argument about legitimacy—namely that the government was illegitimate because the entire state was created by imperialist Britain. Like other Iraqi arguments, this one was fundamentally based on an appeal to nationalism as *the* source of legitimacy.)

All of this leaves us with three fundamental points. First, human rights factors prominently figure in some, but not all, situations characterized by revolutionary behavior. Second, the various and varying sources of legitimacy, including those touching on human rights, that greatly affect governmental stability and revolutionary potential must be analyzed case by case, with an awareness that different actors refer to different sources of legitimacy. Third, views of legitimacy must be combined with an analysis of putative power, and actual power can sometimes be known only after its exercise.

4

Domestic War in Sri Lanka

At first glance, the rise of violent revolutionary behavior or domestic war in Sri Lanka seems perplexing. For decades after independence from the United Kingdom in 1948, the island state of Ceylon, renamed Sri Lanka, was frequently mentioned as the Costa Rica of Asia. Its army was purely ceremonial until the 1970s, marching in parades but manifesting no real fighting capacity. There was, during that same early period, a genuine commitment to political and civil rights. Universal suffrage had existed since 1931, a full seventeen years before independence. From 1948 to 1977, free and fair elections led to a regular change in the political party controlling the government.

Moreover, an extensive welfare state provided relatively generous subsidies for citizens unable to purchase adequate food, shelter, health care, and education. On the Washington-based Overseas Development Council's Physical Quality of Life Index, measuring infant mortality, life expectancy, and literacy, Sri Lanka scored well ahead of Asian neighbors such as India and Pakistan. This scale presumably measures the results of nutrition, health care, and education. These socioeconomic governmental programs were not technically viewed as fundamental human rights that the government was legally obligated to provide, but they were politically permanent in principle—that is, they varied only in the amount spent.

Progressively into the 1970s and even more so during the 1980s Sri Lanka came unglued. Especially from the mid-1980s, security forces increased both brutality in the field and influence in the capital of Colombo; a variety of advisers, nationals of Israel and South Africa, assisted the forces, and officials of the United States served as go-betweens. The political system was increasingly characterized by a blend of democracy and authoritarianism—and at times by gross violations of rights of personal integrity. At times, genocidal attacks and death squad activities were implicitly condoned by the government. Elections and referenda continued to be held, but genuine democracy decreased.

As for socioeconomic matters, according to the World Bank, during 1980–88 the overall Sri Lankan economy (GDP) continued to grow at an annual average rate of 4.3 percent, slightly up from the preceding fifteen years, which is remarkable given the political violence on the island. Defense expenditures increased, as did the national debt, and domestic investment declined, all negative features in the long-term health of the economy. In the 1980s, the Physical Quality of Life Index did not change much for the island as a whole, although life was no doubt more difficult in the Jaffna peninsular and other areas of intense rebel activity.

Great complexity can be captured in the general statement that in the period from 1971 to 1991, two revolutions occurred: one in the north and east by the Sri Lankan Tamil minority and one in the south by radical Sinhalese. India became deeply involved in Sri Lanka politics in an effort to deal with the Tamil revolution, but without decisive results.

The rise of domestic war in Sri Lanka becomes intelligible, at least in hindsight, by focusing on the various sources of state legitimacy, linked to an analysis of power. The absence or weakness of governmental legitimacy stemming from social-ideological and functional sources largely explains both the Tamil and Sinhalese revolutions. Whereas the Sri Lankan government had the power to crush the small but deadly Sinhalese revolution in the south, neither it nor the Indian expeditionary force was able to completely crush Tamil guerrilla fighters in the north. Human rights proved central, particularly to Tamil revolutionary behavior, although in a complex rather than simple way.

THE TAMIL REVOLUTION

Domestic Legitimacy

The Sri Lankan Tamil ethnic minority of Sri Lanka increasingly came to see governing arrangements on the island as illegitimate—that is, incorrect as a system of binding rules and institutions—primarily because of the social history of the area, combined with ethnic nationalism and religion. These social-ideological sources of legitimacy and of its converse, alienation, were intertwined with the issue of governmental performance, especially through policies on language, education, and hydraulic-agricultural development—all of which led to the issue of jobs and who got them. Legal and moral sources of legitimacy were at play as well. Charismatic legitimacy was mostly absent.

The superficial triggering event for widespread Tamil revolutionary behavior occurred on July 26, 1983, when Sinhalese Buddhists went on a genocidal rampage, physically attacking Tamils simply because of their ethnicity. (There had been earlier anti-Tamil riots of a less serious nature, especially in 1977 and 1981.) Mobs from the majority, aided by governmental factions carrying voter registration lists to make identification of Tamils easier, and with no early restraining words or actions from the government, managed in a matter of weeks to kill some 3,000 of the minority, with another 150,000 internally displaced. Some Tamils fled to India. After that event, a larger number of Tamils, whether residing in the north or the east, committed themselves either to a separate Tamil state or to a radically different federal state of Sri Lanka with extensive rights of autonomy for a Tamil province. The politically important group of Tamils residing in the capital of Colombo had been somewhat ambivalent about increased Tamil radicalism, since their positions in the central bureaucracy were at stake. As they were increasingly persecuted, however, they tended to support radical Tamil demands.[1]

Sinhalese nationalists were prone to emphasize that a few Sri Lankan Tamils in the north had been actively pushing for some type of Tamil homeland since the mid-1970s and that immediately preceding the events of July 23, 1983, Tamil rebels had ambushed a governmental patrol made up of Sinhalese Buddhists, killing more than a dozen. Tamils were prone to counter that the Sinhalese-dominated government had already declared a state of emergency in the northern province and was brutally dealing with the local population, raping females and killing Tamil males.[2]

Whatever the immediate causes of the massacre of mid–July 1983 by the Sinhalese Buddhists, after that time most of the various Sri Lankan Tamil elements ceased to regard the unitary state of Sri Lanka as legitimate. Armed insurrection spread throughout the northern and eastern provinces during the rest of the 1980s, spearheaded by the Liberation

Tigers of Tamil Elaam (LTTE)—an armed faction, made up mostly of young northerners, that was fully committed to a separate state. The LTTE fought its Tamil rivals, some of whom were quite strong in the east (the EPRLF), fought an Indian military force as well as the Sri Lankan army to a standstill, and accepted no compromises. Other Tamils, probably most of the Sri Lankan Tamils, entertained the notion of a compromise involving a new federalism with extensive states rights. But they too rejected the legitimacy of a unitary—that is, nonfederal—state.[3]

The violent Tamil revolution of the 1980s, which continued into the 1990s, was rooted in, and explicable by, not just the genocide of 1983 but also, and more fundamentally, a pervasive loss of legitimacy for the unitary state of Sri Lanka, a loss that had been accelerating for almost two decades.

Social-ideological legitimacy. Sri Lankan society is composed primarily of Sinhalese Buddhists, making up more than 70 percent of the population. The dominant strain of Buddhism is a virulent one, with its adherents believing that their version is the purest and most sacred to be found anywhere in Asia. Despite their relatively large numbers, Sinhalese Buddhists are aware of repeated invasions from Dravidian races to the north throughout history; they also manifest some sensitivity about being a Buddhist minority in a region of Hindus. Hence, the overwhelming majority status on the island of the Sinhalese Buddhists has not always produced feelings of security.[4]

Tamil Hindus, by contrast, are a distinct minority, making up less than 20 percent of the Sri Lankan population. They are further divided into two sociopolitical groups. The Sri Lanka Tamils, making up about 12 percent of the total population, are located mainly in the northern and eastern provinces and concentrated in the Jaffna peninsula. The Indian Tamils, about 6 percent of the population, are relatively more recent migrants from southern India and are mostly found on the tea plantations of the eastern region. (Also in the eastern region are Moslems who speak Tamil.)

The Sri Lankan Tamils were full citizens of Sri Lanka from 1948 (and before), were frequently middle class (although most were poor farmers), and were at least initially predisposed to cooperation with the Sinhalese. On the other hand, the Indian Tamils were disenfranchised and denationalized at the time of independence (and thus became stateless, for India did not claim them either) and were mostly common laborers without access to corridors of power in Colombo. Sri Lankan Tamils are proud of their separate kingdoms that existed on the island in the past.

At the time of independence, Sri Lankan politics was characterized above all by a consensus among political elites that the state should be democratic, secular, unitary rather than federal, and multiethnic or pluralistic, with English as the working language of government. The first prime minister, D. S. Senanayake, and his United National Party (UNP), Sinhalese dominated, were committed to these values, as were key Tamil leaders. It seemed that British colonialism had left the island with a legacy of political centrism and moderation. But a more indigenous social history, featuring chauvinistic nationalisms tinged with religion, was to overwhelm this promising start to modern statehood.

The mid-1950s proved crucial. The UNP fragmented, with S.W.R.D. Bandaranaike creating a new party, the Freedom Party (SLFP). The SLFP sought to mobilize the Sinhalese Buddhist masses through appeals to a chauvinistic nationalism. Commentators differ as to whether the primary stimulus to developments was the personal ambition of Bandaranaike, an anti-British sentiment, a genuine ideological fervor, a commitment to mass rather than elitist democracy, a concern for the poor, or some combination of the above. The result, in any event, was that the SLFP won the 1956 general election and moved policies not only further left in socioeconomic terms but also further in the direction of giving the Sinhalese Buddhists political dominance rather than sharing power with the Tamils.[5]

Some said that Bandaranaike was not so much anti-Tamil as he was anti-British and pro–mass democracy. But once he had demonstrated that electoral success could be achieved by appeals to a narrow Sinhalese nationalism linked to Buddhism, the UNP had little recourse but to follow suit if it wished to compete for electoral office in a society overwhelmingly populated by Sinhalese Buddhist voters. When the SLFP was in office and pursued somewhat moderate policies, seen by some as seeking an accommodation with the Tamils, as in the late 1950s, it was attacked by the UNP for selling out majority rule. When the UNP was in office and was seen by some as perhaps being interested in an accommodation with the Tamils, as in the early 1980s, it was attacked by the SLFP for selling out majority rule. Matters worsened in 1972 when the constitution was altered to give formal legal recognition to Buddhism. An act of parliament had made Sinhala the official language in 1956.[6]

From one provocative view, it was mass democracy that led to Tamil revolutionary behavior in Sri Lanka. As long as there was elitist democracy, a transethnic, transreligious consensus held the state together. With the development of mass democracy came an increase in exclusive nationalisms and a quest for greater majority dominance rather than the power-sharing arrangement characterizing 1948–55. From this view, the root cause of political instability was an expansion of political rights. The Sinhalese Buddhist masses did not support a secular and pluralistic state, one with pervasive concern for minority rights—and they voted. Extensive Sinhalese Buddhist literacy did not lead to political tolerance but rather to perceptions of reverse discrimination—namely, that the Sri Lankan Tamil Hindu minority was doing better than the Sinhalese Buddhist majority.

The clear losers in post–1956 developments were the Tamils. The Indian Tamils had always been alienated, having been deprived of both nationality and the franchise in 1948 in a move clearly showing Sinhalese fear of a minority linked, supposedly, to Hindu India. (Many of the Indian Tamils, however, were not recent arrivals, having migrated to Sri Lanka as early as seventy-five years before independence.) But the Indian Tamils, agricultural workers without the vote, had little influence from 1948 through the 1970s. Even in the 1980s, they were not the primary actors in Tamil movements for a homeland.

The Sri Lankan Tamils of the northern province, with both nationality and the franchise, became increasingly alienated after 1956. Their economic and political position in the state eroded, and their efforts to achieve some sort of decentralized or federated state, providing some version of local autonomy, came to naught. There had been, in 1947–48 and after, Sri Lankan Tamils who advocated Tamil Eelam—a Tamil homeland—via either a separate state or a federal scheme with extensive provincial rights. These latter views increased in breadth and depth in direct proportion to the Sinhalese Buddhist push for greater control of the unitary state of Sri Lanka. After 1972 and the constitutional changes in favor of the Sinhalese Buddhists, both peaceful and violent agitation for a Tamil homeland increased, especially in the north.

The social-ideological factors reviewed thus far, principally the emergence of a narrow, exclusive, and chauvinistic Sinhalese Buddhist nationalism, caused the Sri Lankan Tamils to become increasingly alienated from the Sinhalese Buddhist–dominated Sri Lankan unitary state. These same factors fed directly into the related issue of loss of legitimacy for that state, a loss stemming from functional sources—namely, governmental performance.

Functional legitimacy. The Sri Lankan Tamils (as distinct from the Indian Tamils in Sri Lanka) had always done well in finding jobs in the bureaucracy in Colombo, both before and after independence. They had been taught English by American missionaries under British rule, and since English was the language of government, the Tamils had a socioeconomic edge over many Sinhalese who spoke only Sinhala. The harsh geography of the Jaffna peninsular in the north was another factor propelling many Tamils to seek administrative positions. And many Tamils were industrious and achievement-oriented.[7]

As a result of these factors, many Tamils saw a unitary and pluralistic Sri Lanka as no threat to their livelihood, for they had long done well in Colombo. Indeed, some 8 percent of the population of Colombo was Sri Lanka Tamil, which was almost the same proportion they held in the population at large.[8]

Bandaranaike and the SLFP pushed for Sinhala as the language both of education in most of Sri Lanka and of government, directly threatening the economic well-being of a significant part of the Sri Lankan Tamil community. Between 1956 and the violent events of the 1980s, a dual system of education was emphasized (the foundations had been laid during British colonialism), with English being dropped as the preferred language, Sinhala being the language of instruction in most of Sri Lanka, and Tamil being the language of instruction in Tamil areas. A further irritant to the Tamils was the imposition of a quota system for access to higher education; the quotas were designed to increase the numbers of Sinhalese Buddhists in the major universities.

From 1956, Sinhala became the language of the central government under both the UNP and the SLFP, since both were driven by the need to appeal to Sinhalese voters. Thus the Sri Lankan Tamils progressively lost one of their principal economic resources—positions in the state bureaucracy. By the 1980s, Tamil remained the language of education and administration only in the northern province (and in some parts of the eastern province). Sinhala was the official language for education and administration elsewhere, including, and most important, in the bureaucracy in Colombo.[9] The central government also did business in Sinhala in the Tamil areas, an irritant to the Tamils. Much English continued to be used in Colombo, but the official language was Sinhala. From the point of view of many Sinhalese, these developments only reflected majority politics in a nation that was more than 70 percent Sinhalese. The majority, or at least a significant part of it, had long regarded the Sri Lanka Tamils as having undue influence in the bureaucracy because of events associated with colonialism. Thus Sinhalese Buddhist nationalism fed directly into a governmental language policy conducive to more state jobs for Sinhalese who spoke Sinhala. For much of the majority (but not all), the state increased its legitimacy via providing more economic benefits. But this majority was little concerned with the negative impact of the language policy on the Tamil minority.

Whether one conceives of these linguistic developments as involving civil or cultural rights, the result was the same. The Sri Lankan Tamils saw fewer reasons to abide by the laws of a state that disappointed their economic expectations. They had done well in the past via the English language. The adoption of only Sinhala in official Colombo removed one of their primary reasons for allegiance to the state. Here was a case of rising Tamil expectations under both the British and the first UNP government, then the disappointing of these expectations after 1956 and increasingly during the 1970s.

Whereas other multilingual states, like Belgium and Switzerland, had proved stable and prosperous over considerable time, they had achieved that status through careful governmental attention to some sort of mutually acceptable distribution of authority, rights, and benefits among the linguistic groups. Sri Lanka proved incapable of emulating that record. In this respect, Sri Lanka came to resemble Ethiopia, with its deeply divisive linguistic-ethnic-territorial groups.

Other factors contributed to a worsening economic situation in Sri Lanka, making the competition for jobs all the more intense between the Sinhalese and the Tamils. The SLFP under various leaders, believing in more socialism, a large welfare state, and extensive restrictions on foreign investment and trade, undertook policies that slowed economic growth. The rapid rise in the price of imported oil, in 1973 and for a time thereafter, hurt the Sri Lankan economy under both the SLFP and the UNP. Some blamed the continuing British influence on the Sri Lankan economy as one of the factors restraining economic growth. Events in the Persian Gulf in 1990–91 interrupted a flow of money into Sri Lanka via expatriate workers. Rapid population growth intensified the problem of scarce employment. And revolutionary events themselves, especially from 1983, further hurt the economy. The UNP, from 1977, sought to privatize much of the economy and also attract foreign investment, but much damage had already been done, and other negative features remained unchanged.[10]

One of the decisions taken by governments in Colombo was to engage in large-scale hydraulic-irrigation schemes. These governmental programs, designed to increase both domestic sources of energy and agricultural jobs, to some extent affected the eastern region that was Tamil speaking. As part of the governmental plans, Sinhalese Buddhists were moved into these areas for agricultural purposes. While solving some problems, these plans created an important irritant to Tamils, who characterized the entire scheme as Sinhalese Buddhist colonization of part of the Tamil homeland. Thus, in addition to the governmental policy about the interrelated issues of language, education, and jobs, the issue of new settlements in the east gave Tamils added reason to believe they had few reasons for giving allegiance to the unitary state of Sri Lanka.[11]

In general, one can say that from about 1956 to the late 1970s or early 1980s, governmental performance in managing the economy, plus governmental performance in instituting a Sinhala-only language policy, caused many Tamils to become alienated from the state. This governmental performance, detrimentally affecting the economic livelihood of many Tamils, was to a great extent a direct outcome of the social-ideological factors already analyzed. (International events damaging the economy were obviously beyond the control of any Sri Lankan government.)

When discussing governmental performance, one should also note the weakness of the police and military forces in dealing with dissent and rebellion. The ceremonial nature of the Sri Lankan military in the 1950s and 1960s has already been mentioned. The police were almost as badly disciplined and trained. Complicating matters was an uprising in the military in 1962, which had led to the removal of many Sinhalese Christian officers and their replacement with Sinhalese Buddhists. Eventually, military operations led by Sinhalese Buddhist officers in the 1970s and 1980s were ineffective in suppressing Tamil dissent, and the brutality of the operations increased Tamil alienation.[12]

A 1971 coup attempt by radical Sinhalese (discussed below) showed the weakness of the Sri Lankan army. Attempts to improve military effectiveness under the tutelage of Israelis, South Africans, and various mercenaries seemed to encourage the tendency of many Sinhalese Buddhists to engage in brutality toward the Tamils. Some observers believed the Israelis were counseling a scorched-earth policy in the north,[13] patterned on Israeli attacks on Palestinian irregular fighters in the Middle East.

In any event, by the 1980s it was evident that the Sri Lankan police and military were incapable of suppressing increasingly violent Tamil behavior in the northern and eastern provinces. It was estimated that during the 1970s, there were only 200 militant Tamils in the north.[14] From the late 1970s to the late 1980s, the number of Tamil fighters plus their supporters greatly increased. Human rights violations by both the Sinhalese and the Indian army contributed to this increased violence. Indeed, particularly the LTTE proved a match for an experienced, but not very disciplined, Indian expeditionary force that may have reached a peak of about 110,000 troops.[15]

At the time of writing, however, it is possible that Sri Lankan forces have improved their capacity to the point that a separate Tamil state, created by armed force, may be avoided. Governmental forces, with the aid of vigilante groups, managed to suppress a smaller Sinhalese revolution in the south. But events have left open the question of whether Colombo has the power to avoid a new federalism entailing a Tamil homeland in the north through extensive provincial autonomy. Is the only alternative to a new federalism a series of terrorist and counterterrorist steps in which violence and denial of human rights become institutionalized, but without genuine domestic peace?

Legal and moral legitimacy. Had the 1948 constitution remained unchanged, as a legal reflection of the dominant political morality held by political elites, the unitary state of Sri Lanka might have remained legitimate in the eyes of most Tamils. But this is academic speculation, useful only as a point of contrast to analyze what actually happened. The 1946 constitution was supported by only an estimated 10 percent of the population.[16]

The 1972 and 1978 constitutions of Sri Lanka, rather than providing widespread rational or legal legitimacy for the state, became further reasons for Tamils to regard the state as illegitimate. Particularly the 1972 constitution, with its endorsement of Buddhism and reaffirmation of centralization rather than federalism, did much to crystallize a belief in the illegitimacy of the state from the Tamil view. The 1972 constitution also failed to retain that part of the 1948 constitution explicitly proscribing group discrimination. After the adoption of the 1972 constitution, movements for a Tamil homeland expanded. The 1978 constitution, replacing a Westminster parliamentary system with a presidential system resembling the Gaulist Fifth Republic, seemed to many Tamils to be designed to create a much stronger—even partly authoritarian—executive for the explicit purpose of dealing with Tamil demands for some type of homeland.[17]

All of the Sri Lankan constitutions contained long lists of personal rights familiar to Western democrats. The 1972 and 1978 constitutions recognized Tamil as a national language, although Sinhala continued as the sole official language. But many of the civil, political, and cultural rights were offset by contradictory provisions in other parts of the constitutions. The validity of constitutional rights was called into question by the doctrine of parliamentary, then executive, supremacy, which left the courts without the authority to protect personal rights against actions by the "political" branches. States of emergency and the controversial Prevention of Terrorism Act further reduced the influence of the courts in checking executive abuses of human rights. The right of petition for habeas corpus, important in checking detention and prisoner abuse by the executive, existed more on paper than in reality.[18]

Most important, the listing of constitutional rights was contradicted by the actual behavior of the majority population and the governments elected by it. The UNP government headed by President J. R. Jayawardene from 1977 to 1988 was obviously an accomplice to genocidal attacks on the Tamils beginning in July 1983. Public statements by President Jayawardene indicated a disregard for Tamil sensitivities and even their lives.[19] The successor government, also UNP but headed by President Ranasinghe Premadasa, also behaved in ways that raised questions about its commitment to constitutional rights. As one prominent and moderate Tamil concluded, Sri Lankan constitutional rights became "dead letters."[20]

It bears noting that UNP governments from 1978 took action that violated the constitutionally protected rights not only of Tamils but also of others. From 1972, the leaders of the SLFP, in particular Bandaranaike's widow, Sirimavo, had a number of their civil and political rights voided in order to keep them from effectively challenging the UNP. And the parliament was extended by referendum; there were no parliamentary elections between 1977 and 1989 (although there was a 1982 presidential election, which the UNP rigged). The UNP government, after 1987, was brutal in suppressing an attempted Sinhalese revolution in the south (the Indian army was at that time responsible for order in the north).[21] Certainly for the Tamils, but also for others, the 1972 and 1978 constitutions became more bones of contention than legal sources of legitimacy.

Above all, the Sinhalese Buddhists refused to devise a constitution entailing a federalism that might have provided an acceptable degree of local autonomy for the Tamils in the north and east. The leaderships of both the UNP and the SLFP preferred to encourage Sinhalese Buddhist nationalism of a chauvinistic character rather than try to restrain it through a federal constitution with extensive local autonomy—perhaps on a Canadian or Swiss model.

Law is usually a reflection of prevailing or dominant political morality or, if one prefers, political culture. Political attitudes in Sri Lanka, in particular those of the majority of Sinhalese Buddhists, became incompatible with many of the civil and political rights written in the constitutions. On the basis of the social makeup of the island's population, led by short-sighted politicians eager to find issues that would carry them to personal power even at the expense of the political stability of the state, the majority—pushed by a growing population in tight competition for jobs—progressively supported policies, or took action apart from the government, that encouraged Tamil revolutionary behavior.

At best, what can be said in general about Sinhalese Buddhist political morality was that it insisted on more and more majority control and less and less minority rights and benefits. Although civil and political rights and even cultural-linguistic rights were never rejected formally, they were suspended during states of emergency, and majority attitudes were insensitive to the role of the rights of an important minority in producing legitimacy and political stability. Given that the genocidal attacks of July 1983 against the Tamils were at least partially spontaneous on the part of the masses, it could be said that racial and ethnic hatred at that time overwhelmed attention to constitutional rights.

Certainly, no charismatic leadership emerged to save the Sri Lankan state from the policies that the SLFP and UNP leaderships devised. Early Tamil leadership, though not charismatic, had been moderate in seeking cooperation with the majority in a unitary state. The history of the Federal Party, the principal Tamil political party in the 1950s, demonstrated this moderation. Progressively, these moderate Tamil voices, which in the 1970s became supportive of a form of Eelam that could be accommodated within a single federal state, were pushed aside by those willing to use violence on behalf of a separate Tamil state.

Although domestic factors affecting legitimacy, principally social-ideological and functional ones, seemed decisive in Sri Lanka's downward slide, international factors were also at play in a secondary sense. In other words, the development of Sinhalese Buddhist nationalism and governmental insensitivity to the expectations of the Tamil minority proved controlling in the Tamil revolution that accelerated in the 1970s and 1980s. Constitutional developments mirrored these social-ideological and functional factors. Among the international factors, the most important was Indian foreign policy.

International Legitimacy

Neither the unitary state of Sri Lanka nor the Tamil revolution of the 1970s and 1980s occurred in domestic isolation. The international context came to bear on the legitimacy of Sri Lanka in all three possible ways—legal, moral, and political. The most important of these international influences on legitimacy was a combination of moral and political, and the primary agent of action was Indian foreign policy. This policy slightly or temporarily affected the power of both the Tamil revolutionaries and the Sri Lankan government.

Moral-political legitimacy. India, and most of the other states of the world, regarded Sri Lanka as within an unspoken Indian sphere of influence. When the genocidal attacks of July 1983 occurred against the Tamils, no other state took decisive action, whereas India abandoned its official stand of nonintervention in Sri Lankan affairs and adopted a two-track policy. Covertly, it escalated the arming of Tamil fighters and broadened the providing of sanctuary in southern India in the state of Tamil Nadu. Overtly, it sought to broker a deal between the Sinhalese-dominated UNP government and the Sri Lankan Tamils.[22]

The nature of this early policy was both moral and political. Morally, the Indian government of Indira Gandhi did not want to countenance genocide by a state within its sphere of influence. Politically, the federal government of India was pressured by its state of Tamil Nadu to take action to protect Tamil Hindus across the Palk Strait, only twenty-five miles wide. Support for the Sri Lankan Tamils was strong in Tamil Nadu, and Gandhi's Congress Party could not achieve partisan gains and electoral success in that province without taking a strong stand against the massacre of the foreign Tamils.[23]

Just as India had intervened in what was then East Pakistan (now

Bangladesh) for moral and political reasons, so it intervened in Sri Lanka. In 1971 India had intervened in East Pakistan (largely Bengali) to stop genocide carried out by the army of Pakistan (largely Punjabi) and to dismember arch-rival Pakistan by creating the state of Bangladesh. So beginning in 1983, India involved itself more deeply and overtly in Sri Lanka, again to stop genocide and also to make political gains of various sorts. The form of intervention, however, was not exactly the same.

Early Indian foreign policy focused on the protection of Sri Lankan Tamils, who were also Hindus. Indian policy both generated legitimacy for Tamil demands and materially contributed to the power of armed Tamil elements. Arms, supplies, and sanctuary were provided to Sri Lankan fighters, and civilian refugees were given asylum.

Yet there was a second powerful political consideration for New Delhi, one that progressively came into play and that worked to the favor of the Sri Lankan government. India, under various secessionist pressures of its own, did not want to countenance the creation of a sovereign Tamil state in the north of Sri Lanka. This would have been seen almost everywhere as giving support to the Sikhs and others in India who were struggling to carve new states on the Indian subcontinent. Hence, in a crucial shift in Indian policy in the late 1980s, the government of Rajiv Gandhi moved from arming Tamil fighters to trying to disarm them while still attempting to broker a Tamil-Sinhalese political agreement. India also cracked down on the actions of Sri Lankan Tamils in the Indian province of Tamil Nadu; part of this crackdown may have stemmed from the provincial rather than central government, and some Sri Lankan Tamil organizations seemed more restricted than others.[24] New Delhi's policies contributed to the legitimacy of some type of Sri Lankan authority over the entire island.

In 1987 India and the Sri Lanka government reached an accord in which the sovereignty of Sri Lanka on the entire island was reaffirmed. The principal quid pro quo was the creation in the various regions of local councils having some authority over local affairs. Under this accord, India agreed to send, and the government of Sri Lanka agreed to accept, an Indian "peacekeeping" force on the island (IPKF). The tactical problem for India stemmed from the fact that the accord was not negotiated with the various Tamil groups but only with the Sri Lankan government, controlled by the Sinhalese.

The various Sri Lankan Tamil organizations regarded the 1987 accord as a sellout of the demands for a Tamil homeland, with the proposed local councils being seen as too weak. The main practical problem for the IPKF then became how to achieve the disarming of well-entrenched guerrilla forces, particularly those of the LTTE, supported to an important degree by the local population. To meet this challenge, the initial force of Indian soldiers had to be augmented. A very nasty occupation and small war resulted, with much of the northern Tamil population coming to detest the IPKF, even though initial Indian policy had been in favor of protecting Tamils from Sinhalese abuse.

At the same time, a number of Sinhalese Buddhist politicians, including the prime minister at the time the accord was signed, who would become the next president, opposed the accord because it was seen as conceding too much to the Tamils via the local councils and a merged northern and eastern province and/or because it formally accepted the presence of Indian troops in Sri Lanka.[25] (Earlier the Indian government had air-dropped civilian supplies to the Tamils in the north without the consent of the government in Colombo, making it clear that India could use unilateral force if it wished; it was in this context that President Jayawardene agreed to the 1987 accord.)

Thus India, having intervened initially on the side of the Tamils for moral and political reasons but having come to oppose any separate Tamil state because of implications for the territorial integrity of India itself, found the IPKF taking significant casualties while being vigorously opposed by Tamil fighters (and also politically opposed by Sinhalese ultranationalists).[26] Atrocities were committed by the IPKF, as well as against it.[27]

Under these political difficulties, the subsequent Indian government of V. P. Singh finally withdrew the IPKF in 1990. The overall impact of Indian involvement in Sri Lankan affairs was therefore indecisive. India had, in effect, provided international legitimacy first to Tamil causes, then to the sovereignty of Sri Lanka. The bridge between the two concerns had been the 1987 proposal for local councils and hence a weak form of federalism. But this had proved too little for the radical Tamils and too much for important Sinhalese. (Indian policies contributed to the killing of Rajiv Gandhi, since evidence seems to show that Sri Lankan Tamils masterminded his death in 1991.)

Most other states, including the great powers (and the former colonial power, Great Britain), did not regard events in Sri Lanka as of major importance. Both in the United Nations and through bilateral policies, they treated developments mostly as an internal Sri Lankan affair, or they deferred to Indian actions.

The United States, however, was somewhat involved, perhaps because of its interest in naval rights at the port of Trincomalee. Officially, Washington professed nonintervention. Government officials stated that they did not see the United States as a major influence on Sri Lankan events.[28] But Washington definitely tilted toward the government side: maintaining a foreign-assistance program of $75 million, continuing to sell crime-control equipment, concluding a Peace Corps agreement, brokering the introduction of mercenary advisers and fighters, and perhaps actually providing military "advisers." But Washington refused to provide overt military assistance or personnel to the government and said that it had raised human rights issues with Colombo.[29]

Since Britain, the United States, and the Soviet Union, inter alia, refused to provide military assistance overtly to the government (or the Tamils), Colombo turned to the Israeli and South African nationals. Their governments, as the pariahs of the world, seemed only too happy that their nationals were asked for help by a state active in the Non-Aligned Movement. But the presence of Israelis in Colombo did not go unnoticed in the Arab world, and the Sri Lanka economy suffered for it.[30]

Parts of the United Nations system that were concerned with human rights generated some very mild pressure on the government in Colombo to curtail egregious violations of civil rights, but these steps were small, slow, and mostly ineffective.[31] Various private organizations, such as Amnesty International, the International Commission of Jurists, and the International Human Rights Law Group, issued reports condemning actions by all sides. The groups documented extrajudicial killings, forced disappearances, torture by the government's security forces—and death squads. They also listed atrocities by Tamil militants as well as by the IPKF.[32]

Given the pervasive nature of atrocities by the various armed forces and associated vigilante groups, and given the lack of saliency directed to the entire situation by most states, it is difficult for an observer to see much practical impact from these private reports and missions. The activities of the United Nations and the private transnational human rights agencies were intended both to help specific persons and to delegitimize those carrying out human rights violations, but the result is doubtful. India, above all, saw matters in terms of its own territorial integrity, once the genocide against the Tamils was contained.

Colombo did decide in 1989 to admit the International Committee of the Red Cross (ICRC) to its territory for prison visits and related humanitarian activities. This governmental decision was probably the result of growing international pressure on Colombo. Although Amnesty International reported a diminution of violation of human rights in the south during 1990, this probably had more to do with the crushing of the People's Liberation Front (JVP) than with any rapid and broad impact from ICRC action.[33]

Legal legitimacy. The state of Sri Lanka had been accepted in legal terms by the international community, and its various governments had encountered no challenges over credentials in various international groupings. This international legal legitimacy made no difference to the Sri Lankan Tamils. However, Sri Lankan international legal legitimacy may have made India careful initially to clothe its support for the Tamils in covert cover. Even so, that "covert" policy soon became overt in common knowledge, similar to U.S. "covert" support of the contras fighting the Sandinista government in Nicaragua in the 1980s.

International legal legitimacy played a small role in Sri Lankan events after 1983. Most states, including India, titled toward the government side simply because it was the government side. All governments have a general interest in preserving the state system and thus in deferring to the legal principle of nonintervention. Unless some pressing and specific interest arises to the contrary, such as New Delhi's need to carry an election in its state of Tamil Nadu, political calculation usually compels acceptance of state sovereignty and nonintervention. (It is possible for some moral crusade to affect international relations, but such moral crusades without accompanying state interests are more rare than some commentators would have us believe.) This partially explains why Tamil organizations never achieved the status of a "national liberation movement" at the United Nations.

International legal factors, reflecting prevailing political calculations, thus worked to the advantage of Sri Lankan governments. But these political-legal factors were not decisive in Sri Lankan events and did not deter interventionist policies, for a time, by India. Nor did they deter a slight increase in international criticism of human rights violations by the government in the late 1980s. Even Indian foreign policy was not decisive. Domestic factors affecting legitimacy and power were predominant.

THE JVP REVOLUTION

Sri Lanka has actually experienced two sizable "wars," not one. The explanatory factors for the second war are mostly the same, with the exception that the importance of both rights and international influences proved weaker in this case than in the first.

In 1971 the JVP, the Janatha Vimukti Peramuna, a violent political movement, tried to topple the government, but failed. It next resumed the effort in the late 1980s. The trigger for this resurgence was the 1987 Indo–Sri Lankan Accord, which sanctioned Indian troops in Sri Lanka. At the time of writing, the movement seems to have been crushed by brutal methods, with little international involvement. Domestic social-ideological factors, combined with governmental performance, explain the events to a very great extent.[34]

First of all, in social-ideological terms, the JVP is made up of radical Sinhalese Buddhists who are both anti-Tamil and anti-Indian. Second, in ideological terms, many of the members of the JVP are political and social reformers who want to do away with the caste system; some are Marxists of varying stripe. As for the role of governmental performance, the backbone of those taking up arms on behalf of the JVP are unemployed or underemployed and blame governmental policies for their plight. These factors, plus some version of Marxism, account for the violent revolutionary attempts.

The Sri Lankan security forces, working with death squads, managed to suppress this revolutionary movement by 1991. Its main leader, Rohana Wijeveera, was killed in 1989 while under the control of security forces; his body was disposed of before an independent investigation could be made into the cause of death. Although outside private sources, including journalists and human rights groups, publicized and protested the brutality of the repression, no foreign governments expressed great interest in the violence associated with the repression of the JVP.[35]

The fact that the movement was suppressed via summary execution, forced disappearances, torture, and intimidation was perhaps balanced by the equal fact that the rebels had used murder, torture, and intimidation in their own grab for power. India did not have much sympathy for the JVP, considering the movement's anti-Indian posture, and others, such as the United States, regarded it as Marxist. Other outsiders simply did not care. Since the JVP was based to some extent on rural and youthful components of the Sinhalese majority, the issue of minority rights did not arise.

CONCLUSIONS

A study by the Rand Corporation in 1989 noted that revolutionary movements stem from three sources: public resistance to authoritarian rule, ethnic and nationalist aspirations, and economic grievances.[36] The case of Sri Lanka reflects the last two factors more than the first. (In these remarks I emphasize the Tamil, not the JVP, revolution.)

Sri Lanka is certainly not a case of a human rights revolution against an authoritarian regime. The closest that one can come to this version of events is to note that the Tamil revolution evolved into one for collective self-determination, for a Tamil homeland either as a separate state or through extensive local autonomy within a federal state. The two 1966 United Nations Covenants on human rights—covering civil, political, social, economic, and cultural rights—proclaim the right of self-determination to be a collective human right. It is also true that Sri Lankan democracy, based on a commitment to civil and political rights, declined after 1977. And Tamil members of parliament were expelled after the 1983 pogroms. Thus one could argue that the violent Tamil demand for a change in governing arrangements became a human rights movement in the context of declining democracy.

Yet Sri Lanka was clearly a democratic state through 1977. Even after that date, it retained a few democratic elements—elections and referenda—even as authoritarian elements—electoral fraud, intimidation on partisan grounds, states of emergency, emasculation of the courts, and extrajudicial killings and torture informally sanctioned by the state—increased.

But the original central issue as far as the Tamils were concerned was not democratic rights of participation versus authoritarianism. The central issue from 1956 to the mid-1970s was the extent of minority rights and benefits within a democratic state governed by majority rule. Thus the fundamental issue was not rights versus no rights but rather the distribution of rights and benefits—in particular, the limitations on majority control. Free and fair elections may in fact lead to democratic discrimination. Of particular concern to initially moderate Tamils was the decline of police protection in the 1980s under central governments controlled by Sinhalese.

The case study of the Tamil revolution in Sri Lanka, in addition to centering on minority rights and the collective right of self-determination, is also a leading contemporary example of the importance of linguistic rights, whether conceived as civil or cultural. If Switzerland is at one end of the spectrum representing state management of linguistic rights, and Belgium is somewhere in the middle, Sri Lanka from 1956 is at the opposite end. A major cause of the Tamil revolution, or in other terms, a primary precondition for it, was the 1956 statute in favor of only Sinhala in governmental circles. Linguistic rights linked to education, itself linked to jobs, soon followed as important issues.

In summary, fundamental to the Tamil revolution from 1956 through 1972, and certainly after 1983, was a growing view that the unitary state dominated by the Sinhalese Buddhists was illegitimate. But this comes very close to being a truism: many Tamils denied legitimacy to the unitary state of Sri Lanka because they were alienated from it. We can be more analytical.

The unitary state lost legitimacy in the eyes of increasing numbers of Sri Lankan Tamils for two primary and related domestic reasons. The state was seen to reflect only the values of the Sinhalese Buddhists, not the Tamil Hindus. And its governments followed policies emphasizing Sinhala, Buddhism, and jobs for the majority at the expense of the minority. Significant legitimacy, from the Tamil view, was not derived from the three constitutions because they did not reflect the degree of local authority that many Tamils thought was necessary to achieve a homeland. When the minimum was not obtainable, the maximum was pursued with increased fervor. Failure to obtain federalism led to increased demand for a separate state. The political morality of the majority of Sinhalese Buddhists was not sensitive to the emotive aspirations and material expectations of the minority Tamils.

The only important international influence affecting both legitimacy and power in Sri Lanka was Indian foreign policy. It operated first on behalf of the Tamils, from 1983 to 1985, then progressively on behalf of Sri Lankan authority over all of the island. India's search for some political formula short of a unitary state completely dominated by Sinhalese Buddhists, but also short of a separate Tamil state, proved as tortuous as other proffered solutions. Indian foreign policy paid considerable attention to human rights issues after 1983, starting with opposition to genocide and proceeding to some prosecution for violations of civil rights (and the laws of war) by the IPKF. But India's concern for its own territorial integrity was progressively the primary ingredient in its policies toward Sri Lanka, especially after 1987. Ironically, given the origins of Indian policy in opposing genocide, the extensive violations of human rights by the IPKF intensified Tamil opposition to it.

In the case of Sri Lanka, we can explain the general causes or background conditions for the loss of legitimacy for the Sri Lankan state in the Tamil community. These causes, which can be well understood by using the language of human rights, concern the sources of domestic and international legitimacy (and of the converse, alienation). These causes can be combined and roughly ranked to provide an understanding of the Tamil revolutionary movement. We can also discern, at least after the fact, the power put at the service of the various views on legitimacy.

We can also understand a good deal about the related JVP revolution, although both rights and foreign influences were not as important. The JVP revolution too was generally based in social and ideological factors, specifically a Sinhalese Buddhist chauvinistic nationalism combined with Marxism. Governmental performance, specifically widespread unemployment among its youthful members, also played a role. But rights per se played a much smaller role, whether they pertained to self-determination or were of a minority, civil, or political nature. The JVP revolution, being in part anti-Indian, especially after 1987, naturally failed to enlist the support of India, the one state with a sizable interest in Sri Lankan events.

What cannot be explained so well, even with hindsight, and what cannot be predicted with much reliability, are the particular triggers of revolutionary behavior. Also, one cannot precisely predict the outcome of clashes of power; one can only analyze the results after the clash.

Why did genocidal attacks on the Tamils occur during July 1983 and not during November 1982 or at any other specific time? Why did not more Sinhalese Buddhists rally to the JVP instead of sticking with the UNP and SLFP? Why did sizable numbers of Tamils not rally to demands for a separate state but apparently prefer a Tamil province within a federal Sri Lanka? Why did the majority not negotiate for a type of Tamil homeland if it would have meant an end to widespread violence, even if the northern and eastern provinces were merged? Social science has never been able to precisely explain, measure, or predict many intangible factors greatly affecting both legitimacy and power.

Nevertheless, a checklist or typology of general causes is helpful, even if its application to particular cases results in a varying analysis.[37] In the case of Sri Lanka, we see above all that human rights factors were central to Tamil revolutionary behavior. Rights may even have been more important than realized in the JVP revolution, if the motivating causes primarily concerned fighting against the caste system—civil rights—and unemployment—economic rights. But rights were important not in the simple sense that those who demanded rights made a revolution against a regime that denied all rights. Rather, social, ideological, functional, and international factors affected the central conflict in Sri Lanka over the distribution of majority and minority rights—a conflict that evolved into one over collective self-determination in various forms.

5

Domestic War in Liberia

Liberia, which declared its sovereign independence in 1847 and which was one of two black African members of the League of Nations, manifested uncommon political stability for more than 125 years. An intriguing question, therefore, is why Liberia degenerated by 1991 into a vicious domestic war that displaced about 50 percent of the population while destroying much of the economic infrastructure of the country. How could a country that had displayed continuous rule by one political party from 1877 to 1980 change within one decade into a country in which atrocity and starvation came to characterize daily life for much of the population? Some observers believed that the situation in Liberia in 1990 was worse than in Ethiopia during its civil war and famine.[1]

Liberia is an interesting case study in domestic war not only because of the starkness of the changes throughout the 1980s and early 1990s but also because its recent history shows the ambiguity in trying to utilize such analytical concepts as coup and political revolution. In addition, if we could understand the fundamental or structural causes of the Liberian civil disorder of the early 1990s, we might be able to say something about the requisites for a return to political stability in the future. To what extent are human rights factors important in past stability, contemporary unrest, and prospects for a return to stability?

LIBERIAN HISTORY AND THE 1980 COUP

From 1822, when the small Commonwealth of Liberia was created by freed slaves from North America, to the important 1980 coup by Master Sergeant Samuel K. Doe, Liberian politics was dominated by Americo-Liberians (hereafter, the settlers). Even though the descendents of the settlers never totaled more than an estimated 1 to 5 percent of the population (which in 1990 was about 2.4 million), they—and, more precisely, a still smaller elite within the settler community—ruled over the indigenous Africans (hereafter, the indigenes). That roughly 95 percent of Liberians were without significant political influence was the product of several factors: (1) ethnic division (the indigenes were fragmented into sixteen linguistic-ethnic groups); (2) education (until recent times, most indigenes were decidedly undereducated, with 70 percent of the country illiterate as recently as 1965 and with most of these being indigenes); (3) repression (a series of riots, rebellions, and peaceful challenges or potential challenges was met with force and imprisonment); and (4) external support (both the United States and various European states supported the settlers from time to time). Thus, a small but relatively unified, more highly educated, and politically motivated elite was able to control a much larger population.

DOMESTIC FACTORS

The settler community, despite its own experience with slavery, ruled over the indigenous Africans within the expanding borders of Liberia in a manner not unlike that of white colonialists and slavers. Ironically, the philosophy of the "white man's burden" was implemented by the black settlers. "A superior Western civilization [was juxtaposed] to an African 'primitiveness' totally lacking in any redemptive qualities."[2] A special commission from the League of Nations concluded in 1930 that the settler government of Liberia engaged in forced labor and other slave-like practices.[3] Black settlers controlled and exploited black indigenes from the earliest days of the commonwealth and the state until settler rule was ended.

From perhaps about 1880 and certainly from the 1930s to the late 1970s, Liberia was characterized by what Antonio Gramsci would call a hegemonic situation.[4] Not only the settlers but also most indigenes who paid attention to politics in Monrovia assumed that the settlers were the ruling class. From about 1880, colonial intrigues stimulated Liberian nationalism, with its imbedded settler control, among many indigenes. Particularly from the 1930s on, indigenous Africans accepted the state of Liberia and Liberian nationalism as a political frame of reference, along with the existing political elite.[5] Socioeconomic differences between the settlers and the indigenes did not disrupt the political system because of the shared assumption that the settlers *should* govern. This deferential attitude on the part of most politically aware indigenes was encouraged by the carefully thought-out policies of the settler political elite. This elite controlled the indigenes outside of the capital with traditional colonial policies of divide and rule (among the ethnic groups), cooptation of leaders (offering benefits and "perks" for cooperation with the dominant system), and denial of education. The few dissenters, especially in Monrovia, were forcibly repressed.

In other words, historical tradition, carefully cultivated by the settlers from the earliest days through World War II, nurtured an informal ideology with the central precept that the settler class comprised the legitimate rulers of Liberia. This historical-ideological source of legitimacy came to be shared both by the settlers (with power) and by the most politically aware indigenes (without power). Nevertheless, electoral districts were carefully gerrymandered to ensure settler victory, there was a property qualification for voting, and vote tabulations were openly fraudulent.[6]

Deeply divisive splits within the settler community were ameliorated, in part, by marriage between prominent families.[7] Especially after the emergence of the True Whig Party as the dominant political party in 1877, the settlers avoided any fundamental or broad split that would have allowed indigenous political forces to exercise more power. The rise in the mid-1950s of a serious settler opposition party was short-lived.

In this situation, overt repression by military or police force was only sporadic, particularly after the conquering of the hinterland and the stabilization of state boundaries. Although force was certainly used, albeit inconsistently, to pacify the hinterland, thereafter the political history of Liberia was not characterized by large-scale and systematic use of force by the rulers against the ruled. "The military and security forces, though intimidating, would not have been adequate to suppress serious or widespread disorder, had it occurred."[8] Progressively, most indigenes, insofar as they paid any attention to the government in Monrovia, developed a "political conscience" inimicable to their own interests—namely, that the settlers constituted a preferred ruling class. Fundamental legitimacy for settler rule came primarily from an informal ideology, which became part of national history. A liberalization of policies, of sorts, was instituted first by the administration of William V. S. Tubman (1944–71) and then by the administration of William R. Tolbert, Jr. (1971–80). These policies formed an important prelude to, and encouragement of, the striking changes of the 1980s and 1990s. Settler leadership itself set in motion changes that encouraged, although they did not directly cause, loss of settler control.

President Tubman's administration after World War II emphasized a "Unification and Integration" program entailing both a broader educational program and a road network that penetrated, for the first time, at least part of the rural area. As neighboring areas achieved legal independence from their colonial masters, Tubman also encouraged the Africanization of Liberian culture. This latter policy helped undermine the notion of inherent settler superiority over indigenous Africans. A tremendously expanding economy, plus the new road system, led to a migration of indigenes into the cities, especially Monrovia, where enhanced education gave them more positions in the state bureaucracy. The Liberian GNP went from $48 million in 1950 to $367 million in 1969. Government revenues went from $3.9 million to $61.8 million in the same period. Africanization, education, urbanization, and economic growth all stimulated political awareness on the part of more indigenes.[9]

But Tubman controlled the political effects of his socioeconomic policies through a combination of repression and cooptation. Most of the new indigenous middle class was at first content to exchange rising socioeconomic status for political conformity. This acceptance was facilitated by an expanding economy triggered by foreign investment under Tubman's "Open Door" policy. A few indigenes were added to the upper levels of civilian and military positions. The few who were not content with trading improved socioeconomic status for deference to the settlers were repressed, as was, most notably, Henry Boima Fahnbulleh, Sr., a politically prominent indigene convicted of treason on trumped-up charges and detained in 1968.[10]

President Tolbert continued many of his predecessor's policies, but he proved less apt than Tubman in both economic and political management. The overall political system continued to manifest an authoritarian party-state apparatus behind an electoral facade; organizationally, there was a dominant president, a rubber-stamp parliament, and a compliant judiciary.[11] Yet during the early and mid-1970s, press freedoms grew, especially relative to neighboring African states. Moreover, opposition political parties, led by reformist indigenes or a combination of reformist indigenes and settlers, were formed during this period. The two most prominent were the Progressive Alliance of Liberia (PAL), which was headed by Gabriel B. Mathews (a settler) and which later became the Progressive Peoples Party (PPP), and the Movement for Justice in Africa (MOJA), headed by Togba Nah Tipoteh (an indigene). When Amos Sawyer (a settler) of MOJA appeared to be en route to victory in the Monrovian municipal elections in the fall of 1979, those elections where canceled ("postponed") by the Tolbert government.[12]

But traditional settler control was more difficult, and finally impossible, to maintain in the context of a more assertive indigenous population linked to reformist settlers. In the spring of 1979, food riots erupted in Monrovia when Tolbert tried to implement an austerity fiscal program demanded by the International Monetary Fund. These riots occurred in an economy in which a growth rate of about 1.5 percent was negated by an inflation rate of about 15 percent and population growth of about 3 percent. Perhaps equally important, an increasing number of indigenes and settlers were no doubt aware that a very small minority of traditional settlers (perhaps less than 5 percent of the total population) controlled most of the wealth (perhaps more than 60 percent).[13] By early 1980, indigenes and dissatisfied settlers were openly demonstrating for Tolbert's resignation while hard-liners in the True Whig Party were urging repression. "Never before had the traditional state structure of hegemony by the repatriate [settler] core been subjected to such concentrated assault."[14]

Tolbert himself had become something of an egomaniac who increasingly spent the government's meager income on presidential perks, despite the stagnant economic fortunes of the nation. His administration was characterized by greed, corruption, and avarice.[15] In 1979, when he became president of the Organization of African Unity, he spent $200 million on a conference center to host an OAU meeting, symbolizing to many the skewed public-policy priorities increasingly evident during his administration.

In was in this situation—characterized by traditional settler dominance, rising indigene political organization and expectations, declining economic prospects, and presidential extravagance—that seventeen army noncommissioned officers (NCOs), all indigenes, took over the government by force on April 12, 1980. They were led by an eleventh-grade dropout of the Krahn ethnic group, which constituted about 4 percent of Liberians. No one rose in defense of the ancien régime.

If historical and ideological factors, namely the tradition and informal ideology of settler superiority, combined with specific policies pertaining to education and repression, help to explain in general the absence of coup and revolution in Liberia before 1980, what exactly motivated Master Sergeant Doe and his accomplices in their coup? It is now clear that the primary motivation stemmed from previous governmental performance, namely governmental neglect of NCOs, of their training and support. Doe repeatedly stressed the poor living conditions of NCOs and their troops (all indigenes and all divided ethnically) by comparison with the commissioned officers (a mixture of indigenes and settlers) and civilian governmental officials (mostly settlers).[16]

This issue of neglect of the NCOs was inextricably intertwined with the question of ethnic discrimination, which increasingly in the 1970s permeated much of Liberian society. It was the indigenes in the army's lower ranks that were intensely dissatisfied with both military and social conditions. The officer corps fared better. Reportedly, in the food riots in Monrovia in April 1979, the army rank and file refused to fire on the demonstrators. The killing of over one hundred persons was the work of the Monrovian police. Order was restored by the troops and planes of President Sékou Touré of neighboring Guinea, not by the Liberian army.[17] The central point remains that the functional issue of governmental performance in ignoring the conditions of the indigenes in the army cannot be separated from the moral issue of a broader ethnic discrimination. (Most of the enlisted men in the army were Loma, not Krahn. There was no widespread army mutiny in 1980; rather, there was a small coup led by Krahn, who targeted their civilian and military superiors for retribution and removal. But the Loma and other ethnic groups supported these moves. The Loma chief of staff had reportedly considered a coup back in 1971 to block the ascension of President Tolbert.)[18]

In the days after the 1980 coup, Doe and his colleagues gave other reasons for the coup. Some of these statements indicated a supposed interest in correcting the growing authoritarianism, corruption, and mismanagement. And these may have been genuine sentiments at the time. In the light of subsequent events, however, we can say for sure that interest in constitutionalism, human rights, and efficient government soon faded. The Tolbert regime had failed to generate legitimacy in the eyes of the coup makers for functional and moral reasons: neglect of NCOs and ethnic discrimination.

INTERNATIONAL FACTORS

Thus far we have examined Liberian political history and the benchmark year of 1980 almost entirely in terms of domestic factors. This is because these factors were the most important. Yet international factors were not absent.

There has long been a special relationship between the United States and Liberia, sometimes only rhetorical but many times substantial. It was the American Colonization Society, based in the United States that made possible, for better or worse, the permanent introduction of freed slaves into the west coast of Africa. (The first experiment of this kind involved British patrons and what is today Sierra Leone.)[19] But the U.S. government was not officially involved in these transactions and, moreover, lagged behind several European states in recognizing the Liberian proclamation of statehood.

Thereafter, a combination of U.S. governmental support and American private commercial interests sustained both the state of Liberia and the settler community that controlled it. "From 1911 until the mid 1920s, American officials played a crucial role in overseeing Liberia's economy and in organizing and heading the government's administrative apparatus in the hinterland."[20] Characteristic of this growing public and private involvement in Liberian affairs was the Firestone Tire and Rubber Company's loan to Liberia in 1926, which gave the company extensive leverage over the Liberian economy and which was arranged in close consultation with U.S. officials.[21] Also characteristic of the close American-Liberian relations was the fact that former Secretary of State Edward Stettinius, who had private financial interests in oil, saw to it that Liberia adopted a maritime code sympathetic to the registering of oil tankers. Stettinius, his partners, and the Liberian settlers made money while various shipowners evaded the maritime regulations of the United States and other industrialized nations.[22]

Rarely was the United States attentive to Liberian affairs but not supportive of the settler government. Yet in the 1920s the United

States, though not a member of the League of Nations, pushed hard for the League inquiry into slave-like practices in Liberia, an inquiry that led to a critical report of the policies of the Liberian government and to changes in labor practices in Liberia.[23] This tends to be the most notable exception to the general historical rule that the United States supported the Liberian government regardless of the nature of its policies.

At the time of the Doe coup in April 1980, the United States continued to profess a special relationship with Liberia. This traditional bipartisan belief had led to Liberia's receiving the largest per capita allotment of U.S. foreign assistance of any state in sub-Sahara Africa. Although the total amounts of U.S. foreign assistance to Liberia were small ($26.1 million in 1980) relative to assistance to states like Egypt and Israel, compared with other sub-Saharan African states, Liberia was favored. Human rights abuses by the Tolbert administration had been glossed over by the Carter team, despite all the rhetoric in Washington about human rights being the "soul" of Carter foreign policy.[24] (Carter briefly visited Monrovia in 1979.)

At the core of the modern "special relationship" were U.S. perceptions of strategic interests in Liberia. During World War II the United States had built Roberts International Airfield, and the Port of Monrovia provided a good naval harbor. In 1980 Liberia was the only African state to have given the United States access to air and naval facilities on a twenty-four-hour notice. Moreover, the United States had also built in Liberia a "telecommunications station" for diplomatic (and covert) use, the "Omega Navigational Station" for global shipping and aircraft, and a Voice of America transmitter for broadcasting in West Africa.[25] During the cold war, Liberia was definitely in the pro-American camp, and its pursuit of economic growth in the 1950s followed a classical free enterprise model—successfully. (It was successful regarding macrogrowth; distribution of those benefits was another matter.)

These strategic interests were combined with private commercial interests that were important to Liberia but mostly negligible to the United States in macro-terms (Liberia got .5 percent of all American direct foreign investment, worth about $500 million total). However, 75 percent of all American-owned ships were registered via Liberia.[26] Firms based in the United States had important investments in Liberian rubber, iron ore, and banking.

In 1980 there were unconfirmed reports that U.S. military officers discussed a coup against Tolbert, but not with Doe.[27] Such a move would have been uncharacteristic of Carter foreign policy, both in general and in Africa (although some unauthorized and lower-level contacts cannot be ruled out). The Carter administration was supposedly "cool" toward Doe immediately after his takeover,[28] but U.S. officials in Monrovia helped Doe consolidate his power.[29] Whatever the exact U.S. role in the events of 1980, a role that still remains partly a mystery, domestic factors clearly remained more important than international ones. The settler regime headed by Tolbert was so unpopular that no one rose to defend it against seventeen individuals who acted, initially, without foreign support or encouragement. Even some of the lower-class settlers, as well as some of the reformers from the upper-class settlers, had had enough of Tolbert and his repression, corruption, and mismanagement. After 133 years, settler domination in Liberia ended in a concentrated bloodletting. The United States and other outsiders were mostly bystanders in the actual coup.

THE 1980S AND NATIONAL DISINTEGRATION

The violent overthrow of the Tolbert administration was definitely a coup rather than a popular revolution, although the seizure of government by seventeen persons had broad if passive popular support. Did the 1980 coup lead to a political revolution? The answer is both yes and no, depending on time frame and definition. The answer is yes in the sense that between 1980 and 1985, most of the old political organizations and personnel were changed. The answer is no in the sense that by 1989 Liberia was still characterized by authoritarian and minority government, with gross corruption and mismanagement; the only substantive change was the composition of the minority. Most important, the Doe regime never did establish domestic legitimacy beyond the small coterie of Krahn supporters who personally benefited from Doe's rule. And although Doe started out with international legitimacy in the eyes of U.S. foreign policymakers, by the late 1980s even they stood aside as both civil war and regional intervention terminated a decade of Doe's abusive and personally aggrandizing mismanagement.

The First Phase, 1980–1985

Domestic factors. Doe and his colleagues in coup, having killed and sometimes mutilated thirteen high-ranking officials from the preceding settler government, including Tolbert himself, then tried to project themselves as responsible leaders interested in integrating the different sociopolitical factions of Liberia. There was a political revolution of an institutional nature. The old constitution and organizations were scrapped. A Peoples Redemption Council was created as a temporary measure, a constitutional committee submitted a new constitution to the people in a referendum, Doe appointed a provisional national assembly of a fairly broad makeup, and finally, in 1985, national elections were held—without the previous gerrymandered electoral districts and restrictive property requirements. Thus in 1985 the Second Liberian Republic was born, supposedly democratic and presidential.

Beyond this institutional revolution, Doe started out as if he had learned the lessons of the past—principally, the need to avoid minority government in favor of a broad political consensus. In the early 1980s he reached out to indigene and settler reformers, making Gabriel Mathews (PAL) his minister of foreign affairs and Togba Nah Tipoteh (MOJA) his minister of economic affairs and planning. After the televised killings of Tolbert and his colleagues, Doe did not seek vengeance against the established settler community; rather he included several traditional Whig politicians in his inner circle. He did remove a number of settler officers from the military and detained them, while giving the rank and file a substantial pay raise (reflecting the dominant concern in the original coup—the poor pay and conditions of indigene NCOs and enlisted men). Hence, from the coup to just before the elections, it appeared as if a true political revolution were in the making, with the prospect of a substantive change from an elitist one-party state system to a multi-party presidential democracy.[30]

But the electoral campaign as well as the election itself demonstrated that Doe was increasingly determined to hold on to power and to forgo the legal and moral legitimacy derived from free and fair elections. The first indication of Doe's real intentions was when he declared for the new presidency and blocked the major opposition political parties from the elections. The latter was done by preventing them from registering and by harassing their leaders. Only minor, nonthreatening parties were allowed to register, along with Doe's own party.

Second, while the actual voting seemed regular, the counting of the votes was obviously fraudulent. This led to a situation in which, in classic understatement, "the way the voters actually cast their votes bore only a limited relationship to the official results later announced."[31] Protests over the 1985 elections led to further harassment, detention, and exile. A putsch against Doe by one of his original colleagues, Brigadier General Thomas Quiwonkpa, followed shortly after the election but led to many deaths; Quiwonkpa's mutilated body was displayed in public. Doe assumed the presidency in early 1986 and began his "republican" four-year term, relying mainly on repression—and considerable public apathy—to stay in power. At the outset he had virtually no sources of domestic legitimacy. He did have, however, a powerful patron in the Reagan administration.

International factors. Immediately after the 1980 coup, the Doe-led Peoples Redemption Council was denied legal legitimacy by both the Organization of African Unity (OAU) and the Economic Community of West African States (ECOWAS). Both were affected by the dominant policies of Nigeria, which was intensely opposed to Doe and his coup, as were most other neighboring African states. Tolbert had built good personal and political relations with most of his neighboring governments. The latter were shocked by the brutality of the coup, seen as especially egregious because Tolbert at that time was president of the OAU. And several African governments feared a domino effect from the coup, particularly since Jerry Rawlings, likewise an undereducated NCO, had recently seized the government in Ghana.[32]

This initial international opposition in Africa gradually yielded to grudging acceptance and recognition of the Doe regime, especially since the United States made a major economic and diplomatic commitment to Doe from 1981 until the late 1980s. It was Doe's fortune to seize power in Monrovia when the Carter administration was emphasizing security issues in the wake of the seizure of the U.S. embassy in Iran and the Soviet invasion of Afghanistan. Indeed, in Washington in 1980, there was a bipartisan and bibranch consensus that the United States should support Doe both because of the prospects for improvement over the settler regime and because of fear of encroachment by the Soviet Union and its allies. During 1980, the Carter team increased economic and military assistance to the Doe regime; economic aid went from $17.6 million to $23.5 million, military aid from $1.5 million to $2.7 million.[33]

For its part, the Reagan administration initially viewed the world almost solely in terms of the West versus the East and capitalism versus socialism. Doe posed no threat to U.S. strategic installations in Liberia (after a brief flirtation with Libya and others of concern to

Washington), and he proved to have conventional views of economic development—however much they were affected by corruption and personal aggrandizement.

During 1981 the Reagan team, even though working under a budget established by Carter, was able to reprogram funds to begin a U.S. foreign-assistance buildup that was massive by Liberian standards. Economic aid, including Economic Support Funds (ESF), which are closely tied to military purposes, jumped to $55.1 million. Military aid was increased to $6.3 million. This was the beginning of a Reagan policy in Liberia—actually a microcosm of Washington's orientation to many friendly countries during 1981–85—of emphasizing strategic alliances to the exclusion of most other factors. From 1980 through 1985, U.S. foreign assistance to Monrovia increased about 600 percent, with much of this either ESF or outright military assistance.[34]

In the early 1980s Congress supported this foreign policy in general. The Senate was under Republican control during Reagan's early years. The Senate Foreign Relations Committee issued a staff report in 1982 stressing security links and noting in passing that the army was "vital" to Doe's continuation[35] (domestic legitimacy being absent). That report, however, questioned the size of the U.S. military-assistance program, including the number of military advisers that the executive branch wanted in Liberia. There is no record of organized House concern with Liberia during this period.

Therefore, until the fraudulent elections of 1985, international legitimacy was provided chiefly by the United States, building on its special relationship with Liberia. The rationale was primarily political, mainly strategic. Both Carter (in his last two years) and Reagan (especially in his first four years) emphasized military assistance (mainly ESF) to regimes strongly anti-Communist and pro-capitalist. The Carter and Reagan teams could also easily argue, until 1985, that the Doe coup might lead to more democracy and economic "good government" by comparison with the Tolbert period. Doe's actions during his early days of rule did indeed hold out that promise. Thus moral legitimacy was added to the political. Legal legitimacy, as a consequence, fell into place, both within the OAU and United Nations and bilaterally. In the context of a lack of domestic legitimacy for the Doe faction, this international legitimacy—together with its tangible component, foreign assistance—was important. Doe ruled by military force, however much he might speak about a transition to democracy, and the United States provided military assistance, military advisers, and related economic assistance. The United States also strongly supported loans for Liberia via the World Bank and the International Monetary Fund (IMF).

The Second Phase, 1985–1989

Domestic factors. The longer Doe stayed in power, the clearer it became that personal power and clan advantage were the hallmarks of his tenure. Like many others who took office by force of arms, he ruled essentially by that same method. He never cultivated important sources of domestic legitimacy, other than an attempt at a personality cult. His insistence on being called "Doctor Doe" (South Korea awarded him an honorary doctorate) and his other demands for compliance did not, to put it mildly, generate a sense of correctness of rule. Most of those who had cooperated in the 1980 coup were forced from power because they posed potential threats to Doe's personal power; several were killed.[36]

Electoral fraud had deprived his presidency of any sense of legal legitimacy. Moral sources were undermined not only by violation of genuine democratic standards but also by a resumption of the brutalities that had marked his assumption of power. Political murder, mutilation, arbitrary detention, torture, mistreatment, and other violations of civil rights were documented not only by human rights agencies but also by Reagan's State Department and by an increasingly critical Congress.[37] Critical journalistic sources in Liberia were curtailed, shut down, and in one instance burned down.[38]

Doe, rather than breaking with the historical tradition of discrimination on the basis of origin or ethnicity, amplified that tradition, turning the question of minority privilege into the pervasive moral issue that it had been in the late 1970s. Two close observers wrote in 1987, "Not only is there no change of substance [by comparison with the settler regimes], but the worst features of the past have been adopted and extended . . . the 'politics of tribe' *has* come to Liberia since the 1980 installation of military rule."[39]

A microcosm of the broader situation is probably well captured by this description by a dissident from the Gio group:

> I had had many problems at work. Because of my ethnic background, I always had problems with the authorities. This went back to 1985, when they started calling us trouble-makers. [The Krahns associated the Gio and Mano with the Quiwonkpa

putsch of 1985.] After the coup attempt, they made a survey of all the Gio and Mano people working in the government and put us on a list to be fired. They pretended it was due to financial constraints and need to reduce the labor force. My boss told me that in order to keep my position, I should give him a cow. But even after I did that, they stripped me of my authority . . . [and] they took away my car. Other people who were at my level had cars and other benefits, but I wasn't even allowed to ride the bus which picked up my secretaries. It was very frustrating and unfair. When the rebels came, I was happy because our lives were miserable under Doe, and power concedes nothing without a demand.[40]

Functional sources of legitimacy, stemming from positive governmental performance, could not have been more supportive of challengers to Doe's rule. Almost all economic indicators during the 1980s pointed in the negative direction. During the 1980s, the Liberian economy went from bad to worse. According to the World Bank, the GNP declined 1.3 percent from 1980 to 1988. Domestic investment shrunk by 16.7 percent for the same period. The balance of payments deficit had gone from –$16 million in 1970 to –$118 million in 1988. During that same time, the public external debt went from $158 million to $1,101 million. All the while, the population increased by over 3 percent per annum.[41] While global markets in natural rubber and iron ore, Liberia's principal exports, declined, Doe's mismanagement of the economy greatly accelerated the inherent problems. (Historically, neither the indigene nor the settler community had been known for remarkable entrepreneurship. The settlers had contracted out to Americans, Indians, Lebanese, and other foreigners much basic economic activity, getting a share of the returns via governmental regulation.)[42]

In addition to the World Bank, other external sources certified the extent of domestic economic chaos. In 1986 the General Accounting Office of the United States indicated that $66.5 million in U.S. foreign assistance to Liberia could not be accounted for.[43] In 1987, the International Monetary Fund declared Liberia in default of its obligations and suspended further drawing rights, having already given up, back in 1985, on efforts to get the government to agree to reforms. At about the same time, the World Bank suspended loan possibilities.[44] In 1986–87 the Reagan administration got an agreement from Doe for a U.S. team of financial managers to take a look at, and presumably help correct, the governmental finances; the team left after one year, having declared the figures a hopeless mess.[45] In the midst of all this economic decay, Doe spent lavishly on automobiles, airplanes, and other presidential perks.[46] Exactly how much Doe siphoned off to himself and his cronies will probably never be firmly established.

Somehow out of this economic mismanagement and corruption, several socioeconomic indicators turned up positive numbers. The number of doctors per inhabitants went up, as did the calorie supply, and infant mortality went down.[47] These factors pertaining to health and nutrition may have helped deter further challenges to the government; they certainly did not generate much real legitimacy in the face of the larger economic decline.

From the time of the 1985 elections until late 1989, there was a series of alleged and sometimes real coup attempts against the Doe regime. The difficulty of separating fact from government-inspired fiction (to justify repressive rule) makes it impossible to say just how many attempts. But starting in December 1989, an armed rebellion gathered support. This eventually became a tricornered civil war, complicated further by the introduction of outside troops. The bloody and complex situation eventually led to the torture and killing of Doe.

In 1980 Doe had promised, "We have not taken over this government only to bring back the same kind of government that we removed."[48] Yet he had done precisely that. Moreover, just as Tolbert had spent lavishly in the context of a declining national economy, so had Doe. And in 1990 Doe met the same type of brutal death that he and his cohorts had inflicted on Tolbert and most of his cabinet. Doe's government had become essentially the same as Tolbert's, only worse. Doe's demise was similar to Tolbert's, only worse. At least Tolbert had not been tortured to death.

The failure of Doe's repressive actions to maintain his rule turned Liberia into a killing field throughout 1990 and into 1991. Around Christmas 1989, Charles Taylor, with a mixed ancestry partly in the settler community, had launched a rebellion. Moving back into Liberia from Sierra Leone with a very few supporters, he utilized anti-Doe and anti-Krahn feeling in Nimba County, dominated by the Gio and Mano peoples. The Liberian army then carried out repressive measures in Nimba, involving attacks on civilians. Taylor's rebels responded in kind against the Krahn and their close allies, or their perceived allies, the Mandingos. Most of this initial violence in late 1989 and early 1990 was therefore interethnic, with little involvement by settlers.

Doe's lack of legitimacy, when added to the brutality and indiscriminate nature of army operations, contributed to Taylor's success, despite allegations linking Taylor to corruption when he had held government office in Monrovia. His forces, initially perhaps only fifty but enlarged by those galvanized by atrocities into a force of perhaps ten thousand, steadily advanced toward Monrovia during early 1990. Taylor's National Patriotic Front for Liberia called for Doe's resignation, but Doe refused.

Complicating matters was the fact that the rebel movement splintered in February. Prince Johnson, of uncertain ancestry, led a breakaway faction, also relying on mainly Gio and Mano support and eventually calling itself the Independent Patriotic Front for Liberia. As Taylor's forces were finally being stymied by the Krahn remnant of the army, Johnson's forces continued to advance. Johnson and his forces captured Doe, who had repeatedly refused to yield the presidency despite the magnitude of the opposition against him; Johnson then made a videotape of the torture and murder of Doe (September 1990).[49] As a result two private armies, Taylor's and Johnson's, with comparable records of brutality and atrocity, competed for power, with both leaders claiming the presidency.

The bifurcated armed rebellion, though generating thousands of supporters, had nevertheless failed to enlist massive popular support. Perhaps 50 percent of the Liberian population had either fled as war refugees (probably over six hundred thousand) into neighboring countries, principally Guinea, the Ivory Coast, and Sierra Leone, or had become internally displaced.[50] The Gio and Mano groups had been terrorized by the Krahn-dominated army; the Krahn and the Mandingos had been terrorized first by Taylor's forces and then by Johnson's; and the other ethnic groups, including many settlers, had been caught in the cross fire. In Monrovia, for example, Krahn members of the Liberian army entered areas supposedly "protected" by the Red Cross symbol and systematically murdered six hundred civilians, including women and children. Given these indiscriminate brutalities, it is no wonder that many Liberians fled from the three armies rather than join them.

Therefore, unlike some other domestic upheavals (e.g., in Iran, Nicaragua, or the Philippines), the revolution in Liberia did not consist of a broad opposition front united in immediate goals. There was not one popular revolution against Doe and his Krahn-based rule but rather two armed rebellions heavily influenced by personal ambition and ethnic friction, with most of the population fleeing the action. In the process, much of the economic infrastructure—including dams, farms, rubber plantations, mines, and banks—was destroyed. Perhaps 80 percent of Monrovians were malnourished during 1990.

Complicating the situation still further was the introduction of military troops from certain African states, acting under the name of ECOWAS. International factors came to play an increasingly important role in the disintegration of Liberia during 1990–91, although such international factors had never been totally absent.

International factors. Although the United States, under the rubric of a "special relationship," had been Liberia's most important foreign patron, as we saw in an earlier section, this did not prevent other states from taking an active role in Liberian developments. Progressively, the United States deferred to military action by ECOWAS, refusing to engage in structural military intervention to affect the basic power relationships in Liberia. Rather, the United States resorted to diplomacy supportive of Nigeria and ECOWAS, plus humanitarian intervention (in August 1990) to rescue Americans and other foreigners whose lives and basic human rights were at risk. This was in marked contrast to U.S. structural interventions in Grenada, Nicaragua, and Panama.

Somewhat surprisingly, given the professed U.S. strategic interests in Liberia, the Bush administration did not try to control events in Monrovia—at least not directly. This may have been because no contender could claim any degree of moral legitimacy, given the atrocities committed. It was probably also because of the end of the cold war and the disintegration of the Soviet Union.

In fact, the Bush team did not have a free hand in dealing with Liberia. Congress had been trying to restrict U.S. foreign assistance on human rights grounds ever since the fraudulent elections of 1985. Before that election, there were sufficient votes in Congress to state clearly that the only legitimate government in Monrovia would be that government based on free and fair elections (the standard moral-legal source of legitimacy). In the 1985 Security and Development Cooperation Act, Section 807, Congress had stated: "U.S. interests in a stable, friendly regime will best be served by legitimate civilian rule in Liberia. . . . [Congress] is basing its approval of security assistance . . . on the expectations of a successful completion of free and fair elections on a multiparty basis . . . and a return to full civilian, constitutional rule as a consequence of such elections."[51]

Subsequently, Senator Howard Wolpe asked the Reagan administration in 1986, somewhat rhetorically, "In light of the recent developments which include reported election irregularities, the postelection attempted coup, and the reported reactions by the Liberian People [street demonstrations in support of the erroneously reported coup success], is the Doe government perceived by the general Liberian public as a legitimate government?"[52] In 1986–88, Congress, believing that the Doe government was not legitimate, passed various restrictions on U.S. bilateral aid to Liberia.

The Reagan administration, by contrast, tried to put a positive gloss on Liberian events. In 1985, the assistant secretary of state for Africa, Chester Crocker, told Congress, "Election day was a remarkable achievement, given the history, given the lack of experience."[53] One year later, Crocker was still seeing matters in a positive light: "We believe there is reason to keep trying to work with the Doe government to make the promise of Liberia's Second Republic succeed. There is in Liberia today a civilian government, a multiparty legislature, a journalistic community of government and nongovernment newspapers and radio stations, an ongoing tradition among the citizenry of speaking out, a new constitution that protects freedoms and a judicial system that can help enforce those provisions."[54] Secretary of State George Shultz visited Monrovia in 1987, tried to sweep the facts of repression and mismanagement under the diplomatic carpet, and gave a de facto "pat on the back" to Doe.[55] This venture in cover-up diplomacy displeased private human rights agencies closely watching the situation, and they worked with a bipartisan group in Congress. By 1988, U.S. foreign assistance to Liberia had dropped to $23.7 million (having reached a high of $82.3 million back in 1985).

The 1990 restraint in Bush policy—that is, in not trying directly and militarily to control Liberian events—may have stemmed not only from congressional pressure over human rights (and moral-legal sources of legitimacy) but also from a changed perception of strategic need, given a different foreign policy by the Soviet Union. Moreover, Taylor was seen as having links to Libya via Burkino Fasso, and both Taylor and Johnson had threatened to take foreign hostages or had actually taken them. Moreover, the United States seemed not to want to get involved in perhaps a series of African military interventions (it also avoided one in the Somalian civil war), preferring to let African states make the decisions about direct, structural intervention.

Also important to Bush policy was the fact that no major actor in the Liberian civil war had been able to maintain legitimacy, whether from a legal, moral, or political point of view. U.S. advisers had been with the Liberian army when it had first sought to pacify Nimba County.[56] But the Bush administration came to effectively withdraw legitimacy from the Doe regime, despite U.S. foreign assistance of over $500 million since 1980, aside from comparable multilateral assistance from the World Bank and IMF. When Taylor demanded Doe's resignation in 1990, the United States claimed it offered its good offices to arrange safe passage for Doe,[57] thus indicating a lack of support for Doe. Washington had done the same vis-à-vis Anastasio Somoza Debayle in Nicaragua in 1979, facilitating his removal from Managua.

As the carnage increased, Nigeria took the lead in a regional military arrangement of dubious legality and unclear objective. An economic group of sixteen states, ECOWAS had no explicit authority to engage in security or military operations and certainly no explicit authority to intervene in a state that had not requested outside involvement. But its Military Observer Group (ECOMOG), a fighting force initially of six thousand troops, was quickly augmented to ten thousand. As a consequence of these legal and political uncertainties, several member states, most of them Francophone, objected to the Liberian intervention.

Nevertheless, under Nigeria's leadership if not dominance, ECOMOG in August 1990 went forward, or at least went into Monrovia, where it was militarily stalemated on the ground and politically stalemated in general. It was criticized for triggering the killing of civilians who were nationals of states participating in ECOMOG, for defending the Krahn, for fighting Taylor's forces but not Johnson's, for shelling the port of Buchanan and causing considerable civilian damage, for not defending the Krahn sufficiently, and for supporting a third political force—namely an interim government headed by Amos Sawyer. Progressively, however, ECOMOG helped to end the actual fighting and attacks on civilians, which had claimed more than ten thousand lives, at least in and around Monrovia. Yet the decline in shooting was not accompanied by a clear and rapid movement toward a peaceful resolution of questions of governance.

At the time of this writing, Liberia remained without effective government, with Charles Taylor, Prince Johnson, and Amos Sawyer all claiming the presidency. Personal ambition by the first two, or in the words of a U.S. official, "some big egos,"[58] had stymied the search for a consensus. Nigeria, with U.S. diplomatic support, had thrown its weight behind Sawyer, at least as an interim measure, but this inter-mestic (international and domestic) alignment had failed to cause Tay-lor and Johnson to alter their ambitions. It came down to a question of power, and Taylor and Johnson still had enough military force to back their unbending claims.

CONCLUSIONS

Viewed in hindsight, the disintegration of Liberia, once an African model of political stability, into bloody and inconclusive domestic war is reasonably understandable, even though the actual dates of coup and rebellion could not have been predicted with exactitude. Both the demise of the Tolbert-settler regime and the overthrow of the Doe-Krahn regime are understandable in terms of the absence or weakness of legitimacy. That the Doe regime lasted as long as it did is due as much to international legitimacy awarded by the Reagan administra-tion for political reasons as to the effectiveness of Doe's internal re-pressive measures. But these indiscriminate and ethnically oriented measures eventually contributed to his downfall too.

The settler dynasty persisted as long as it did—for over 130 years—principally because of the Liberian informal ideology, reinforced by historical tradition, which awarded legitimate governing status to Americo-Liberians and their descendents. This political conscious-ness was carefully nurtured by the ruling elite, but the elite's domin-ion over political attitudes was seriously undermined by Tubman's policies of unification and integration after World War II. The Africa-nization, urbanization, increased wealth, and education of Liberia in the 1950s and 1960s changed views on legitimate government. More indigenes resisted automatic settler rule, demanding more attention to moral-legal sources of legitimate government via democratic elec-tions and associated civil rights that were supportive of indigene ma-jority rule.

The Doe coup of 1980, which took place in the context of a more as-sertive indigene community, could not have been predicted in the sense that social science cannot predict the actions of seventeen indi-viduals with no record of political activity. One might have expected some type of political activity from the Loma in the military, but not from a few Krahn. Yet almost all sources of legitimacy for the Tolbert regime were clearly weakening, and it seemed only a matter of time until the settler hegemony would yield, either peacefully or violently. The failure of the Tolbert government to control the rice riots of early 1979, without outside help, showed the lack of both the legitimacy and the repressive power of Liberia's traditional ruling group—a group that had become badly split over power sharing versus a repressive status quo. But Doe learned nothing from Liberian—or any other—history. He progressively eschewed cultivation of domestic sources of legitimacy, ultimately resting his rule on feeble attempts at a personality cult and repression by his ethnic kin. He broke with historical tradition and rejected the previous informal ideology sustaining settler rule. But he failed to generate domestic legitimacy from positive governmental performance, Liberian nationalism, adherence to legal rules, or commitment to widely shared views of political morality. After the fraudulent elections of 1985, it was clear that his regime lacked domestic legitimacy in the eyes of most politically active Liberians, and he was able to rely only on repression and political apathy for his continuation in office.

In this situation, the support of the Reagan administration was crucial in keeping Doe in power, especially since a number of neighboring states had first opposed the Doe group and tried to deny it international legal and moral legitimacy. But U.S. foreign policy during the Reagan years was heavily affected by political alignment in the East-West, capitalist-socialist struggle. Because of Doe's pro-Washington, pro-capitalist policies, the Reagan team provided sizable amounts of military assistance, including military officials on the ground, which helped to sustain Doe's rule. This executive orientation was increasingly challenged by Congress, relying on a moral-legal standard of legitimacy at variance with the Reagan team's political standard. In the context of civil war, and in the context of reduced East-West tensions, the Bush administration eventually withdrew legitimacy from Doe and apparently offered to escort him out of the country.

Given that diplomatic signal, Nigeria pushed ahead with a controversial military intervention, via ECOWAS, that was designed to move Doe aside. Both Nigeria and the United States, with their supporters, tried to arrange for an interim government led by Sawyer, pending installation of a government whose legitimacy would be derived from internationally supervised elections. But Taylor and Johnson, largely devoid of legitimacy themselves, nevertheless retained blocking power.

A return to political stability in Liberia would be facilitated by combining important sources of domestic legitimacy—principally, democratic elections leading to a broad-based government functioning effectively for the benefit of Liberians regardless of origin, language, and ethnicity. Such a government would receive international support, from both Nigeria and the United States. Such a government would thus combine domestic and international sources of legitimacy centering on law, morality, and performance. In historical fact, Liberia never had such a government. Whether it could develop one in the 1990s, and how it could overcome the various "big egos" that wanted to continue personal rule linked to ethnicity, remained uncertain.

6

Domestic War in Romania

The year 1989 marked the changing of the Communist guard throughout Eastern Europe. From Prague to Sofia, Communist regimes swiftly collapsed. In Romania, however, the removal of the old guard was not achieved with the same ease and completeness as in several other former Eastern bloc nations. The Romanian political revolution of 1989 was in some ways like the French revolution of 1789, although on a smaller scale. Both were violent and incomplete, leaving a residue of bitterness and confusion for years afterward. Both contained an important human rights component, although again on a smaller scale in Romania.

On December 15, 1989, several hundred ethnic Hungarians gathered in the western city of Timisoara to protest the forced eviction of the Hungarian Reformed pastor Laszlo Toekes from his parish. Toekes was an outspoken critic of President Ceausescu for his record on human rights and specifically the rights of minorities. On the following day, protests over Toekes's eviction by Romanian authorities broadened in size and in scope to include ethnic Romanian students and workers. As the demonstration grew, protesters began to call for the end of Communist rule and chanted anti-Ceausescu slogans. On the afternoon of December 17, the increasing momentum of protests in Timisoara was met by the army and the Securitate (the special security force or palace guard), who fired on the crowds of demonstrators.

When Ceausescu returned from a state visit to Iran on the twentieth, he declared a state of emergency in western Romania and blamed the protests in Timisoara on the work of outsiders from both the East and the West. As foreign radio broadcasts spread the news of the killings in Timisoara, demonstrations erupted in Romania's major cities. These demonstrations spread to Bucharest on the twenty-first as a planned rally of support for Ceausescu turned on the Romanian president. The following day, elements of the Romanian army joined the side of the protesters as a group calling itself the Council of National Salvation announced the overthrow of Ceausescu. But fighting in Romania continued as army troops loyal to the provisional government fought members of Ceausescu's Securitate. In Bucharest, fighting was heavy around the television station as the provisional government fought to keep control of the state media. On December 23, Romania's Front for National Salvation announced the capture of Ceausescu and his wife in a town north of Bucharest. On December 25, 1989, the Romanian media reported the execution of Nicolae and Elena Ceausescu after a secret trial found them guilty of "genocide."

Although it is relatively easy to re-create a superficial description of events, it is much more difficult to explain definitively why events transpired as they did and what these events imply for the future. Some of the difficulty in analyzing the key concept of political legitimacy in Romania can be seen in the fate of Ceausescu, the president and general secretary of the Romanian Communist party. Unanimously reelected to that post in late November 1989 with public displays of broad support, within a month Ceausescu and his wife, Elena, were the objects of an even broader ridicule and were shot by firing squad. Rights to life, peaceful assembly, religious freedom, and minority protection were central to spiraling events. Yet the Ceausescus were removed from power in a very irregular process by persons whose commitment to human rights was highly suspect.

DOMESTIC LEGITIMACY

In late 1989 Nicolae Ceausescu seemed to be a firm bulwark against the currents of pluralistic reform sweeping the USSR and Eastern Europe. In celebration of his reelection as party general secretary, large crowds of workers waited for four hours to hear Ceausescu speak for ten minutes about Romania's glowing prospects for the future.[1] This controlled and orchestrated gathering epitomized the situation of regime stability, but without genuine political legitimacy for probably the majority of Romanians.

The absence of revolutionary behavior against Ceausescu before late December 1989 can be explained first by a set of interrelated domestic factors: (1) attempts to create a personality cult; (2) the merger of this cult with policies pursuing national autonomy; (3) the implicit linkage of these policies with appeals to nationalism, despite an official Marxist dogma stressing international class solidarity; and (4) a dominant national political morality strong on deference to authority and weak on assertions of individual and group rights.

These domestic sources of regime stability were eventually undermined by disastrous policies that, since Ceausescu was clearly the person responsible, destroyed his image of a wise leader committed to the good of the nation. General dissatisfaction with the economy and with lack of power sharing provided the background for an outbreak of demonstrations protesting the absence of minority and religious freedoms.

The events of 1989 showed, at least in retrospect, that a deference to dictatorship combined with active repression was not a substitute for positive sources of legitimacy. Encouraged by international developments, many Romanians finally revolted to throw off twenty-four years of absolute dictatorship. As usual, there was no one cause of revolutionary events. Nevertheless, the different forces or factors feeding into decisive events can be identified.

Personal Legitimacy

Rarely does any one individual penetrate the life of an entire nation in the manner in which Nicolae Ceausescu appeared to penetrate every aspect of Romanian life. A Romanian author explained quite simply, "When you say Ceausescu, you say Romania."[2]

The first Communist dictator of modern Romania, Gheorghe Gheorghiu-Dej, was apparently impressed by Ceausescu's Communist activism and thus fostered a close relationship that was to facilitate Ceausescu's rise through the party ranks.[3] Gheorghiu-Dej spoke of Ceausescu as the "perfect embodiment of the Stalinist apparatchik."[4] Such favor from Gheorghiu-Dej did not, however, guarantee Ceausescu's succession to the leadership of the Romanian Communist party following Gheorghiu-Dej's death in 1965. During a period of collective leadership after Gheorghiu-Dej's death, Ceausescu worked to discredit his opponents and consolidate his power. Ceausescu took an important step in this consolidation process at the Central Committee Plenum in April 1968. In the same tradition in which Nikita Khrushchev renounced Stalin, Ceausescu attacked the excesses of Gheorghiu-Dej and launched a purge of the former leader's sympathizers. As a result of this purge, Ceausescu was able to eliminate his major rivals, especially the secret police chief, Alexandru Draghici, and move further toward supremacy over the party apparatus.

Other events in the spring of 1968 provided Ceausescu with the opportunity to present himself as a national hero. In Czechoslovakia, Alexander Dubček's "socialism with a human face" raised the threat of Soviet military intervention. Ceausescu asserted Romania's national independence by refusing to allow Romanian troops to participate in the planning of or action by the Warsaw Pact of Communist armies.

On August 21, 1968, after the Soviet-led invasion of Czechoslovakia, Ceausescu addressed a large and enthusiastic crowd in Bucharest's Palace Square and rejected the Brezhnev Doctrine by denouncing Soviet interference in the internal affairs of another socialist state.[5] Clearly Ceausescu's refusal to send troops to Prague came not from support for Dubček's liberal reforms but from fear that Ceausescu's own independent course might lead to similar action on the part of the Soviets. Yet conventional wisdom holds that Ceausescu's fear of a Soviet move into Romania was greatly exaggerated. Although Dubček and Ceausescu, not to mention Tito in Yugoslavia, were deviating from Soviet policies, Ceausescu was doing so in ways that did not threaten Soviet totalitarian control within the USSR. By contrast, had Dubček been successful in implementing civil and political rights within a largely socialist Czechoslovakia, pressures would have grown for domestic political reform in the Soviet Union. Ceausescu, being clearly Stalinist, presented no such threat to Moscow, however much of a nuisance his foreign policy might have been in the Middle East, East Asia, and elsewhere.

For the Romanian population, however, the fear of a Soviet invasion in 1968 was real. This perception of fear created a national hero out of Ceausescu, not only for his refusal to send troops to Czechoslovakia but also for his determination to defend Romania against a similar Soviet threat. On the strength of his nationalistic stand in 1968, Ceausescu consolidated his personal power at the Tenth Party Congress in 1969.[6] Thus he merged the start of a personality cult with an appeal to Romanian nationalism.

In March 1974, Ceausescu became the president of the Romanian

Socialist Republic. An element of royal pageantry surrounded the new president as he was sworn into the office created especially for him.[7] In other ways too, the portrait of Ceausescu painted by the artisans of his cult of personality is distinguished not only by its creativity but also by the depth to which it penetrated Romanian society. For every letter of the alphabet, there was an adjective or a phrase to illustrate Ceausescu's greatness.[8] On the sixty-fifth anniversary of the unification of Romania at the end of World War II, "even the folk dancers and ballerinas who performed somehow managed to weave Mr. Ceausescu's virtues into their pageantry."[9] These adjectives and phrases formed rhythmic chants, which greeted Ceausescu at party functions and national celebrations.

Ceausescu's image as a revolutionary and a true interpreter of the science of Marxism-Leninism-Stalinism is detailed in volume upon volume of cult propaganda. One such volume was published on the occasion of Ceausescu's sixtieth birthday in 1978. The work, entitled *Omagiu*, makes a 664-page tribute to the life and accomplishments of the Romanian leader. The visual image of Ceausescu created by the cult was always ten years younger and at least several inches taller than Ceausescu's actual age and stature. Ceausescu's wit and intelligence were attested to in the honorary degrees he received not only from Romanian universities but from universities throughout the world. In reality, Ceausescu had minimal formal education. Ceausescu was given credit either for the substance or for the inspiration of every good idea generated in Romania. Nothing in Romania could be written or created without reference to Ceausescu's guiding intellect or motivation.[10]

The cult of personality that deified Nicolae Ceausescu became a family affair in the early 1970s as it embraced Ceausescu's wife, Elena. Elena's increased adulation in the press corresponded to her elevation in the party ranks and to her heightened political position. In the early 1970s, Nicolae Ceausescu created a policy to increase the labor force by promoting women's participation in the workplace. The design of this campaign was not so much to elevate the position of women in general as it was to promote Elena to the Romanian Communist Party Executive Committee in 1973.[11] One of her most important steps to power in the party was her 1979 promotion to the position of chair of the Central Committee commission for state and party cadres. Through this position, Elena was able to manipulate the appointments of Romania's top party and state officials. In 1980 she became deputy first prime minister, achieving a position of power second only to that of her husband.[12] Only with her blessing were individuals elevated to Ceausescu's inner circle.

The Romanian royal family had not only a king and a queen but also a favorite prince. This prince was the Ceausescus' son, Nicu, who, like his mother, climbed the ranks of the party on the tails of his father's cult of personality.[13] The rise of both Elena and Nicu obviously showed the extent of nepotism in the Romanian regime. When combined with other policies, it had a damaging effect on public policy.

Party and state cadres were rotated often so as not to allow any individual or group to establish a base of power independent from that of the leader and his family. This constant rotation of officials, to protect the "royal" family, was marked by incompetence and inefficiency. Individuals were placed in positions for which they had no knowledge or ability to succeed.

Challenges to the primacy of the dictator and his family simply were not tolerated. For example, a party member, Constantin Pirvulescu, was openly critical of Ceausescu at the Twelfth Party Congress in 1979. Pirvulescu censored Ceausescu "for having usurped political power, transformed the party into a mere instrument for his glorification, and imposed a family dictatorship."[14] Ceausescu responded to this outburst with a heavy hand, as well as with a further flurry of pro-Ceausescu cult propaganda. The same pattern held a decade later, when six party members who had lost their senior positions sent a letter to Ceausescu criticizing various aspects of his policies. Again, the dictator ignored their complaints and responded with repressive measures.[15]

Ceausescu's rule by cult and clan had certain negative consequences for his efforts to generate legitimacy on a personal basis. A growing personality cult did not translate well into genuine legitimacy for his rule. Increasingly from the late 1970s, he was unable to meet a number of widespread expectations held by many Romanians, including demands for "increased discussion and 'participation,' socialist legality and rapid economic development."[16] When these expectations were not realized, the gulf between Ceausescu's policies, particularly in the area of the economy and power sharing, and the wishes of the Romanian people broadened. This gulf then led to renewed efforts at a personality cult.[17]

One of the most important negative consequences was the alienation of some members of the party and/or army. For these people, the royal image of the Ceausescus was fundamentally incompatible with a broader elite.[18] Just as some Soviet Communists, like Khrushchev, had professed a dislike for the elevation of Stalin over the party, so some Romanian Communists were alienated by the elevation of the Ceausescu clan over the primacy of the party. But the occasional open criticism by some party members yielded only negative results for them personally.

Ceausescu was able to repress others in official positions because of the loyalty to him of the Securitate, who enforced his repressive commands. Ceausescu won their allegiance with relatively higher salaries, better military equipment than possessed by the regular army, and other perks. This situation naturally offended senior members of the regular army, who were shortchanged on training, equipment, and even control over their subordinates. Decisions were made that affected the army in several ways, such as assignment to civilian construction projects, without the concurrence of the army high command.

As Ceausescu and his family eclipsed others holding official positions, policy was made by dictatorship and not by oligarchy. Beneath the public show of support for the dictator was significant, if quiet, alienation by those who wanted a broader elite—but who were by no means democrats wanting to transfer more power to the people.

Another important consequence of Ceausescu's highly personalized rule was the direct blame he (and his family) received for all of Romania's ills. It was widely known, because it was widely advertised, that Ceausescu was at the very center of every important decision made. No major policy initiative could be taken without his approval. For example, response to the 1977 earthquake lagged because Ceausescu was out of the country; not even disaster relief could go forward without the guiding hand of the dictator. As a result, the social and economic problems that plagued Romania, especially during the 1980s, fell right into Ceausescu's authoritarian lap. Personal leadership increasingly became a liability rather than a widely accepted source of legitimate rule.

Functional Legitimacy

Romanian governments from about 1960 sought both industrialized growth and national autonomy. The 1964 "Statement on the Stand of the Romanian Worker's Party Concerning the Problems of the International Communist and Working Class Movement" was a clear economic declaration of independence from the Soviet Union and its plans, via the Council for Mutual Economic Assistance (CMEA), to emphasize Romanian agriculture within regional economic planning. The declaration openly stated that Romanian Communists would not sacrifice autonomy and industry for the sake of a Soviet master plan seen as beneficial to Moscow.

It was overstated, but generally correct, that under the direction of Ceausescu, the push for "multilateral industrialization became the ultimate purpose of the Romanian leadership."[19] The ultimate purpose of Romanian leadership was to hold and exercise power. Beyond that fundamental purpose, Ceausescu pursued industrialized growth for the nation with as little reliance on any one other state as possible. Romania's pattern of economic development, as well as its problematic results, is reflective of a combination of Stalinist procedures and a relatively autonomous orientation.

As early as 1947, the party sponsored a program of rapid industrialization.[20] The process of industrialization and modernization in Romania advocated the Stalinist practices of central planning, collectivization of agriculture, and development of heavy industry. This program of development initially achieved some measure of success for the Romanian economy, which boasted a high rate of growth between about 1950 and the late 1960s. Industrial workers in Romania saw a relative improvement in their standard of living during this era as the mostly rural work force migrated to larger urban areas for employment.

Thus, for the first decade of Ceausescu's personalized rule, considerable macro-economic growth was achieved, with some trickle-down effect for the population.[21] Some success could also be measured in terms of Romania's relative autonomy from the Soviet Union and the CMEA. By 1970, Romanian trade with the Soviet bloc fell to less than one half its previous total.[22]

In addition, Romania was internationally rewarded, for deviation from the Soviet orbit, with a host of foreign credit opportunities. Romania found the capital as well as the technology needed for its rapid industrialization from sources in the United States, Canada, and Western Europe. Ceausescu's identification of Romania as a "socialist developing state" in the early 1970s increased Romania's economic opportunities for new markets in the Third World and gave it a new preferential status with the European Economic Community.[23]

Romania's economic success was soon beset with a host of problems. In addition to the inefficiencies inherent in a command economy, the international oil crisis of 1973 and a damaging earthquake in 1977 converged to turn macro-growth and limited trickle-down into negative growth and declining real income for the vast number of Romanians. Partly due to increased oil prices, the period from the mid-1970s to the early 1980s was marked by a shift in trade away from Western sources and toward Eastern Europe and the Soviet Union. Romania was forced to rely on the Soviet Union for deliveries of crude oil for the first time in 1979.[24] Because Romania had distanced itself from the CMEA, it did not enjoy a favorable rate of exchange for crude oil from the Soviets. Romania's favorable balance of trade with the Third World declined after 1976.[25] In 1981 Romania requested IMF refinancing of its $11-billion debt when it became unable to meet the schedule of payments.[26]

Romania's extensive debt marred the domestic economy not so much because of the total dollar amount of indebtedness but because of Ceausescu's highly accelerated program of repayment. He blamed his country's economic situation on mistakes both by other Romanians and by foreign capitalists.[27] As a result, Ceausescu's plan for "fixing" Romania's economic situation did not include reform of outdated Stalinist methods but rather the swift elimination of debt through domestic austerity. The basic premise of Ceausescu's plan to retire Romania's foreign debt required drastic cuts in imports in addition to increased exports of anything that could be exchanged for hard currency.

The economic policies of Ceausescu's regime reflected his own elevated sense of worth (he continued to spend lavishly on himself and his family, as in the construction of a new presidential palace), his pursuit of national autonomy at any cost (he demanded export of foodstuffs while malnutrition was prevalent in his country), and his disdain for the plight of his citizens (who were reduced to the lowest standard of living in Europe, with the exception of Albania). One does not lack for examples of the ill effects of Ceausescu's forced austerity on Romania's standard of living. Drastic cuts in energy consumption forced Romanians in 1983 to limit their use of electricity to 50 percent of the previous year.[28] Heat for homes and businesses was cut to only seven hours per day. Diners in Bucharest's restaurants were often seen wearing big fur hats; the Romanian joke quipped, "Do not open the window—a passer-by might catch a cold."[29]

Low investment in agriculture during Romania's push for industrialization created problems for the Romanian economy, problems that were magnified by enforced austerity. In an attempt to cover the shortage of basic food staples, many of which were exported for hard currency, Ceausescu created a "scientific diet," which, for example, tried to reduce drastically the consumption of meat.[30] The scarcity of basic foodstuffs as well as other consumer goods led to the proliferation of black market transactions and corruption.

Economic problems were not unique to Romania but were shared by the majority of command systems by the end of the 1980s. These problems were magnified in Romania, however, because of Ceausescu's drastic methods of debt reduction and his refusal to abandon Stalinist economic practices. Ceausescu's firm stance against economic reform, combined with violations of civil and political rights, increasingly isolated Romania from foreign help for its desperate economic plight, especially when independence from the USSR meant less and less to the West.

Given the situation of the Romanian economy by the late 1980s, little legitimacy could be derived from that source. Indeed, as suggested above, the Romanian economy had the political effect of undercutting attempts to generate legitimacy from a personality cult. The dictator was centrally responsible for the economy, and everyone knew it.

Ideological Legitimacy

From the end of World War II until 1989, all Romanian governments professed to be some version of Marxist. Like other Communist regimes, Romanian governments ostensibly sought political legitimacy through an appeal to Marxism as "scientific socialism," asserting a right to rule because of knowledge of the economic "laws" driving persons and classes. Law in the conventional sense, law derived from procedures, meant little, since the party was effectively above the law. The dictator, in turn, was above both law and party. Much has been written for and against the proposition that Marx's claim to "truth" inevitably led to dictators like Lenin, Stalin, Brezhnev, Mao, Castro, and Ceausescu. After all, if Marxism equates with a secular religion, most religions need an authoritative interpreter or "pope." Presumably, scientific truth cannot have multiple meanings. Thus, according to this argument, there is a logical connection between Marxism and dictators.

Regardless of this connection, from as early as the 1950s all Romanian governments informally stressed nationalism more than any formal version of Marxism. In other words, although formal appeals were made to Marxism (or Leninism, or Stalinism, etc.), real legitimacy or a sense of correctness was frequently sought through an appeal to nationalism. This was certainly true for the ill-fated Ceausescu, whose Marxist rhetoric was increasingly a fig leaf for personal power linked to nationalism. In this sense he was probably not very different from Stalin, whose appeals to the Soviet people during World War II were couched more in terms of defense of the Russian empire than of Marxism-Leninism.

Initially, the Romanian Communist party (RCP) appealed to a very small sector of Romanian society. Since its founding in 1921, the party's association with ethnic minorities and Jews, as well as its support for the Soviet Union's claim to Bessarabia, ran against strong currents of opinion in Romanian society. Of the four parties sharing power in Romania after the 1944 coup against the Iron Guard marshal, Ion Antonescu, the Romanian Communist party had the smallest popular support. Membership in the RCP grew dramatically, however, from the end of 1944. The presence of Soviet troops in Romania sent a strong message that the party was an up-and-coming political force.[31]

The RCP, on consolidation of power thanks to the Soviet military, took its place in the Soviet orbit through a process of the Russification of its culture and the initial subordination and coordination of its goals to those of the Soviet Union. However, Ceausescu's predecessor began very early to spin Romania away from its close association with the Soviets—most notably after Khrushchev's denunciation of Stalin. Under the leadership of Gheorghiu-Dej, the process of "desatellitization" included the negotiated withdrawal of Soviet troops in 1958 and the purge of the "Muscovite" faction in the party. The 1964 declaration of economic independence carried an unmistakable nationalistic flavor, even as the command economy remained in place.

Following in Gheorghiu-Dej's footsteps, Ceausescu pursued the path of Romanian nationalism. Clearly, Ceausescu's 1968 renouncement of the Soviet-led invasion of Czechoslovakia was a powerful means to this end. In 1969 the Romanian president translated popular support for his nationalist stance against the Soviet Union into a new defense platform. At the Tenth Party Congress, Ceausescu announced the "popular war" doctrine as the basic document of Romanian defense policy. According to this doctrine, any threat to Romanian sovereignty would be countered by a coordinated response by the entire Romanian population. The doctrine of "popular war" was codified in July 1972. In this way, Romania wrote its rejection of the Brezhnev doctrine into law and further rewrote the Marxist-Leninist conception of the waning power of the territorial state.[32]

As the Romanian leadership "nationalized" its defense platform, it worked for a nationalization of its cultural agenda as well. From 1969 to 1971, a certain relaxation of censorship allowed Romanian artists to throw off the dictates demanded by the previous period of Russification. The RCP kept careful watch over the artistic community during this period of "liberalization" and began to narrow the focus of Ceausescu's "mini cultural revolution"—lest artistic expression take on an antiparty or anti-Ceausescu air. Following this period of cultural liberalization, the official purpose of Romanian culture became the expression of Romanian nationalism defined in such a way as to lend legitimacy to Ceausescu's regime. Some of Romania's creative intelligentsia were encouraged to use this new creative license to defile traditional enemies such as the Hungarians and even the Russians.[33]

Ceausescu's nationalism was clearly chauvinistic.[34] This chauvinistic nationalism was especially reflected in his policies toward Romania's ethnic minorities. Of Romania's twenty-two ethnic minorities, the Hungarians represent the largest group with a population of between 1.7 and 2.0 million.[35] Historical animosity with the ethnic Hungarians centered in the area of Transylvania. Ceausescu increased discrimination, especially against this ethnic Hungarian population.

In 1968, a year when Ceausescu was engendering support at home and abroad for his nationalistic postures, the RCP worked to erode the last traces of Hungarian autonomy by eliminating the Hungarian Autonomous Region. Although the establishment of the region in 1952 had not come to represent any true measure of political autonomy for the Hungarians living in Transylvania, its abolition was—at a minimum—a symbolic statement of the regime's disinclination to prevent discrimination against the Hungarian minority. According to official party policy, the rights of all minorities would be protected through the process of modernization.[36]

Despite this assertion, Romania's minority populations faced discrimination and limited opportunities in the area of education as a result of the educational law of 1973. This law emphasized technical education, for which textbooks written in the languages of Romania's ethnic minorities were rarely, if ever, available.[37] Economically, Romania's minorities were affected by the movement of ethnic Romanians into areas with large minority populations. In these areas, ethnic

Romanians often displaced Hungarians and Germans from their positions in the workplace.[38] In 1977 a former party official, Karoly Kiraly, wrote three letters to members of the party elite, charging that the Hungarian minority was being "forcibly assimilated." Kiraly was arrested by Romanian officials and was subjected to strict police surveillance after his release.[39] Progressively into the 1980s, the Ceausescu regime continued economic "modernization" and "planning" in such a way that ethnic Hungarian villages were razed and their residents "relocated."[40] All of this discrimination against minorities, especially Hungarians, attracted considerable international attention. Nevertheless, Ceausescu pursued his policies of ethnic discrimination until the very end.

The point to be stressed here is that most minorities, as well as their few supporters among ethnic Romanians, had ample reason to regard Ceausescu's rule as illegitimate because of the internal effect of his chauvinistic nationalism. Clearly, ethnic Hungarians came to strongly detest Ceausescu's rule. At the same time, this nationalism was a two-edged sword, for it allowed Ceausescu to appeal to his like-minded conationalists on emotive-ideological grounds. Perhaps for some of the ethnic Romanians, who made up 80 percent of the overall nation, this appeal to nationalism helped to offset economic hardship and political powerlessness. For ethnic Romanians in official positions, nationalism may have seemed a good thing as long as their special privileges were not threatened.

With hindsight we can say that Ceausescu's chauvinistic nationalism created a key problem: it was ethnic Hungarians who protested, setting in motion the events that toppled Ceausescu. Although his nationalistic policies were popular in the 1960s, especially when directed against the Soviet Union, these policies eventually antagonized internal minorities and their international supporters while not providing enough support or legitimacy to offset other negative feelings.

Historical-Moral Legitimacy

"As perhaps nowhere else in the world, history is politics in east-central Europe. The past is always present."[41] In Romania, moral and historical factors, or if one prefers, elements of national political culture, contributed to twenty-four years of absolute rule by Nicolae Ceausescu. If one uses the distinction between civic and deferential political cultures to get at the issue of assertiveness or participation linked to democratic values, Romania historically was clearly a deferential culture. Other than one mass uprising of peasants in 1907, the recent Romanian history has not been one of either participation or mass political mobilization. Indeed, in longer perspective, Romanian political culture calls to mind "feudalism and autocracy."[42]

When Communist rule came to Romania, peasants accounted for the majority of the population. Even well into the 1980s, over 60 percent of the urban work force was composed of people with rural roots.[43] Although peasant revolts are not unheard of, and indeed some occurred in Romania, a predominant view is that peasant culture tends to exhibit qualities of conformism and fatalism not conducive to civil and political rights, much less to assertiveness in bringing about the practice of those rights in the face of powerful opposition.[44] Moreover, the history of foreign rule in Romania, especially of Turkish rule, is often cited as having lingering effects on Romanian attitudes about authoritarian rule and submission to it. Romanian history shows not only a pattern of authoritarian rule but also an important place in the political process for powerful elites like the landholders of the nineteenth and twentieth centuries.[45]

Traditional relationships between the rulers and the ruled in Romania created a strong sense of fatalistic cynicism about politics. A tradition of adversarial relationships between the elites and the masses afforded Romanians little sense of citizenship or of the granting or accepting of the concept of natural rights.[46] A poll by Radio Free Europe in the mid-1980s indicated that only 17 percent of Romanian respondents felt that the Ceausescu regime would liberalize.[47]

These historical and moral factors of fatalistic deference were institutionalized. Critics, dissidents, and would-be reformers had great difficulty in building broad, cooperative coalitions for democratic change—especially in the face of a police state. When liberal challenges to or criticisms of Ceausescu did occur, and they did periodically, they were small and fragmented and thus rather easily neutralized by Romania's apparatus of repression. Moreover, beyond deference, there have been periodic efforts to glorify antidemocratic people and movements.

Unlike religious institutions in Poland, those in Romania proved no serious challenge to Ceausescu's personalized rule. They proved pliable and mostly supportive of the authoritarian regime, with the exception of ethnic Hungarian elements. In 1948 the "Law on Religious Confessions" recognized only fourteen of the sixty religious groups that had been active in Romania before World War II. In December of that same year, the Romanian authorities eliminated the Romanian United church by forcibly unifying it with the Romanian Orthodox church. This "unification" was brought about with the help of the Romanian Orthodox church, which was widely recognized for its collaboration with the party. Such collaboration between the church and Romanian authorities led to the arrest in March 1979 of Father Gheorge Calciu-Dumitreasa, who had become outspoken on the subject of the regime's atheism. The Romanian Orthodox priest was released from prison in 1985 after much international pressure, but very little internal religious pressure, was focused on his case.[48]

And unlike trade unions in Poland, those in Romania never posed a concerted challenge to the ruling elite, although they were periodically troublesome, as in East Germany. The very process of urbanization and industrialization, however, with perhaps some role for Marxist rhetoric about rule by and for the proletariat, contributed to increased assertiveness by blue-collar workers. Political cultures do change; history is not stagnant; different moral values are informally learned.[49] Russian political culture too had been widely regarded as deferential over the years, but that did not prevent important demonstrations for democratic rights in Moscow and Leningrad in 1991 in dangerous opposition to Stalinist forces attempting a coup.

As was typical of other Communist regimes, the Romanian regime created the appearance of independent trade unions. Like neighboring Yugoslavia, Romania sought to create the image of extensive economic democracy or self-management. This was all mostly a sham, since worker organizations were tightly controlled from the top. As a result of these political factors, and with a deteriorating economic situation, Romanian workers became increasingly dissatisfied with the approved channels of participation.[50]

In August 1977, worker dissatisfaction erupted among miners in Jiu Valley with a widespread strike for increased benefits and safety standards. But the Ceausescu regime contained the unrest with harsh repression. Perhaps as many as four thousand workers lost their jobs. Strike organizers were arrested without trial and were kept under police scrutiny.[51]

The creation of the Free Trade Union of Romanian Workers in February 1979 did not lead to fundamental change. The trade union's goal of improved working conditions, as well as its calls for the end of special privileges for party officials, never came to fruition; its leaders were either arrested, forced to leave Romania, or in at least one case, confined to a psychiatric hospital.[52] In the early 1980s, Ceausescu kept an increasingly tight lid on the Romanian workplace to show his determination that worker assertiveness in Poland would not affect Romania.[53] The Romanian workplace remained relatively quiet for the next several years.

In 1987 a mass demonstration of workers occurred in Brasov. Workers from the Red Flag truck-and-tractor factory marched to the Communist party headquarters and the mayor's office, where they burned files and pictures. Numerous protests followed the events in Brasov as students in Timisoara and Cluj showed their support for workers in Brasov as well as their dissatisfaction over economic conditions. These demonstrations were clearly symptoms of the growing sense of dissatisfaction with the Communist regime, but they did not lead to a broader democratic or liberal movement to challenge Ceausescu's rule.[54]

In addition to a compliant church and a restricted labor movement, a deferential intelligentsia also contributed to an overall situation of macro-stability without legitimacy. Romania, for example, did not have the tradition of *samzidat*, or underground "publishing," found in other East European countries. The regime found it fairly easy to co-opt intellectuals. The case of the writer Dumitru Rada Popescu was typical. Popescu dropped his independent line after his election to the Writer's Union in 1981.[55] There were dissident intellectuals, of course, just not very many of them. The writer Paul Goma's critical position on Romania's human rights practices led to his arrest in April 1977. Because of international attention to his case he was finally allowed to go abroad. A "joke" about dissent among Romania's intellectual community explained that Romanian dissent "lives in Paris and his name is Paul Goma."[56]

As late as November 1989, the Romanian activist Doina Cornea wrote a sharp letter of criticism against colleagues in the intellectual community. Cornea censured intellectuals in various fields for their largely passive and "moderately obedient" response to the regime's restrictions on freedom of expression.[57] In general, Romania's intellectuals fit into the traditional roles of acquiescence and submission to authority.

The overall condition of deference in Romania continued through

November 1989 as small sparks of dissent were controlled by the apparently efficient apparatus of repression. Even as the rest of Eastern Europe mobilized to overturn Communist regimes, the mass mobilization of Romanians did not appear imminent or inevitable. In fact, one of the continuing problems for Romania, after the violent events of late 1989, was the spontaneous, disorganized, and fragmented nature of the Romanian domestic war.

Even after the fall of Ceausescu, the succeeding National Salvation Front was composed of a large number of former Communists, many of whom seemed in the Stalinist rather than Gorbachev wing of the party. If true, this would suggest that authoritarian rather than democratic elements in Romanian political culture were still strong. In turn, this would suggest that human rights values, though important, especially to ethnic Hungarians, in triggering the 1989 revolution, were not widespread or consolidated. There was even some official effort to refurbish the image of Marshal Ion Antonescu.[58]

INTERNATIONAL LEGITIMACY

From the international point of view, after 1955, when Romania was admitted to the United Nations, there was never any question about the legal legitimacy of either the state of Romania or its various governments. But it is important to observe that this international legal legitimacy was largely irrelevant to the survival of the Ceausescu regime. In addition, the moral and political aspects of this international legitimacy changed over time.

At first, the USSR deferred to, or acquiesced in, an independent Romania that presented no threat to Soviet totalitarian control within the USSR. The Soviets deferred to Ceausescu much as did most Romanians. The U.S.-led West also granted political legitimacy to Ceausescu, as a reward for his nationalistic foreign policy. Official U.S. foreign policy, as determined by the executive branch, did not focus very much or seriously on the denial of human rights or any other moral question within Romania. This was pointed out with some vehemence by David Funderburk, the U.S. ambassador to Romania for a time during the first Reagan administration.[59] What counted for the U.S. government was global strategic alignment, and as long as Ceausescu was nonaligned, he reaped Western rewards.

Yet various international actors had been trying to deny Ceausescu legitimacy on moral grounds by focusing on various human rights in Romania. With the decline of the cold war, and indeed with the decline of communism in the rest of Europe, this moral concern became more important. By the late 1980s, the West had largely withdrawn political legitimacy from Ceausescu and substituted demands for radical change on grounds of political morality. Thus, finally, the lack of moral legitimacy proved damaging to Ceausescu, although it was still primarily domestic rather than international events that spelled his doom. The changing international climate was seen in the fact that in the midst of the Romanian revolution, the Soviet Union under Mikhail Gorbachev discussed with the United States the wisdom of armed intervention to guarantee the triumph of non-Communist forces.

Political Legitimacy

Ceausescu's Romania earned a reputation for independence and non-alignment in the international community in 1967 for maintaining diplomatic relations with Israel after the Yom Kippur War and for being the first East bloc country to recognize West Germany. The Romanian president's defiant stand against the Soviet invasion of Czechoslovakia in 1968, and other independent foreign policies including his refusal to join the Soviet boycott of the Summer Olympic games in Los Angeles in 1984, solidified Ceausescu's international political legitimacy as far as the West was concerned. We have already noted how in the 1970s and early 1980s, Ceausescu was able to obtain Western credit and technology. This was tangible evidence of the dictator's political legitimacy in Western eyes. In particular, the United States provided economic credits under policies of détente in return for continued Romanian independence from the USSR.

This dynamic of Romanian-American relations was previewed by Richard Nixon's trip to Bucharest in August 1969. For President Nixon, "Romania appeared to be a prime candidate" to serve as a liaison between the United States and China. Nixon wanted to use improved Sino-American relations as part of his larger foreign policy plan of issue "linkage" with the Soviet Union, including the use of the Soviet Union to end the Vietnam War.[60] Ceausescu consented to the role as liaison between the United States and China in the hope that in return, Romanian exports would receive Most Favored Nation (MFN) status in U.S. markets.

Romania did not receive MFN trading status until August 1975, as part of the Romanian-American Trade Agreement.[61] Congress attached conditions to MFN status for all command economies on the initial grounds of endorsement of the right to emigration. Yet despite this effort of Congress, along with the efforts of various private organizations to focus on the denial of human rights in Romania (not just the right to emigrate but religious and minority freedoms as well), the U.S. executive tried to continue the basic policy of rewarding Ceausescu's independence with economic "carrots." This orientation in bilateral relations lasted until 1988.

Thus, both Republican and Democratic administrations in Washington saw Ceausescu as legitimate for reasons of political alignment. They did not try to deny legitimacy because of morality—namely, gross violations of human rights for Romanians. For example, despite mounting opposition to Romanian MFN status from private circles and from members of Congress, Ronald Reagan's waiver request, allowing MFN status despite inadequate progress on emigration and other rights matters, avoided formal disapproval from Congress through 1987.[62]

In June 1987, Reagan submitted what would be the last request to extend MFN status to Romania. The assistant secretary of state for Human Rights and Humanitarian Affairs, Richard Schifter, made the relatively new argument that MFN status was a viable vehicle for human rights change in Romania and that in the past, MFN status had been responsible for increased emigration and family reunion.[63] Once again, the president's waiver request extended Romania's MFN status through July 1988 in the absence of the formal disproval of both houses.[64] Even the second Reagan administration, despite its anti-Communist credentials, played the standard game of endorsing Ceausescu because of his independence, although it had to graft new human rights arguments onto its strategic position.

In February 1988, the U.S. administration sent Deputy Secretary of State John C. Whitehead to Bucharest with a "special Presidential message for Ceausescu" concerning the status of human rights in his country.[65] On February 26, 1988, U.S. State Department Spokesperson Phyllis Oakley announced that Romania no longer wished to accept MFN status from the United States under the conditions imposed by the Jackson-Vanik amendment.[66] MFN status for Romania was allowed to expire in July 1988. As far as U.S. policy toward Romania was concerned, those emphasizing moral legitimacy, principally through attention to human rights, had finally won the day.

Moral Legitimacy

There were always foreign entities that stressed the denial of human rights in Romania and tried to deny the government legitimacy on moral grounds. Private groups such as Amnesty International, parts of governing systems such as the U.S. Congress from 1974, certain governmental spokespeople such as those meeting under the CSCE (Conference on Security and Cooperation in Europe) process, the Hungarian government from the early 1970s, on occasion a United Nations body, and even the Soviet Union under Gorbachev all stressed the need for political reform centering on the implementation of internationally recognized human rights. Implicitly, they all sought to undermine at least some of the legitimacy of Ceausescu's personalized rule on moral grounds.

As political reform progressed in the Soviet Union and Eastern Europe, Romania's nonalignment became less important in the West. Therefore, greater stress could be placed on moral questions like human rights. There is no doubt that the international climate changed drastically, and in late 1989 more attention was given not just to change in specific rights but to removing authoritarian communism in Eastern Europe. This changing climate may have encouraged various elements inside Romania to assert themselves against the Ceausescu regime, although this is difficult to prove definitely.

It is relatively easy to document international concern with human rights in Romania, even if it is much harder to establish the impact of this concern. For example, reports from private human rights organizations, such as Helsinki Watch and Amnesty International, outlined a pattern of gross violations of human rights in the Romanian Socialist Republic. On July 7, 1987, Amnesty International issued a major report on the state of Romanian human rights, citing Romanian authorities for their inhuman methods of silencing dissent.[67]

Likewise, concern for the implementation of human rights in Romania was voiced in the United Nations, and this attention to Romania's situation intensified during the 1980s. (As far back as 1949, Australia had temporarily blocked Romania's admission to the U.N. General Assembly because of denial of religious rights.) In the 1980s the question of rights in Romania came full circle as the U.N. Subcommission on the Prevention of Discrimination and the Protection of Minorities commissioned a Romanian expert, Dumitru Mazilu, to prepare a report on the status of human rights and youth in Romania. Romanian authorities repeatedly harassed Mazilu and finally prevented him from appearing before the subcommission in 1988.[68] In 1989, Mazilu's report was smuggled out of Romania and published by the subcommission as a "highly critical" indictment of Romania's human rights practices.[69]

In 1989 the parent U.N. Commission on Human Rights made the decision, relatively important for that agency, to establish a Special Rapporteur to investigate the situation of Romanian human rights. This is a form of diplomatic pressure not lightly undertaken by state members of the commission. On December 18, 1989, the Special Rapporteur submitted his first report as the situation in Romania started to show its first signs of unraveling.[70] Clearly, U.N. pressure did not directly cause revolutionary events in Romania in 1989, but U.N. developments were symptomatic of the growing international pressures on Ceausescu.

Hungary, even under Communist governments, took an active role in criticizing Ceausescu's treatment of minorities, naturally focusing on ethnic Hungarians. Transylvania is a disputed region between the two states, and as far back as 1971, Hungary publicly denounced Romanian policies toward minorities. A 1977 agreement on minorities between the two states was not implemented on the Romanian side to Hungarian satisfaction. By 1984, the question of ethnic Hungarians in Romania was being handled at the level of the Central Committee of the Hungarian Communist party. In 1988, tens of thousands of Hungarians demonstrated in front of the Romanian embassy in Budapest, protesting the razing of Hungarian villages in Romania and the relocation of the residents. Hungary took a leading role in criticisms of Romania within the United Nations.[71] These and other actions by the Hungarian government and by nationals in Hungary, actions such as working with the U.N. Office of the High Commissioner for Refugees in providing for ethnic Hungarians fleeing Romania, clearly provided moral encouragement to some of those in Romania challenging Ceausescu's policies.

Probably most important, Ceausescu was increasingly squeezed by both the United States and, eventually, the USSR. In Washington in 1974, Congress attached the Jackson-Vanik amendment to the trade bill authorizing MFN status. The amendment required all command economies, which meant Communist economies, to permit reasonable emigration as the price tag of MFN status. Whereas the Soviet Union preferred not to seek MFN status in order not to have its emigration policies scrutinized by Congress, Romania persistently sought that status—and became the focal point for those trying to apply the Jackson-Vanik amendment.[72]

When President Gerald Ford proposed MFN status for Romania in 1975, there was considerable opposition. Many American Jewish groups joined with members of Congress to try to block this presidential determination. Included in the Jackson-Vanik legislation was a provision allowing for a presidential waiver of emigration requirements if the country in question could provide assurances of freer emigration practices in the future. Thus, as in other U.S. statutes pertaining to human rights abroad, reasonable progress could be shown even if some vague standard of achievement had not yet been reached. Because Ceausescu refused to give any written assurances about the future of his emigration policies, President Ford successfully submitted the initial waiver on an unwritten and vague Ceausescu promise.[73]

This process—in which the president would submit a waiver request to extend Romania's MFN treatment and then Congress would hold hearings on the request—continued annually during the Carter and the Reagan administrations. In this way, "the real rhythm of Romanian-American relations was set by the language of the Jackson-Vanik amendment."[74] But in the 1980s, as the focus of congressional hearings about Romania's emigration record expanded to a broader discussion of Romania's human rights record, this process became increasingly important. A shift became apparent at the 1985 hearings as objections to extending Romania's MFN status focused on Ceausescu's record on minority and religious rights more than on emigration issues.[75] Yet despite growing congressional opposition to Ceausescu's human rights record, President Reagan was able to get his waiver through each year after much acrimonious debate, relying on party loyalty combined with considerable congressional sympathy for American business interests in Romania. In 1988, however, Romania finally lost MFN status. Those wishing to pressure Ceausescu on human rights grounds won out. This loss of an important economic benefit probably had some impact on the thinking of some Romanians responsible for economic management.

Similarly, a more coordinated Western pressure was increasingly focused on Romania through debate in the Conference on Security and Cooperation in Europe (CSCE). In January 1989, Romania openly rejected human rights clauses in the final document adopted by follow-up conference in Vienna. Romania explicitly renounced any obligation in the areas of religious rights and the rights of ethnic minorities, maintaining "that the question of nationalities had been solved once and for all under socialism."[76] This Romanian stonewalling did not block continued Western pressure. By early 1989, some Romanian critics were citing CSCE stands on human rights violations in their urging of changes on Ceausescu.[77]

With the rise of Gorbachev to power in the Soviet Union in 1985, Ceausescu faced a second major source of pressure for change. Whereas in the past many Romanians had feared a military invasion from Moscow, now the threat from Moscow became an invasion of "new thinking." Ceausescu's rejection of Gorbachev's platforms of *perestroika* and *glasnost* was clearly evident during the Soviet leader's visit to Bucharest in 1987. RCP members sat in silence as Gorbachev outlined his package of reforms, which he suggested were needed in Romania as well as in the USSR. The two leaders showed their disapproval for each other during this meeting. Ceausescu pointedly refused to follow the Romanian text of Gorbachev's speech, and the Soviet leader tried to cut off the audience's rhythmic approval of Ceausescu.[78]

According to some observers, the cool response that Gorbachev received at party meetings was not shared by many Romanians, who had begun to look to Gorbachev as a "symbol of hope" for their own country's liberalization.[79] Some party members, such as Ion Iliescu, were sympathetic to Gorbachev's reforms, which is precisely why Ceausescu had Iliescu sent out of the country during Gorbachev's visit. No doubt a broader range of party members, if interested in saving the preferred position of the party, favored reform communism, even if they were required to support an unbending Ceausescu in public.

Soviet-Romanian relations continued their downward slide as the Soviets began to voice their concerns over Romania's human rights practices. At a human rights conference in Paris in May 1989, Soviet representatives were openly critical of Romania's attempt to build a barbed-wire fence along its border with Hungary.[80] In November 1989, Gorbachev sent only token congratulations to Ceausescu on his reelection as general secretary of the RCP, damning him with faint praise.[81]

The international shift from a grant of legitimacy to Ceausescu for political reasons to a denial of legitimacy for moral and human rights reasons is clear. What is not so clear is the impact of this shift on Romanian actors in the 1989 events, actors besides ethnic Hungarians. The suspicion lingers that many officials after 1989 were just as uninterested in internationally recognized human rights as Ceausescu had been. After all, much of history shows that political leaders do not learn from history.

CONCLUSIONS

Many questions remain about the events of December 1989 and thereafter. The most basic of these questions asks whether Nicolae Ceausescu's fall from power was the result of a popular uprising or of a coup that somehow "hijacked" the Timisoara demonstrations. Many interpretations, some fanciful, have attempted to answer this question.[82] Jonathan Eyal offers one of the more persuasive interpretations. He wrote, "The Romanian revolution was spontaneous, but this does not preclude the existence of certain plotters both within and outside the Communist Party."[83]

Despite unresolved questions, the known events that led to Ceausescu's fall from power reflect different participants holding different views about the legitimacy of his regime and the ability of these participants to influence the final outcome. It is clear that ethnic Hungarians triggered decisive events and that they regarded the Romanian government as unfit to rule because of human rights violations. But Romanian students and workers joined in the protests because of concerns for other than minority rights and indeed for other orientations, such as lack of a bright economic future.

Certainly, key political and military figures threw their support to the protesters not primarily because they felt solidarity for human rights improvements but rather because they saw Ceausescu as having brought the state, the Communist party, and the military to a ruinous impotence. Most of these disaffected members of the formal elite regarded Ceausescu's personalized rule as illegitimate, but more for functional reasons than for human rights reasons. After the National Salvation Front took over, a number of politicians who were concerned with human rights left the ruling coalition because of the lack of attention given to human rights reform.

Ceausescu's efforts to rule via personal legitimacy, linked to appeals to nationalism, failed in the face of economic policies that both led to disaster and excluded most of the formal elite from power sharing. Appeals to nationalism were popular in the 1960s, when they were directed externally against the Russians and internally against the ethnic Hungarians. But as the economy declined from about 1973 to 1989, a national historical tradition of deference yielded, at least temporarily, to assertiveness in opposition to dictatorial mismanagement. The only group that fought for Ceausescu was his special police, who had been pampered and allowed to act without restraint, but that was too narrow a base for survival of the government.

Given the long decline of the national economy, which of course affected the infrastructure of military power, and given that Ceausescu used the military for economic construction despite opposition from military leaders, and given that the equipment and training of the army had been neglected, it is not surprising that much of the army fought for the rebel side. It is noteworthy that the army's leadership did not oppose Ceausescu on moral, democratic, or human rights grounds. The leaders opposed the dictator on pragmatic, functional grounds, as reflected in the statement that the army gave its support to Romania's provisional government "on the condition that 'serious politicians' took over instead of 'a few crazy poets and intellectuals.'"[84] This did not indicate strong solidarity with students and leaders of the Hungarian minority.

Iliescu became the head of this group of "serious politicians" not only as the leader of Romania's provisional government but also as the first president of the new Romanian Republic. Iliescu seems to have split with Ceausescu back in the 1970s more over the concentration of power in the "royal family," and the detrimental policies resulting therefrom, than over a fundamental opposition to authoritarian rule or minority discrimination. Iliescu and others like him seem to blame Romania's problems on Ceausescu alone and not on inherent problems in elitist rule or a command economy.[85] With the obvious exclusion of most officials from real power and the growing poverty of the country, however independent, it would have been surprising if there had been no reports of planned coups, whether from within or outside the party.

Official actions after Ceausescu's death involved extralegal use of workers called to the capital to violently suppress peaceful demonstrations, secretive control over communications media, failure to release all sorts of information into the public domain, and other indications of a lack of respect for the rule of law and internationally recognized human rights. All of this confirmed the fear that the new leadership in Romania was as insensitive to human rights and to moral-legal sources of legitimacy as was the ancien régime.

International sources of legitimacy had been important first in support of and then in opposition to Ceausescu's rule. Western grants of legitimacy because of his nonalignment with or independence from the USSR had allowed Ceausescu to obtain the capital and technology needed for his economic programs. But the denial of legitimacy by outsiders because of human rights violations, a denial that built to a peak in 1988 and 1989, certainly encouraged the Hungarians and perhaps some workers and students to call for the dictator's ouster. Although domestic factors were primary, international factors were not absent.

It will be interesting to see if these same international factors can support what is at best a shaky post-Ceausescu commitment to human rights, thus helping the new Romanian Republic to maintain what legitimacy it now has from legal-moral sources. It will be unfortunate for all concerned if the new governing arrangements again rely on traditional Romanian deference to an authority still lacking genuine legitimacy.

Conclusion:
Reflections on Human Rights and Peace

At the start of 1991, the world was fixated on international war in the Persian Gulf, first by the continuing Iraqi invasion of Kuwait and then by the armed response of an international coalition as authorized by the United Nations Security Council. But at the start of 1992, international war was hard to find anywhere in the world—at least in its classical form. (Some Palestinians did continue to "war" with Israel.) On the domestic level, some "wars" wound down during 1991–92, as in El Salvador, while others continued, as in Peru, Sri Lanka, and Somalia, inter alia.

Beyond such changing specifics, can we now say that there is a body of knowledge available about peace and war, international and domestic, that sheds light on these and other particular situations? Can we now say that we know the general causes of international and domestic wars, or know their patterns, or know what factors have what results in what situations? What role, if any, do we find for human rights factors in the causes of international and domestic war?

Some things we know, or think we know for now, and some remain question marks. We know that the realist school of thought—traumatized by World War II and the cold war, times of intense hostility—stressed the pursuit and use of power, especially military power, to the almost total exclusion of a remarkable relationship between democracy and peace. The stable implementation of civil and political rights within a territorial state over time leads to the absence of overt war among similar polities. Thus liberalism, much discredited during an age of international hostility, actually turns out to be a valid understanding of at least part of, or one type of, international relations. Democratic states, which by definition are relatively serious about implementing civil and political rights, compose a community within the larger international society, a community whose operating code includes renunciation of force, serious attention to legal rules, including those on human rights, and extensive cooperation.

It should be noted, however, that democratic interest in human rights does not mean that human rights standards are not violated. This paradox is demonstrated by the situation in Western Europe. All members of the Council of Europe are genuinely democratic, yet the international regional system for protection of human rights under the European Convention on Human Rights has not withered away for lack of cases. Both the European Commission and the European Court of Human Rights have active caseloads. Compared with authoritarian states, democracies can be serious about civil and political rights and at the same time violate, on occasion, international standards of human rights. The situation in the Council of Europe provides an important antidote to those Americans who say that the United States does not need to become a party to human rights treaties because the country is already committed to human rights under the U.S. constitution.

Not all of international relations meets the standards of the international democratic community. The liberalism of the 1920s and 1930s did indeed overstate some states' interest in rational cooperation and the resultant role of international law and organization in moderating bellicose foreign policies. Thus realism was correct in its emphasis on power considerations for that part of international relations affected by authoritarian rather than democratic states. When authoritarians and democrats interact, peace does not stem from attention to human rights but rather primarily (though not entirely) from calculations about the exercise of power. The condition of civil and political rights within states explains much less about the presence or absence of international war in these mixed situations. Some authoritarians prove to be as "peace loving" as any democrat, as far as aggressive foreign policy is concerned. And some democrats prove as war-prone and aggressive as any authoritarian, since democrats— some of them powerful—fight many wars and cause some of them.

Realism and liberalism, two major schools of understanding international relations in the West, may be insufficient for understanding the pattern of international war among developed states, however. As John Mueller argues, there is considerable, if incomplete, evidence that *developed* states, whether democratic or authoritarian, do not war among themselves. Industrial-technocratic development makes wars among developed states extremely costly. In addition, a certain moral development—holding major war to be obscene—also forms a barrier against war among developed states. The two types of development may be linked historically. Industrialized states have usually had a period in their history of fighting major wars, which may help to produce a moral development holding such wars objectionable. Thus developmentalism, in addition to realism and liberalism, appears to shed light on overt international war among great powers.

Socioeconomic rights seem to play only an indirect role in overt international war. Most of the industrially developed states are also democracies, and all of these democracies—with the exception of the United States—accept socioeconomic as well as civil-political rights. The second generation of socioeconomic rights may play an indirect and minor role in contributing to a national consensus that war is debasing. All human rights contribute to human dignity in principle, and thus all human rights feed into the notion that major war among developed states is to be avoided, on moral as well as material grounds. But socioeconomic rights do not seem to correlate in any direct way with the presence or absence of overt international war.

It has not been generally appreciated that democracies, although they do not engage in overt international war among themselves, seem capable of undertaking covert international "war" against other democratic governments. The leading example of this remarkable phenomenon is the United States during the cold war with the Soviet Union. Even allowing for the gray areas of what is and is not a democratic government (say, in Indonesia circa 1960 or in Nicaragua circa 1985), clearly, on more than one occasion, the United States covertly intervened, sometimes with threat or use of force, to bring down or harass an elected government that was paying considerable and genuine attention to civil and political rights. Mossadeq in Iran, Arbenz in Guatemala, Goulart in Brazil, and Allende in Chile were all overthrown with active U.S. leadership or support for threatened or employed violence. All of these heads of government not only were elected but also were genuinely sympathetic to many civil and political rights. There were other examples of "peaceful" covert U.S. intervention against the policies, if not the existence, of democratic governments, mostly in the Western Hemisphere.

Just as we cannot scientifically prove why democracies do not fight overt international wars among themselves, so we cannot prove all the reasons for this U.S. pattern of covert behavior. The surface or superficial cause of U.S. covert international "war" against certain democratic governments seems clear. Washington feared that the practice of civil and political rights in certain states would lead to a situation advantageous to the Soviet Union and thus detrimental to U.S. security. Serious attention to many economic and social rights by these targeted governments only confirmed Washington's fears that elected leaders would strike deals with the leaders of "scientific socialism."

The possible deeper underpinnings of this policy of covert international "war" against elected leaders sympathetic to many human rights are not very clear. As Michael Hunt argues, it is probable, but difficult to prove definitively, that an "American ideology" greatly exacerbated U.S. security fears. All of the overthrown leaders were non-European, sympathetic to a national social revolution involving redistribution of wealth, and recalcitrant about doing what Washington wanted done. An American predisposition to view critically other races, social revolutions, and nonalignment with U.S. policy may have contributed to an extremely broad conception of the needs of U.S. security—in some cases, security needs very far from the territorial United States, as in Iran and Indonesia.

I find persuasive the argument that the United States defined its national security in terms of a way of life inhospitable to toleration of social revolution in other states. If such revolutions took place outside the North Atlantic area and within a self-defined U.S. sphere of influence, the United States moved against the revolutionary government, whether or not it was democratic. A U.S. fear of social reform, which could have international repercussions via "falling dominoes," was equated by Washington with an advance in Soviet influence. The circle was complete. Cultural predispositions merged with surface reasoning on behalf of "national interest" and "national security."

But a general theory competes with Hunt's sui generis interpretation of U.S. diplomatic history. If we go back to Immanuel Kant, we find an intriguing distinction between mature and barely participatory democracies. Only among mature democracies is forcible foreign policy ruled out. Mature democracies are those following the principle of separation of institutions, alignment with other democracies, and a mostly private economy. Other democracies, although genuinely elected, are not "members of the club." That is, they are not part of the community of stable democracies in which forceful action is rejected according to democratic norms and procedures. According to Kantian views, there is an important difference between elected governments and mature democracies. Only among the latter is forceful foreign policy abjured.

Despite this Kantian theory of democratic foreign policy, it is not yet completely clear whether covert "war" against foreign elected leaders is characteristic of democracies in general or only of the United States during the cold war. Aside from Britain's active help in the overthrow of Mossadeq, no evidence has been found indicating a broad democratic pattern of covert "war" against democracies since 1945.

The causes of domestic "war" have long proved elusive. This is extremely unfortunate, since probably more people have been killed and wounded since 1945 in domestic rather than in international wars. If we had some idea about an ordering of causes, or even about some contributing factors in certain situations, much of the mayhem of the world might be ameliorated.

The many studies of internal armed conflict and violent political revolution, which together make up my category of domestic war, have not had much success in identifying general causes across national situations. That being the case, there seems to be a slight trend away from grand theories of revolution and toward a series of national case studies. In the second part of this work, I have tried to bridge these two traditions. Taking the core notion of political legitimacy, defined as the correctness of governing arrangements, I have presented an interpretation of domestic and international sources of legitimacy, followed by three illustrative case studies.

As for my framework of analysis centering on legitimacy, a concern with human rights leads to the following observations. There are many sources of legitimacy, both domestic and international. Universal human rights, as moral rights translated into legal form, compose but one of the sources—and not necessarily the most important. Both national conceptions of political morality, encompassing judgments about human rights, and international standards of those rights can, but do not have to, exert considerable influence in situations of domestic war. Increasingly, national and international human rights standards seem to be merging as universal rights are increasingly being incorporated into national discourse about rights.

For those concerned with the role of human rights in situations of potential or actual domestic war, one of the key issues remains the linkage between concern for rights and political power. If there is a national or international actor concerned with human rights in a national situation, what is that actor's power to generate influence in support of a rights orientation?

Each of the case studies, chosen almost randomly but with a concern for different geographical and cultural representation, shows a relationship between human rights and domestic "war," but in ways that differed in each case. Nevertheless, the overall framework centering on political legitimacy seems vindicated as an aid to understanding, even if it does not lead to precise prediction.

In the case of Sri Lanka, it is important to emphasize that the principle of the right to political participation gives rise to further specific questions about majority versus minority rights. This became the central issue in Sri Lankan political stability after independence. Despite broad and serious attention to civil and political as well as social and economic rights, disruptive questions arose. Most important, were the majority Sinhalese Buddhists prepared to share power and benefits with the minority Tamil Hindus in ways acceptable to the latter?

The derivative questions of Tamil rights to education in the Tamil language and access to jobs fed directly into the domestic war that continues to the time of this writing. Since much of the Tamil minority became increasingly dissatisfied with linguistic rights and job opportunities, a violent movement for ethno-national self-determination eventually arose, directed toward the creation of a separate state. Awareness of a series of rights enhances our understanding of the violence in Sri Lanka, even if we still cannot either explain or precisely predict why one group of Tamils chooses violence and another favors peaceful negotiation.

A concern for human rights also explained important international influences on the Sri Lanka situation. India militarily intervened to stop genocidal attacks on the Tamils in Sri Lanka (as propelled by Tamil influences in southern India). But India altered its policy in large part because Sri Lankan Tamil demands for full self-determination in the form of a separate state were perceived by New Delhi as negatively affecting the territorial integrity of India. Faced with its own separatist movements, the government of the late Rajiv Gandhi shifted its policy from efforts to militarily protect the Tamils in Sri Lanka to efforts to mediate the dispute for a peaceful satisfaction of some of their demands—and finally to efforts to disarm the Tamils.

Thus in Sri Lanka in the 1980s and 1990s, although an analysis focusing on economics and ethnicity provided numerous insights into domestic war, a focus on several human rights clearly helped explain the basic causes of the Tamil-Sinhalese conflict. This focus on rights did not substitute for an analysis of power, in the sense of political as well as military capability. Rather, issues of rights had to be juxtaposed to issues of power. For example, how many of the Tamil communities in Sri Lanka were prepared to fight for the Tigers of Tamil Elaam? How effective were the Sri Lankan and Indian armies in contesting the Tigers? Would a compromise solution centering on Tamil local autonomy within a single federal state undercut violent options?

Central to the case of domestic "war" in Sri Lanka was the following basic question: what made governing arrangements correct, and in whose view? The language of human rights aided analysis by calling attention to minority rights, educational rights, perhaps the right to work, and ultimately the collective human right to self-determination of peoples.

In the case of Liberia, again the central question properly addressed political legitimacy: were governing arrangements correct, and in whose view? A concern with human rights enhanced at least a partial understanding of the increasing political instability and violence of the 1980s and early 1990s. Whereas majority rule in Sri Lanka had been established at independence, majority rule in Liberia had long been denied by the settler community arriving from North America. Indigenes and reformist settlers were increasingly disenchanted with both the political repression and the socioeconomic discrimination that characterized the Tubman and Tolbert governments. Important background conditions for the Doe coup of 1980 included not only the need for increased economic status, education, and urbanization for the indigenes but also the government's performance in ignoring the welfare of the noncommissioned officers of the army and the broader moral issue of ethnic discrimination, which was related to human rights standards.

Domestic factors were primary in both Doe's coup of 1980 and his subsequent demise in the late 1980s (politically) and early 1990s (physically). In fact, the immediate domestic causes of violent behavior against the Tolbert and Doe governments remained essentially the same: poor government performance understood in both a positive (socioeconomic) and negative (repressive) sense. The Doe regime was almost a textbook example of how not to govern: deny genuine elections, discriminate on the basis of ethnicity, promote graft and corruption rather than sound economic policies, and engage in political murder and torture.

In Liberia, as in Sri Lanka, international sources of legitimacy, including moral-legal ones concerned with human rights, proved important, if not fully decisive. The most important outside players were the United States and Nigeria. Initially, both the Carter and the Reagan governments were insensitive to rights issues, emphasizing instead short-term U.S. security interests. But as Tolbert yielded to Doe and as Doe yielded to domestic war, the Bush administration preferred to remain mostly on the sidelines rather than support any of the Liberian factions. (By that time, the perception of Soviet threat was receding in all of Africa.) Since the Taylor, Johnson, and Doe factions all seemed unattractive in both moral and political terms, the United States tended to defer to Nigeria and its leadership of ECOWAS. Had one of the competing Liberian factions been clearly democratic and free from atrocities in combat, it would have been easier for international factors to coalesce behind a definite favorite.

In Liberia, the central question of political legitimacy and the constituent issue of moral and legal rights highlighted factors pertaining to majority rule, ethnic discrimination, the ineffectiveness of brutal but intermittent repression, and the difficulty of retaining international support in the face of gross violations of human rights. In addition, governmental economic policies, rather than being based on pursuit of socioeconomic rights without discrimination, much less on pursuit of sheer macro-economic growth, proved disastrous, hastening the downfall of leaders, particularly Doe. Any number of actors, both domestic and international, were at times willing to disregard serious human rights issues in the pursuit of personal or national power. This was true not only of Taylor and Johnson but also of Reagan and Shultz. But this ignoring of rights proved neither conducive to political stability nor beneficial for most Liberians.

As for Romania, the central importance of political legitimacy remained the same, but as expected, the precise issues and train of events differed. One could use the same nine sources of political legitimacy to clarify the causes of domestic revolution and violent behavior, although judgments were still required concerning exact interplay and weight of importance.

In Romania, as in Sri Lanka and Liberia, domestic factors were paramount, but international sources of legitimacy were important. At both levels, human rights considerations eventually proved influential. Domestically, Nicolae Ceausescu's discrimination against the ethnic Hungarian minority, along with infringements on religious freedom, triggered violent events in December 1989. The broadening of demands for Ceausescu's resignation (and of course such demands reflected the fundamental view that his dictatorial rule was illegitimate) involved other factors such as the denial of participatory rights, the disastrous condition of the economy, and rule by personality and family. These views about moral-legal rights, governmental functioning, and attempted personality cults helped produce an assertiveness (possibly temporary) on the part of many Romanians, an assertiveness that ran counter to the Romanian history of deference to various types of authoritarian authority.

Although several human rights concerns were important to several different types of actors in the decisive December 1989 events that chased Stalinist rule from Romania, those concerns did not seem uppermost in the minds of other important players. Some of those who seized on the moment of unrest and who finally, by force of arms, defeated the dictator's supporters and killed Nicolae and Elena Ceausescu had once been part of the ancien régime. Being perhaps reform Communists or believers in oligarchy, they seemed more interested in a broadening of power within the traditional elite than in a broadening of rights involving genuine mass participation and various other individual and group freedoms. This partly explains the indecisiveness of the Romanian 1989 revolution and the continuing political instability in that state.

International sources of legitimacy were also important. The West in effect granted legitimacy to Ceausescu on political grounds, rewarding him for his independence from the Soviet Union in international relations. This Western view led to important material help in his domestic economic programming. Later, however, most foreign actors of any importance to Romania shifted stands. In 1988 and 1989 they withdrew legitimacy from Ceausescu's personalized rule for moral reasons linked to human rights. By that time his independence from the USSR was of little importance, and so various international actors increased pressure for radical governmental change in Romania. Thus, international action for human rights came to play a larger role, over time, in matters affecting Romania.

This shift was no doubt perceived by various members of the formal elite who, seeing that international support had dissipated, moved against the dictator. No further foreign help could be expected from any important source to alleviate Romania's economic debacle. And this international shift was certainly realized by ethnic Hungarians and other dissidents, who were aware of support for their cause from the Hungarian government, the CSCE process, the United Nations, and other international sources. Views about political legitimacy in Romania thus resulted in an intermestic process, part international and part domestic, in which concern for various human rights was merged with other considerations.

In the case of Romania, it is interesting how little either the ideology of Marxism or basic legal factors affected political stability and/or domestic war. Ceausescu's personality cult was linked more to Romanian nationalism than communism, and the same priorities could be found in those who moved against him. Most "rebels" did not act because he had misinterpreted Marxism but because he had ruined the national economy and/or negatively affected various groups within the state. Some Romanians, of course, were strongly opposed to communism, but until the late 1970s, authoritarian communism was widely if passively deferred to in Romania because it produced macroeconomic growth and trickle-down benefits on a reasonably broad scale.

Whereas some of Ceausescu's domestic critics certainly wanted more constitutional rule in Romania, international legal recognition of Ceausescu's government meant nothing in practical terms. The important sources of legitimacy, both domestic and international, were not so much purely legal as moral, functional, and political.

Are there any valid generalizations about human rights and domestic war that transcend our few case studies and/or that might be validated by other cases? As other recent studies of revolutions and internal wars have concluded, one cannot overlook the diversity of this subject matter and the sheer variety of factors at work in states such as Peru, Somalia, the Sudan, Guatemala, Ethiopia, Angola, Myanmar, Cambodia, "Soviet" Georgia, Chad, El Salvador, Colombia, India, China, Iraq, Turkey, and elsewhere—including Sri Lanka, Liberia, and Romania. I would posit the following five hypotheses as worthy of further examination.

1. In an era of human rights rhetoric, particularly after the discrediting of European authoritarian socialism, legal-moral factors centering on human rights should increase in relative importance, both nationally and internationally, at least in the near future. On the eve of the

twenty-first century, considerable intermestic (international and domestic) pressures are growing for some version of democratic state capitalism. I am not sure that this represents what some have termed "the end of history." But endorsement of democratic state capitalism is the general import of the two generations of internationally recognized human rights, especially if one recalls the endorsement of private property in the Universal Declaration of Human Rights (Article 17).

International standards indicate that there should be broad participation in all of public policy (which requires civil as well as political rights) and that economic policy should be managed or regulated by public authority to provide basic needs for the least well off. According to a broad international consensus, economic growth is most productive if ownership is primarily private, but public regulation is needed to alleviate the harshness for those who do not fare well under competition. The Western industrialized states have been affluent and stable not only because of freedom but also because of a welfare state that usually accepts economic and social rights. *Long-term domestic peace cannot successfully avoid fundamental human rights questions.*

2. This means that governing arrangements, as in Kenya, will likely come under increased domestic and international pressure to try to change in favor of democratic and civil rights. The trend will not be linear, as in China and Saudi Arabia, where domestic pressures for change can be bought off and/or resisted for a time and where international pressures can be reduced in favor of strategic and economic advantage.

Immensely complex situations can arise, as in Algeria. There, the movement toward increased participatory rights seemed certain to lead to a government violative of other internationally recognized rights—for example, rights for women and for religious freedom. Thus those within and outside Algeria, observing the army's move against an anticipated electoral victory by Islamic fundamentalists, faced a dilemma about how to protect a wide range of universal rights. Implementing some rights could lead to violations of others, a not altogether unusual situation. Nevertheless, in the near future, the movement will occur even in historically deferential nations like Russia and Algeria. *Domestic peace will be sought through some form of participatory rights.*

3. For much of the world, a liberalization in favor of political pluralism and a wide range of legally recognized civil rights will entail delicate efforts to satisfy various minority and ethnic groups. Compro-

mise and tolerant solutions will have to be reached regarding linguistic, religious, and representational rights. Political compromise may be in short supply, not only in places like Sri Lanka, Liberia, and Romania but also in places like Algeria and "Soviet" Georgia.

Considerable local autonomy within federalism may have to be tried broadly. Extensive forms of self-determination of peoples within a state may become the rule of the day, as has been true for some time in the United Kingdom, Belgium, and Switzerland—to cite three illustrative stable democracies. In some rare cases, the creation of a new state may be the only path to peace, as in the case of Eritrea and Ethiopia, Ireland and the United Kingdom, and Slovenia and Yugoslavia.

Nothing inherent in rights codes gives precise guidance on the best way to implement civil-political principles. Useful political compromises vary from situation to situation. *Participatory rights lead to a need to tolerate and/or reward various groups, perhaps entailing the creation of new states as a last resort. There is no general formula for appropriate tolerance or compromise.*

4. Governing arrangements that not only respect internationally recognized civil and political rights and manage resulting intergroup competition, but also acknowledge economic and social rights stand a better probability of stability and prosperity than others. Gross inequalities in social and economic conditions tend to encourage, but do not seem to definitely cause, domestic violence. The recognition of socioeconomic rights, as minimum standards to which all people in the state are entitled, helps to mitigate violence stemming from inequality.

Few are the stable democracies that do not have extensive welfare programs for the underclasses, even if they do not formally accept fundamental economic and social rights. Even if socioeconomic *rights* are not implemented, pursuing a policy of balanced socioeconomic development may prove conducive to civil-political rights. Romania is by no means the only example of a country in which a large economic gap between elite and mass contributed to violent behavior.

Even in normally democratic states, groups glorifying violence have thrived in times of severe economic distress. Even Britain had a lively Fascist movement during the global depression of the 1920s and 1930s. Economic difficulties in the West in the 1990s have been the context for renewed racism and scapegoating, in the United States, France, and the united Germany for example. Thus declining income or economic hardship in general, rather than simply a particular gap or particular level of income, may undermine the stable practice of civil and political rights. *Civil and political rights do not survive well in a socioeconomic context characterized by gross inequality.*

5. Governmental repression can produce domestic peace for a time. But repression alone fails to deal with the fundamental causes of dissatisfaction and potential unrest. There is no reliable way to predict how long repression can undergird an authoritarian and discriminatory regime. Intervening variables concern the deferential nature of a people and the power capabilities of ruling despots, as well as the nature of international pressure for change. We cannot precisely predict the future of China or Myanmar, just as we did not precisely predict the changes in South Africa. *All repressive regimes lacking major sources of legitimacy in the view of large numbers of citizens face an uncertain future. Growing attention to universal human rights exacerbates this problem.*

There is a possible, and indeed sometimes an actual, linkage between international and domestic war through the use of foreign force in a situation characterized by domestic unrest. However, this does not seem to be a prevalent feature of international relations. Frequently, foreign involvement in situations of domestic unrest is political or diplomatic. Only infrequently is foreign force overtly used. And very rarely are human rights factors the reason for such uses of force.

In several situations, violations of human rights have contributed to what I have called domestic war, and foreign armed participation has then occurred. We have studied the cases of Sri Lanka (forceful involvement by India) and Liberia (forceful involvement by Nigeria via ECOWAS). In Romania, forceful intervention was discussed between the USSR and the United States.

The Indian armed incursion into East Pakistan, soon to be Bangladesh, in 1971 was triggered in part by Pakistani murderous attacks on political dissidents. Iraq attacked Iran in 1979, when Iran was destabilized by a political revolution. Tanzania ordered an armed incursion into Uganda in 1978, when the Idi Amin government was "at war" with several armed rebel movements (but only after Ugandan governmental forces had carried out a military raid into Tanzania). South African and Cuban military forces participated directly in the civil war in Angola, although the causes of that domestic war were complex and not centered on internationally recognized human rights. The United States used force in Grenada, when Washington claimed domestic instability on that small island. A tripartite Western coalition used force in Lebanon in 1983, and Syria used force in that same situation. Undoubtedly, domestic unrest, whether related to human rights violations or not, can on occasion attract foreign use of force.

Yet in a number of situations, political revolution if not internal armed conflict, whatever the causes, was not characterized by foreign armed intervention. We studied the case of Romania, where collective armed involvement was actively considered by several states but was finally eschewed. In the case of the downfall of Marcos in the Philippines, geography made foreign force difficult to exercise in that mostly peaceful political revolution. During the prolonged domestic war in Ethiopia, there was no overt forceful foreign involvement, either because more powerful states were geographically removed or because they were not sufficiently interested. The same was true in the neighboring Sudan, characterized for several decades by an armed contest between the government and a rebellious south. One could cite other cases in which domestic war did *not* attract foreign use of force.

Occasionally, though not often, the United Nations Security Council will authorize the use of force in response to gross violations of human rights essentially within territorial states and in a situation of domestic war. The Council came close to explicitly doing so in the spring of 1991 with regard to the plight of the Kurds in Iraq. Yet I rather doubt that the moral interdependence of peoples, or a political consensus on the part of state members of the Council, will often lead to this type of centralized authorization of force to protect the international rights of people. I would be happy to be proven wrong on this score, but the loss of life and other costs of such forceful international humanitarian action would seem to mitigate against frequent use.

Moreover, many developing states still prefer state autonomy to more organized international relations. It is, after all, the sovereignty of the developing states that will be overridden by such Council action most of the time. It is in the developing states of the Southern Hemisphere, and perhaps in the unstable states emerging from the old Soviet Union, that gross violations of human rights in situations of domestic war will most likely attract international attention. Whether the debate has been about humanitarian relief in general, peacekeeping in Yugoslavia, or other subjects, most developing states in the early 1990s have been unenthusiastic about an active and authoritative Council. Numerous Council resolutions, even when dealing with pariahs or near pariahs like Iraq and Libya, have used wording reaffirming state sovereignty and jurisdiction.

All of this means that although there may be a link between domestic and international war, and although various human rights may be central to triggering domestic unrest (as shown in our case studies), there is certainly nothing automatic about the overall process. Domestic war has many causes, and such situations may or may not attract foreign uses of force depending on such factors as geography, calculations of power, moral solidarity, and respect for legal rules. For example, Western European states did not use force to correct human rights violations in authoritarian Greece in the late 1960s and early 1970s, even though they were geographically close with a collective power superiority. They felt restrained by moral and legal obligations, and perhaps by economic costs.

The phrase "human rights and peace" comprises more than just two "motherhood" concepts juxtaposed for reasons of politically correct semantics. It is still true that the two concepts are tossed about in erroneous bromides, such as when political leaders toss off statements like, "Democracies do not engage in aggression."

Human rights, particularly in the form of civil and political rights, are powerfully correlated with peace within a community of democratic states. These same civil and political rights, however, even within a grouping of democratic states, do not always block covert international "war." It seems that some elected governments are not always viewed as part of a democratic community, although we have yet to prove that U.S. covert policy during the cold war was typical of all powerful democracies. I suspect that Americans are indeed exceptional, but not always in the sense that "American exceptionalism" is equated with admirable qualities.

I have shown that at least in some cases of domestic war, using the language of rights can facilitate an understanding of complex situations. It may yet be that those developing states of the Southern Hemisphere, or of Eastern and Central Europe for that matter, that combine civil and political rights with economic and social rights, or at least with a program of balanced development in which great inequality of economic and social "goods" is avoided, will turn out to be more stable than otherwise. On this subject in particular, one would do well to be wary of easy generalization. The case of Sri Lanka reminds us that even states with decades of political pluralism and with considerable social and economic advances can still come unglued. There are many sources of political legitimacy, and a determined minority, viewing the government or state as illegitimate, can wreck great havoc.

Domestic peace may be even more difficult to establish than international peace. It would indeed be ironic, as well as profoundly depressing, if an increase in international peace coincided with more domestic war. We have explored the possibility that a combination of factors is at work reducing major war among major states: implementation of civil-political rights, attention to socioeconomic rights, material development, and the war experience itself, leading to moral revulsion. It is not out of the question that the disintegration of the Soviet Union and its European empire, combined with the myriad difficulties facing the developing states of the Southern Hemisphere, could produce endemic domestic war in many places. The challenges of state and nation building, political compromise, toleration of peoples long hated, and pursuit of economic growth with equity may prove more than a match for the wisdom of both elite and mass.

The international bill of rights, covering civil-political and socioeconomic rights for all people without discrimination, provides a recipe for the pursuit of domestic as well as international peace. But rights do not implement themselves. Politics drives law. A series of political decisions is required to adapt legal rights to particular circumstances. And we have yet to see whether some form of democratic state capitalism writ large, providing not just participation but also minimal socioeconomic needs, can provide political stability beyond its traditional area of success.

Notes

INTRODUCTION

1. The United Nations Charter and the Universal Declaration of Human Rights, along with other legal and quasi-legal human rights documents, can be found in Albert P. Blaustein, et al., eds., *Human Rights Source-Book*. New York: Paragon, 1987

2. See, e.g., Katrina Tomasevski, "The Right to Peace," *Current Research on Peace and Violence* 5, no. 1 (1982): 42–69.

3. See, e.g., Pascale Kromarek, ed., *Environnement et droits de l'homme* (Paris: UNESCO, 1988).

4. *The Realization of the Right to Development* (New York: United Nations, 1991), 44. Some scholars endorse, and some reject, the right to development.

5. In my book *The Internationalization of Human Rights* (Lexington, Mass.: Lexington Books for D.C. Heath, 1991), chap. 2, I discuss the efforts to both endorse and specify international civil and political rights.

6. See ibid. I refer to the Expert Committee charged with supervising the United Nations Covenant on Economic, Social, and Cultural Rights and also to the European Social Charter with its monitoring process. There is also renewed attention to socioeconomic rights in the Organization of American States.

7. See, e.g., Johan Galtung, "Nonterritorial Actors and the Problem of Peace," in Saul Mendlovitz, ed., *The Creation of a Just World Order* (New York: Free Press, 1975), esp. 151–52.

8. See, for example, Jeane J. Kirkpatrick and Allan Gerson, "The Reagan Doctrine, Human Rights, and International Law," in Louis Henkin et al., *Right v. Might: International Law and the Use of Force* (New York: Council on Foreign Relations, 1991), 19–36, and W. Michael Reisman, "Sovereignty and Human Rights in Contemporary International Law," *American Journal of International Law* 84, no. 4 (October 1990): 866–77.

9. The historical situation regarding the United Nations Security Council and threats to the peace involving human rights violations is nicely covered in Vernon Van Dyke, *Human Rights, the United States, and International Community* (New York: Oxford University Press, 1970). For the situation of the Iraqi Kurds, see United Nations, Security Council, *Resolution 688* (April 5, 1991).

CHAPTER I

1. See, among others, Hedley Bull, *The Anarchical Society: A Study of Order in World Politics* (New York: Columbia University Press, 1977), and Robert Gilpin, *War and Change in World Politics* (Cambridge: Cambridge University Press, 1981). For an overview of different versions of realism, see Robert O. Keohane, ed., *Neorealism and Its Critics* (New York: Columbia University Press, 1986).

2. For an overview of different versions of liberalism, see Mark W. Zacher and Richard A. Mathew, "Liberal International Theory: Common Threads, Divergent Strands" (Paper presented to the annual meeting of the American Political Science Association, Chicago, September 3–6, 1992).

3. Keohane, *Neorealism*.

4. Geoffrey Blainey, *The Causes of War,* 3d ed. (New York: Free Press, 1988), 113.

5. Ibid., 114.

6. Ibid., 123.

7. Melvin Small and J. David Singer, eds., *International War: An Anthology and Study Guide* (Homewood, Ill.: Dorsey Press, 1985), 17. See also J. David Singer, ed., *The Correlates of War: Vols. I and II* (New York: Free Press, 1979, 1980). And see J. David Singer and Melvin Small, *Resort to Arms: International and Civil Wars, 1850–1980* (Beverly Hills, Calif.: Sage, 1982).

8. Seyom Brown, *The Causes and Prevention of War* (New York: St. Martin's Press, 1987), 16.

9. John G. Stoessinger, *Nations in Darkness: China, Russia, and America,* 5th rev. ed. (New York: McGraw-Hill, 1990).

10. Jack Levy, "Historical Trends in Great Power War, 1495–1975,"

International Studies Quarterly 26, no. 2 (June 1982): 278–300.

11. Melvin Small, *Was War Necessary: National Security and U.S. Entry into War, 1812–1950* (Beverly Hills, Calif.: Sage, 1980).

12. The definition of *aggression*, as a legal term, is fraught with many dangers. Its core meaning is the wrongful first use of armed attack, unless authoritative bodies determine otherwise. See Louis Henkin et al., *International Law: Cases and Materials* (St. Paul, Minn.: West, 1980), 908, 916.

13. T. V. Paul, "Asymetric Conflicts: A Study of War Initiation by Lesser Powers," Ph.D. dissertation, University of California–Los Angeles, 1991.

14. David P. Forsythe, *The Internationalization of Human Rights* (Lexington, Mass.: Lexington Books for D.C. Heath, 1991, 173–78.

15. "Safeguarding Human Rights," *Current Policy*, no. 775, December 10, 1985. For a scholarly rediscovery of Kant's thoughts about democracy and peace, see George Modelski, "Is World Politics Evolutionary Learning?" *International Organization* 44, no. 1 (Winter 1990): 1–25.

16. Michael W. Doyle, "Liberalism and World Politics," *American Political Science Review* 80, no. 4 (December 1986): 1151–69.

17. Nils Petter Gleditsch, "Democracy and Peace," *Journal of Peace Research* 29, no. 4 (November 1992): 369–76.

18. Benjamin Jowett, *Thucydides, Book V* (London: Oxford University Press, 1900).

19. Doyle, "Liberalism and World Politics."

20. United States Institute of Peace, *Journal* 3, no. 2 (June 1990): 4. See Bruce Russett, "Democracy and Peace," in Bruce Russett et al., *Choices in World Politics: Sovereignty and Interdependence* (New York: Freeman, 1989), pp. 245–60.

21. Zeev Maoz and Bruce Russett, "Normative and Structural Modes of the Democratic Peace" (Paper presented at the annual meeting of the American Political Science Association, Chicago, September 3–6, 1992).

22. See Glen Fisher, *Mindsets* (Yarmouth, Maine: Intercultural Press, 1988), 83–84 and passim, regarding basic assumptions not subject to scientific explanation.

23. William D. Coplin, "The World Court in the International Bargaining Process," in Robert Gregg and Michael Barkun, eds., *The United Nations and Its Functions* (Princeton, N.J.: Van Nostrand, 1968), 317–32.

24. See Thomas M. Franck, *Judging the World Court* (New York: Priority Press, 1986), for the Twentieth Century Fund. And "Nicaragua v. the United States," *International Legal Materials* 25 (1986): 1023.

25. Maoz and Russett, "Normative and Structural Modes."

26. Research findings are reviewed in Steve Chan, *International Relations in Perspective* (New York: Macmillan, 1984), chap. 3.

27. David P. Forsythe, *The Politics of International Law: U.S. Foreign Policy Reconsidered* (Boulder, Colo.: Lynne Rienner, 1990).

28. See William V. O'Brien, *Law and Morality in Israel's War with the PLO* (New York: Routledge, 1991), chap. 5.

29. Walter S. Jones, *The Logic of International Relations*, 6th rev. ed. (Glenview, Ill.: Scott, Foresman, 1988), chap. 11, lists many possible causes. Kenneth N. Waltz, *Man, the State and War: A Theoretical Analysis* (New York: Columbia University Press, 1959), lists three generic causes. See also James E. Dougherty and Robert L. Pfaltzgraff, Jr., *Contending Theories of International Relations: A Comprehensive Survey*, 2d ed. (New York: Harper and Row, 1981).

30. John Mueller, *Retreat from Doomsday* (New York: Basic Books, 1989).

31. Mueller, *Retreat*, p. 220.

32. William Ebenstein, *Today's Isms*, 7th ed. (Englewood Cliffs, N.J.: Prentice-Hall, 1973).

33. Mueller, *Retreat*, p. 11 and *passim*.

CHAPTER 2

1. Steven Van Evera, "The Case against Intervention," *Atlantic Monthly*, July 1990, 72. As is natural in journalism, this essay is short on extended proof and analysis.

2. J. L. Brierly, *The Law of Nations: An Introduction to The International Law of Peace* (Oxford: Oxford University Press, 1963), 403–4.

3. Policymakers and participants have admitted to these interventions. On Iran, see the memoirs of the principal CIA agent involved, Kermit Roosevelt, *Countercoup: The Struggle for the Control of Iran* (New York: McGraw-Hill, 1979). On the democratic nature of Iran, or at least of the Mossadeq era, see Fakhreddin Azimi, *Iran: The Crisis of Democracy, 1941–1953* (London: I. B. Tauris and Co., 1989); Bahman Nirumand, *Iran: The New Imperialism in Action* (New York: Monthly Review Press, 1969); Saikal Amin, *The Rise and Fall of the Shah* (Princeton, N.J.: Princeton University Press, 1980); and William A. Dorman and Mansour Farhand, *The U.S. Press and Iran* (Berkeley: University of California Press, 1987). On Guatemala, see Stephen Schlesinger and Stephen Kinzer, *Bitter Fruit: The Untold Story of the American Coup in Guatemala* (New York: Doubleday, 1982); Marta Cehelsky and Henry Wells, *Guatemala Election Factbook* (Washington, D.C.: Institute for the Comparative Study of Political Systems, 1966); and Georges A. Fauriol and Eva Loser, *Guatemala's Political Puzzle* (New Brunswick, N.J.: Transaction Books, 1988).

4. William Blum, *The CIA: A Forgotten History* (London: Zed Books, 1986), chaps. 9–10; Richard H. Immerman, "Guatemala as Cold War History," *Political Science Quarterly* 95, no. 4 (Winter 1980–81): 629–54; Mark J. Gasiorowski, "The 1953 Coup d'etat in Iran," *International Journal of Middle East Studies* 19, no. 3 (August 1987), 261–86.

5. Blum, *The CIA*.

6. Piero Gleijeses, *Shattered Hope: The Guatemalan Revolution and the United States, 1944–1954* (Princeton, N.J.: Princeton University Press, 1991), 379.

7. John Prados, *Presidents' Secret Wars: CIA and Pentagon Covert Operations Since World War II* (New York: William Morrow and Co., 1986), 103.

8. Blum, *The CIA*; see also Gleijeses, *Shattered Hope*.

9. Gleijeses, *Shattered Hope*, 365.

10. In addition to Blum, *The CIA*, Prados, *Secret Wars*, and Thomas Powers, *The Man Who Kept the Secrets: Richard Helms and the CIA* (New York: Washington Square Press, Pocket Books, 1979), see John Ranelagh, *The Agency: The Rise and Decline of the CIA* (London: Weidenfeld and Nicolson, 1986). Gleijeses, *Shattered Hope*, is very good in researching the tendency of American newspapers and magazines to accept governmental statements at face value during the early and mid-1950s.

11. Gleijeses, *Shattered Hope*, 365–66, emphasis added.

12. Blum, *The CIA*, 73, 98.

13. Gleijeses, *Shattered Hope*.

14. Blum, *The CIA*; Prados, *Secret Wars*; Powers, *The Man*; and Ranelagh, *The Agency*, all agree on this point.

15. Herbert Feith, *The Decline of Constitutional Democracy in Indonesia* (Ithaca, N.Y.: Cornell University Press, 1962).

16. Ibid.; Baladas Ghoshal, *Indonesian Politics, 1955–59: The Emergence of Guided Democracy* (Calcutta: K. P. Bagchi and Co., 1982); Jon Reinhard, *Foreign Policy and National Integration: The Case of Indonesia* (New Haven, Conn.: Yale University Press, 1971).

17. Powers, *The Man*, saw the U.S. policy as one of harassment and pressure rather than a serious overthrow. But compare Julie Southwood and Patrick Flanagan, *Indonesia: Law, Propaganda, and Terror* (London: Zed Press, 1983). The U.S. ambassador to Indonesia at that time confirms the intervention but pleads ignorance as to cause and details; see Howard Palfrey Jones, *Indonesia: The Possible Dream* (New York: Harcourt, Brace, Jovanovich, 1971).

18. See especially Prados, *Secret Wars*, 106.

19. Blum, *The CIA*, chap. 14.

20. Ibid., chap. 27.

21. Ibid; Ranelagh, *The Agency*, 390.

22. There is no question about a broad range of U.S. covert interventions in Brazilian politics in the early 1960s through such actions as providing funding to particular candidates during electoral campaigns. The only points remaining concern exactly what U.S. officials said to Brazilian military officials and thus whether the United States engineered the coup or just supported it. Even the latter role constitutes intervention.

23. For background, see Frederico G. Gill, *The Political System of Chile* (Boston: Houghton Mifflin Co., 1966). For the Allende period, see Arturo Valenzuela, *The Breakdown of Democratic Regimes: Chile* (Baltimore: Johns Hopkins University Press, 1982).

24. Henry A. Kissinger, *Years of Upheaval* (Boston: Little, Brown and Co., 1982), chap. 9.

25. Quoted in Roger Morris, *Uncertain Greatness: Henry Kissinger and American Foreign Policy* (New York: Harper and Row, 1977), 240–41.

26. In addition to Kissinger, *Years*, see Powers, *The Man*, chap. 13, and Cole Blaiser, *The Hovering Giant: U.S. Responses to Revolutionary Change in Latin America, 1910–1985*, rev. ed. (Pittsburgh: University of Pittsburgh Press, 1985).

27. Mark Falcoff, *Modern Chile, 1970–1989: A Critical History* (New Brunswick, N.J.: Transaction Pubs., 1989), 31 and passim. See also Valenzuela, *Breakdown*, esp. chap. 4.

28. Powers, *The Man*.

29. Dennis Gilbert, *Sandinistas: The Party and the Revolution* (New York: Basil Blackwell, 1988), esp. 34–36.

30. Ibid., 121–23. U.S. Department of State, *Country Reports on Human Rights Practices for 1984* (Washington, D.C.: Government Printing Office, 1985), 608–24. (This source is not fully reliable on Nicaragua for the period covered, given attempts by the executive to remove the government whose record is being reported.)

31. Sam Dillon, *The Commandos: The CIA and Nicaragua's Contra Rebels* (New York: Henry Hold, 1991), chronicles both the Sandinistas' and the contras' violations of human rights.

32. I have researched the details in David P. Forsythe, *The Politics of International Law: U.S. Foreign Policy Reconsidered* (Boulder, Colo.: Lynne Rienner, 1990), chap. 3.

33. For an overview, see Thomas W. Walker, "Nicaraguan-U.S. Friction: The First Four Years, 1979–1983," in Kenneth M. Coleman and George C. Herring, eds., *The Central American Crisis: Sources of Conflict and the Failure of U.S. Policy* (Wilmington, Del.: Scholarly Resources, 1985), 179. See also Michael E. Conroy, ed., *Nicaragua: Profiles of the Revolutionary Public Sector* (Boulder, Colo.: Westview Press, 1987), esp. chap. 6 on health policy.

34. See Forsythe, *International Law*, chap. 3.

35. Anastasio Somoza's Nicaragua proves that one can have elections without democracy, as was equally true in other Latin states such as Guatemala, Honduras, and El Salvador and in the previous Stalinist states of Europe. In the Latin states mentioned, there were even multiple parties and an absence of formal curbs on the press. In those states, the central problem was that the civilian winners of elections did not make basic policy; rather, the authoritarian military did. Thus the polity remained essentially authoritarian, despite the facade of technically free and fair elections.

36. Eliott Abrams, "Keeping Pressure on the Sandinistas, *New York Times*, January 13, 1986, 15.

37. Aryeh Neier, "Flimflam on Central America," *New York Times*, December 14, 1985, 15.

38. Van Evera, "The Case against Intervention."

39. Charles D. Ameringer, *U.S. Foreign Intelligence: The Secret Side of American History* (Lexington, Mass.: Lexington Books, 1990).

40. Ralph McGehee, *Deadly Deceits: My Twenty-five Years in the CIA* (New York: Sheridan Square Pubs., 1983), 59.

41. Ranelagh, *The Agency*, 390n.

42. Blum, *The CIA*, chap. 11; Ranelagh, *The Agency*, 275–76; McGehee, *Deadly Deceits*, 27.

43. Blum, *The CIA*, chap. 25; McGehee, *Deadly Deceits*, 59.

44. Philip Agee and Louis Wolf, eds., *Dirty Work: The CIA in Western Europe* (Secaucus, N.J.: Lyle Stuart, 1978), 184–88.

45. Rustem Galiullin, *The CIA in Asia: Covert Operations against India and Afghanistan* (Moscow: Progress Publishers, 1988).

46. Michael H. Hunt, *Ideology and U.S. Foreign Policy* (New Haven, Conn.: Yale University Press, 1987).

47. David Mayers, *George Kennan and the Dilemmas of U.S. Foreign Policy* (New York: Oxford University Press, 1988).

48. Michael W. Doyle, "Kant, Liberal Legacies, and Foreign Affairs," *Philosophy and Public Affairs* 12, no. 4 (1983): 226–29.

49. Ibid., 335.

50. Ibid., 331.

51. Michael W. Doyle, "Liberalism and World Politics," *American Political Science Review* 80, no. 4 (December 1986): 1162.

CHAPTER 3

1. Thomas H. Greene, *Comparative Revolutionary Movements: Search for Theory and Justice* (Englewood Cliffs, N.J.: Prentice-Hall, 1990), 12.

2. Robert Darnton, "Did East Germany Have a Revolution?" *New York Times*, December 3, 1990, A13.

3. Samuel P. Huntington, *Political Order in Changing Societies* (New Haven, Conn.: Yale University Press, 1968), 264.

4. Robert H. Dix, "Varieties of Revolution," *Comparative Politics* 15, no. 2 (April 1983): 281–94.

5. See, e.g., Crane Brinton, *The Anatomy of Revolution* (New York: Vintage, 1938, 1965); Karl Marx and Friedrich Engels, *Manifesto of the Communist Party* (New York: International Publishers, 1932); Ted Robert Gurr, *Why Men Rebel* (Princeton, N.J.: Princeton University Press, 1970); Charles Tilly, *From Mobilization to Revolution* (Reading, Mass.: Addison-Wesley, 1978); Huntington, *Political Order*; Theda Skocpol, *States and Social Revolutions* (Cambridge: Cambridge University Press, 1979); and Jack A. Goldstone, ed., *Revolutions: Theoretical, Comparative, and Historical Studies* (New York: Harcourt, Brace, Jovanovich, 1986).

6. Matthew Soberg Shugart, "Patterns of Revolution," *Theory and Society* 18, no. 1 (January 1989): 249.

7. Jack Goldstone et al., eds., *Revolutions of the Late Twentieth Century* (Boulder, Colo.: Westview Press, 1991).

8. Greene, *Revolutionary Movements*, 192. Emphasis in the original.

9. James B. Rule, *Theories of Civil Violence* (Berkeley: University of California Press, 1988), 256. Emphasis in the original.

10. Lucian W. Pye, *Aspects of Political Development* (Boston: Little, Brown, 1966), 134.

11. Darnton, "East Germany.".

12. Ernst Haas, *When Knowledge Is Power: Three Models of Change in International Organizations* (Berkeley: University of California Press, 1990).

13. The argument is made clearly by James A. Bill in "U.S. Foreign Policy and Iran: A System of Reinforced Failure," in David P. Forsythe, ed., *American Foreign Policy in an Uncertain World* (Lincoln: University of Nebraska Press, 1984), 419–52. See also Farideh Farhi, "State Disintegration and Urban-Based Revolutionary Crisis," *Comparative Political Studies* 21, no. 1 (April 1988): 231–56, for a discussion of "permissive world context." And see Gary Hawes, "Theories of Peasant Revolution: A Critique and Contribution from the Philippines," *World Politics*, 42, no. 2 (January 1990), 261–98.

14. The usage is borrowed from Kenneth N. Waltz, *Man, the State, and War: A Theoretical Analysis* (New York: Columbia University Press, 1959).

15. Ted Robert Gurr, "War, Revolution, and the Growth of the Coercive State," *Comparative Political Studies* 21, no. 1 (April 1988): 46.

16. See Barry M. Schutz and Robert O. Slater, eds., *Revolution and Political Change in the Third World* (Boulder, Colo.: Lynne Rienner, 1990), 7.

17. See Goldstone, *Revolutions*.

18. Susan M. Miller, ed., *Max Weber: Selections from His Work* (New York: Thomas Y. Crowell, 1963), 63. See also Robert Cotterell, "Legality and Political Legitimacy in the Sociology of Max Weber," in David Sugarman, ed., *Legality, Ideology, and the State* (London: Academic Press, 1983).

19. For a discussion of how one nation may manifest at least five different "cultures" and how these cultures compete for dominance, see Michael Thompson et al., *Cultural Theory* (Boulder, Colo: Westview Press, 1990).

20. For the argument that the concept of charisma has been much overrated as an explanatory idea, see William Spinrad, "Charisma: A Blighted Concept and an Alternative Formula," *Political Science Quarterly* 106, no. 2 (Summer 1991): 295–312.

21. For a highly theoretical discussion, see Ronald Rogowski, *Rational Legitimacy* (Princeton, N.J.: Princeton University Press, 1974).

22. Zehra F. Arat, *Democracy and Human Rights in Developing Countries* (Boulder, Colo.: Lynne Rienner, 1991).

23. T. David Mason, "Indigenous Factors," in Schutz and Slater, *Revolution and Political Change*, 31–48.

24. See David P. Forsythe, *The Internationalization of Human Rights* (Lexington, Mass.: Lexington Books for D.C. Heath, 1991), chap. 4.

25. Geoffrey Blainey, *The Causes of War*, 3d rev. ed. (New York: Free Press, 1988).

26. Raphael Zariski, "Ethnic Extremism among Ethnoterritorial Minorities in Western Europe," *Comparative Politics* 21 (April 1989): 253–72; John B. Londregan and Keith T. Poole, "Poverty, the Coup Trap, and the Seizure of Executive Power," *World Politics* 42, no. 2 (January 1990): 151–83.

27. See, e.g., Brinton, *Anatomy of Revolution*, 32–33. But compare Mark Irving Lichback, "An Evaluation of 'Does Economic Equality Breed Political Conflict' Studies," *World Politics* 41, no. 4 (July 1989): 431–70.

28. Londregan and Poole, "Poverty." Recall Arat, *Democracy and Human Rights*.

29. Gurr, "War, Revolution," 45–65.

30. Theda Skocpol, for example, has modified her views over time.

CHAPTER 4

1. A very concise review of factors involved in the Tamil revolution, covering the massacre of July 1983, is contained in the presentation of W. Howard Wriggins, former U.S. ambassador to Sri Lanka, in House Committee on Foreign Affairs, *The Human Rights Implications of the*

Sinhalese-Tamil Conflict in Sri Lanka: Hearings before the Subcommittees on Human Rights and International Organizations and on Asian and Pacific Affairs, 98th Cong., 2d sess., August 2, 1984, 6–24 (hereafter cited as *Hearings*).

2. Useful reviews of the events are found in the following: Chandra Richard De Silva, *Sri Lanka: A History* (New Delhi: Vikas Publishing House, 1987); James Manor, ed., *Sri Lanka in Change and Crisis* (London: Croom Helm, 1984); Rajiva Wijesinha, *Current Crisis in Sri Lanka* (New Delhi: Navrang, 1986); K. M. de Silva, *Managing Ethnic Tensions in Multi-Ethnic Societies: Sri Lanka, 1880–1985* (Lanham, Md.: University Press of America, 1986 ; Mohan Ram, *Sri Lanka: The Fractured Island* (London: Penguin, 1989); A. J. Wilson, *The Breakup of Sri Lanka: The Sinhalese-Tamil Conflict* (London: C. Hurst and Co., 1988); Russell R. Ross and Andrea Matles Savada, eds., *Sri Lanka: A Country Study* (Washington, D.C.: GPO, 1990); S. J. Tambiah, *Sri Lanka: Ethnic Fratricide and the Dismantling of Democracy* (Chicago: University of Chicago Press, 1986); Satchi Ponnambalam, *Sri Lanka: The National Question and the Tamil Liberation Struggle* (London: Zed Books, 1983).

3. It does not seem necessary for the purposes of this chapter to go into a detailed description of the differences among the various Tamil organizations.

4. The role of Buddhism and Hinduism in Sri Lanka is covered in depth in Bruce Kapfered, *Legends of People, Myths of State* (Washington, D.C.: Smithsonian Institution Press, 1988), in addition to the literature cited in note 2.

5. In addition to the literature cited in note 2, see especially Marshall R. Singer, "New Realities in Sri Lanka Politics," *Asian Studies* 30, no. 4 (April 1990): 409–25.

6. Ibid., inter alia.

7. See note 2.

8. Ibid.

9. See esp. Wijesinha, *Current Crisis,* 18–20.

10. Economic factors are well covered in ibid., 30–31, and in Mick Moore, "Economic Liberalism versus Political Pluralism in Sri Lanka?" *Modern Asian Studies* 24, no. 2 (1990): 341–83.

11. The issue is well covered in C. R. de Silva, *Sri Lanka,* starting at page 238.

12. Among other sources, see Marshall R. Singer, "Sri Lanka in 1990: The Ethnic Strife Continues," *Asian Survey* 31, no. 2 (February 1991): 140–46.

13. Wijesinha, *Current Crisis,* 102–3.

14. Statement of Ms. Amy Young, International Human Rights Law Group, in *Hearings,* 25. Compare the similar statement of U.S. officials in the same hearings.

15. See Singer, "New Realities," 422–25, among other sources.

16. Wilson, *Breakup of Sri Lanka*, chap. 1.

17. Constitutional issues are well treated in C. R. de Silva, *Sri Lanka*, 226–35.

18. Amnesty International, *Sri Lanka: Extrajudicial Executions, "Disappearances," and Torture, 1987 to 1990* (New York: Amnesty International U.S.A, 1990).

19. See *Hearings*, 112.

20. Wilson, *Breakup of Sri Lanka*, 50–54.

21. Amnesty International, *Sri Lanka*. And see Shantha K. Hennayake, "The Peace Accord and the Tamils in Sri Lanka," *Asian Survey* 24, no. 4 not just Tamils, (April 1989): 401–15, who makes the point that many Sinhalese, were victimized by the UNP governments after 1977.

22. See Wilson, *Breakup of Sri Lanka*, chap. 7, and Singer, "New Realities," 416, inter alia.

23. C. R. de Silva, *Sri Lanka*, 244–45.

24. *Washington Post*, National Edition, June 3–9, 1991, 20.

25. House Committee on Foreign Affairs, *The Indo–Sri Lankan Agreement: Hearings before the Subcommittee on Asian and Pacific Affairs*, 100th Cong., 1st sess., August 6, 1987 (hereafter cited as *Agreement*).

26. The *Washington Post*, June 3–9, 1991, 20, reported twelve hundred deaths for the IPKF by the time it was withdrawn.

27. Amnesty International, *Sri Lanka*.

28. *Agreement*, 14. See also *Hearings*, 81; U.S. officials saw no Soviet role in Sri Lanka (83).

29. *Hearings*, statements of Mr. Schaffer.

30. The countries of the Non-Aligned Movement, mostly lesser developed, avoided formal alliance with the two superpowers and sought influence through unity; Wijesinha, *Current Crisis*, 103.

31. U.N. action is reviewed in Amnesty International, *Sri Lanka*.

32. Ibid.; *New York Times*, March 31, 1990, 4; Paul Siegart, *Sri Lanka: A Mounting Tragedy of Errors* (Geneva: International Commission of Jurists, 1984); Virginia Leary, *Ethnic Conflict and Violence in Sri Lanka* (Geneva: International Commission of Jurists, 1981).

33. Amnesty International, *Sri Lanka*.

34. The JVP revolution is in need of further in-depth analysis, with more concentration on the Tamils.

35. Compare the record of private groups cited at note 32.

36. Jeffrey D. Simon, *Revolutions without Guerrillas* (Santa Monica, Calif.: Rand, 1989). Of course, Sri Lanka manifested both Tamil and JVP guerrillas.

37. See Ernst Haas, *When Knowledge Is Power: Three Models of*

Change in International Organizations (Berkeley: University of California Press, 1990), for an argument in favor of typologies, but not full-blown theories, of certain political developments.

CHAPTER 5

1. Africa Watch, *Liberia: A Human Rights Disaster* (New York: Africa Watch, 1990), 22.

2. D. Elwood Dunn and S. Byron Tarr, *Liberia: A National Polity in Transition* (Metuchen, N.J.: Scarecrow Press, 1988), 82. Franz Fanon spoke of "peau noire masques blancs," quoted in Michel Galy, "La guerre civile, loin de Monrovia," *Le Monde Diplomatique*, July 1990, 3.

3. See, among others, Stephen S. Hlophe, *Class, Ethnicity, and Politics in Liberia* (Washington, D.C.: University Press of America, 1979), 119–24.

4. See, for example, Roger Simon, *Gramsci's Political Thought* (London: Lawrence and Wishart, 1982).

5. Hlophe, *Class*, 110, 125–34, 206–55.

6. John A. Wiseman, *Democracy in Black Africa* (New York: Paragon, 1990), 144; Yekutiel Gershoni, *Black Colonialism: The Americo-Liberian Scramble for the Hinterland* (Boulder, Colo.: Westview Press, 1985), 104.

7. Gus Liebenow, "The Libyan Coup in Perspective," *Current History* 80, no. 464 (March 1981): 104.

8. Martin Lowenkopf, *Politics in Liberia: The Conservative Road to Development* (Palo Alto, Calif.: Hoover Institution Press, 1976), 171.

9. Ibid.

10. Ibid., 164–66.

11. Dunn and Tarr, *Liberia*, 50.

12. Liebenow, "Libyan Coup," 105.

13. Ibid., 104.

14. Dunn and Tarr, *Liberia*, 67.

15. Liebenow, "Libyan Coup," 104.

16. Ibid., 131.

17. Ibid.

18. Dunn and Tarr, *Liberia*, 69. See also Julius Emeka Okolo, "Liberia: The Military Coup," *World Today* 37 (April 1981): 149–57.

19. Gershoni, *Black Colonialism*, 6.

20. Ibid., 100.

21. Hassan B. Sisay, *Big Powers and Small Nations: A Case Study of United States–Liberian Relations* (Lanham, Md.: University Press of America, 1985), chap. 8.

22. Carlisle Rodney, "The 'American Century' Implemented: Stet-

tinius and the Liberian Flag of Convenience," *Business History Review* 54 (Summer 1980): 175–91.

23. In addition to Hlophe, *Class*, see Sisay, *Big Powers*, chap. 4.

24. For an example of a whitewashed report reflecting the special relationship, see U.S. Department of State, *Country Reports on Human Rights Practices for 1979* (Washington, D.C.: GPO, 1980), 106–9. "While there is residual tension . . . Liberia's political dynamics now reflect the normal third world strains of rich/poor and urban/rural" (106). "President Tolbert has been a leading advocate of human rights" (109).

25. Senate Committee on Foreign Relations, *Liberia and Ghana—Policy Challenges in West Africa*, 97th Cong., 2d sess., June 1982, 1–2 (hereafter cited as *Liberia and Ghana*); William Lacy (U.S. ambassador to Liberia), "Liberia: The Road to Recovery," *Current Policy*, no. 343 (October 28, 1981).

26. Lacy, "Liberia."

27. Dunn and Tarr, *Liberia*, 91.

28. Liebenow, "Libyan Coup," 102; Sisay, *Big Powers*, 167.

29. Dunn and Tarr, *Liberia*, 93.

30. See esp. Lacy, "Liberia."

31. Wiseman, *Democracy in Black Africa*, 147–48.

32. Amadu Sesay, "The OAU and Regime Recognition: Politics of Discord and Collaboration in Africa," *Scandinavian Journal of Development Alternatives* 4 (March 1985): 25–41. See also Joseph E. Holloway, *Liberian Diplomacy in Africa: A Study of Inter-African Relations* (Lanham, Md.: University Press of America, 1981).

33. A good review of congressional and Democratic support for Doe is found in Sisay, *Big Powers*, 167–70.

34. Particular figures on U.S. foreign assistance can be found in U.S. Department of State, *Country Reports on Human Rights Practices* (Washington, D.C.: GPO, annual).

35. *Liberia and Ghana*.

36. Events are reviewed in Dunn and Tarr, *Liberia*. On attempts at charismatic rule, see Henry Bienen, "Populist Military Regimes in West Africa, *Armed Forces and Society* 11, no. 3 (Spring 1985): 367, which also covers Doe's elimination of rivals.

37. Lawyers Committee for Human Rights, *Liberia: A Promise Betrayed* (Washington, D.C.: Lawyers Committee, 1986); Africa Watch, *Liberia: Flight from Terror* (New York: Watch Committees, 1990); Africa Watch, *Liberia: A Human Rights Disaster*; House Committee on Foreign Affairs, *Foreign Assistance Legislation for Fiscal Years 1990–91: Hearings and Markup before the Subcommittee on Africa*, 101st Cong., 1st sess., March 8, 9, April 25, 1989, 207–12, 244–50. The annual reports compiled by Reagan's State Department and reviewed by Congress became increasingly candid over time; see esp. U.S. Department

of State, *Country Reports on Human Rights Practices for 1989* (Washington, D.C.: GPO, 1990). See also Ernest Harsch, "Amos Sawyer: Fighting for Rights," *Africa Report* 32 (July/August 1989): 27–30.

38. See Lewis Smith, "Liberia: Muzzling the Media," *Africa Report* 32 (March/April 1987): 11; Momo K. Rogers, "The Liberian Press: An Analysis," *Journalism Quarterly* 63 (Summer 1986): 275–81.

39. Dunn and Tarr, *Liberia*, 136, 199.

40. Quoted in Africa Watch, *Liberia: Flight from Terror*, 17–18.

41. World Bank, *World Development Report* (New York: Oxford University Press, 1990).

42. Liebenow, "Libyan Coup," 103.

43. N. Brian Winchester, "United States Policy toward Africa," *Current History* 87, no. 529 (May 1988): 194.

44. Kenneth B. Noble, "Doe Leads the Good Life as Liberia Grows Poorer and Its People, Fractious," *New York Times*, March 26, 1990, A4.

45. Gordon C. Thomasson, "Liberian Disaster: Made in the U.S.A.," *New York Times*, July 14, 1990, A15.

46. Noble, "Doe Leads the Good Life."

47. World Bank, *World Development Report*; Bienen, "Populist Military Regimes," 364–65.

48. Quoted in Dunn and Tarr, *Liberia*, 95.

49. Africa Watch, *Liberia: A Human Rights Disaster*. See also Holly Burkhalter and Rakiya Omaar, "Failures of State," *Africa Report* 35 (November/December 1990): 27–29.

50. Africa Watch, *Liberia: Flight from Terror*.

51. Quoted in House Committee on Foreign Affairs, *Liberia: Recent Developments and United States Foreign Policy: Hearings and Markup before the Subcommittees on Human Rights and on Africa*, 99th Cong., 2d sess., January 23, 28, 29, 1986, 1 (hereafter cited as *Liberia: Recent Developments*).

52. Ibid., 2; see also p. 61.

53. Senate Committee on Foreign Relations, *Liberia and United States Policy: Hearings before the Subcommittee on African Affairs*, 99th Cong., 1st sess., December 10, 1985, 5. See also Suzanne Cronje, "Doe's a Dear . . . a Reagan Dear," *New Statesman* 110 (December 6, 1985): 17–18, and Bienen, "Populist Military Regimes," 370.

54. *Liberia: Recent Developments*, 32.

55. David K. Shipler, "Shultz Is under Fire for Asserting Liberia Has Made Gains on Rights," *New York Times*, January 16, 1987, A1; Michael H. Posner, "Shultz's Liberia—and President Doe's," *New York Times*, January 25, 1987, A25; Winchester, "United States Policy," 194; "Honesty Watch," *Economist* 305 (November 28, 1987): 46.

56. Senate Committee on Foreign Relations, *Emergency Situations in Sudan and Liberia: Hearings before the Subcommittee on African*

Affairs, 101st Cong., 2d sess., November 27, 1990, 78–79, testimony by Chester Crocker.

57. Ibid., 3–4.

58. Ibid., 21.

CHAPTER 6

1. Alan Riding, "In Rumania, the Old Order Won't Budge," *New York Times,* November 25, 1989, A7.

2. Dan Ionescu, "An A to Z of Personality in Romania," *Radio Free Europe Research,* Romanian SR/11 (February 1989): 9–17.

3. Edward Behr, *Kiss the Hand You Cannot Bite: The Rise and Fall of the Ceausescus* (New York: Villard Books, 1991), 109; Mary Ellen Fischer, *Nicholae Ceausescu: A Study in Political Leadership* (Boulder, Colo.: Lynne Rienner Publishers, 1989), 28.

4. Behr, *Kiss the Hand,* 136.

5. For a review of Ceausescu's involvement in the 1968 crises in Czechoslovakia, see Fischer, *Nicholae Ceausescu,* 141–46; Daniel Nelson, ed., *Romania in the 1980's* (Boulder, Colo.: Westview Press, 1981), 124–26.

6. Nelson, *Romania,* 125.

7. Fischer, *Nicholae Ceausescu,* 160.

8. Ionescu, "A to Z," 16.

9. John Kifner, "In Rumania, All Hail the Chief and Dracula, Too," *New York Times,* December 24, 1983, A2.

10. Behr, *Kiss the Hand,* 169, 171, 176.

11. Fischer, *Nicholae Ceausescu,* 175.

12. Behr, *Kiss the Hand,* 182.

13. Ceausescu's rule "by clan" was often referred to as a case of "dynastic socialism" or "socialism in one family" and was compared to North Korea under Kim Il-sung.

14. Pirvulescu quoted in Vladimir Tismaneanu, "Personal Power and Political Crisis in Romania," *Government and Opposition* 24, no. 2 (Spring 1989): 184–85.

15. Michael Shafir, "Former Senior RCP Officials Protest Ceausescu's Policies," *Radio Free Europe Research,* Romanian SR/3 (March 29, 1989): 3–13.

16. Nelson, *Romania,* 131.

17. This point is made especially by Fischer, *Nicholae Ceausescu,* 161–65.

18. Nelson, *Romania,* 131.

19. Ibid., 6.

20. Trond Gilberg, *Nationalism and Communism in Romania: The*

Rise and Fall of Ceausescu's Personal Dictatorship (Boulder, Colo.: Westview Press, 1990), 111.

21. For a useful review of the Romanian economy as it progressed into the 1980s, including the problems in analyzing Romania's economic statistics, see Nelson, *Romania*, chap. 9.

22. Ibid., 221.

23. Michael Shafir, *Romanian Politics, Economics, and Society: Political Stagnation and Simulated Change* (London: Frances Pinter, 1985), 112.

24. Ibid., 116.

25. Ibid., 114.

26. John B. Oakes, "Ceausescu on Rumania, the West and East," *New York Times*, August 4, 1982, A23.

27. Ibid.; among others, see also Shafir, *Romanian Politics*, 121.

28. Kifner, "In Romania."

29. Quoted in "Cold Comfort," *Economist* 297 (October 21, 1985): 5–12.

30. Gilberg, *Nationalism*, 125.

31. Ibid., 45; see also Shafir, *Romanian Politics*, 33.

32. For a complete discussion, see Ari Chaplin, "The 'Popular War' Doctrine in Romanian Defense Policy," *East European Quarterly* 17 (September 1983): 267–81.

33. Shafir, *Romanian Politics*, 148.

34. Among others, see Gilberg, *Nationalism*, esp. 174.

35. Official figures vary.

36. Shafir, *Romanian Politics*, 158, 159.

37. Ibid., 163.

38. Ibid.; Gilberg, *Nationalism*, 157.

39. Amnesty International, *Romania: Human Rights in the Eighties* (London: Amnesty International, 1987), 6–7.

40. Per Ronnas, "Turning the Romanian Peasant into a New Socialist Man: An Assessment of Rural Development Policy in Romania," *Soviet Studies* 41 (October 1989): 443–558. Ronnas provides an excellent overview of the rural resettlement plan. He argues, however, that the plan was not necessarily discriminatory against predominantly Hungarian villages.

41. Charles Gati, "East-Central Europe: The Morning After," *Foreign Affairs* 69, no. 5 (Winter 1990/91): 130.

42. Karen Dawisha, *Eastern Europe, Gorbachev, and Reform* (Cambridge: Cambridge University Press, 1988), 41.

43. Shafir, *Romanian Politics*, 140.

44. Michael Shafir, "Political Culture, Intellectual Dissent, and Intellectual Consent: The Case of Romania," *Orbis* 27 (Summer 1983): 403–20.

45. Fischer, *Nicholae Ceausescu*, 173.

46. Gilberg, *Nationalism*, 3, 13.

47. "Romanian Expectations Concerning Domestic Developments," *Radio Free Europe/Radio Liberty, East European Area Audience and Opinion Research* (December 1984): 1–10.

48. Amnesty International, *Romania*, 6, 8.

49. Michael Thompson et al., *Cultural Theory* (Boulder, Colo.: Westview Press, 1990).

50. Nelson, *Romania*, 174–97, esp. 183.

51. Amnesty International, *Romania*, 7.

52. Ibid., 7.

53. *New York Times*, April 7, 1981, A8; Marvine Howe, "Rumania Determined to Avoid Poland's Plight," *New York Times*, November 1, 1981, A21.

54. Vladimir Socor, "Social Protests Continue," *Radio Free Europe Research*, Romanian SR/1 (January 1988): 21–23.

55. Shafir, *Romanian Politics*, 147.

56. Ibid., 168.

57. Quoted in Crisula Stefanescu, "Human Rights Activist Doina Cornea Complains about the Position of the Romanian Intellectual," *Radio Free Europe Research*, Romanian SR/8 (November 1989): 13–15.

58. Gati, "East-Central Europe," 135–36.

59. David B. Funderburk, *Pinstripes and Reds: An American Ambassador Caught Between the State Department and the Romanian Communists* (Raleigh, N.C.: Edwards and Broughton Co., 1988).

60. Joseph F. Harrington and Bruce J. Courtney, *Tweaking the Nose of the Russians: Fifty Years of American-Romanian Relations* (Boulder, Colo.: East European Monographs, 1991), 290, 291.

61. Ibid., 392.

62. A comprehensive review of congressional hearings concerning Romanian MFN is provided in ibid.

63. Ibid., 572; Lawyers Committee on Human Rights, *The Reagan Administration's Record on Human Rights* (Washington, D.C.: Lawyers Committee, 1987), 134.

64. Harrington and Courtney, *Fifty Years*, 577.

65. Ibid., 580–81.

66. Paul Gafton, "Romania Renounces MFN Trade Status with the USA," *Radio Free Europe Research*, Romanian SR/4 (March 1988): 3–5.

67. Amnesty International, *Romania*.

68. Michael Shafir, "The Mazilu Riddle: Romanian Official Fails to Appear before UN Body," *Radio Free Europe Research*, Romanian SR/10 (August 1988): 23–26.

69. Michael Shafir, "The UN Publishes Mazilu's Report on Human Rights and Young People," *Radio Free Europe Research*, Romanian SR/7 (September 1989): 15.

70. U.N. ECOSOC/CN.4/1991/30, *Report on the Situation of Human Rights in Romania,* January 8, 1991, 1.

71. Dan Ionescu, "Romania's Diminishing International Standing," *Radio Free Europe Research,* Romanian SR/3 (March 1989): 31–36.

72. Harrington and Courtney, *Fifty Years,* 371.

73. Ibid., 384.

74. Ibid., 396.

75. Ibid., 540.

76. Vladimir Socor, "Romania Rejects Final Document Adopted by CSCE," *Radio Free Europe Research,* Romanian SR/1 (February 1989): 20.

77. Shafir, "RCP Officials Protest," 4.

78. Henry Kamm, "Gorbachev Speaks to Rumanians on 'Openness' to a Cool Response," *New York Times,* May 27, 1987, A1.

79. Henry Kamm, "In Rumania, Gorbachev Is Gone and So Is Food," *New York Times,* May 31, 1987, A5.

80. Steven Greenhouse, "Soviets, at Rights Parley, Assail Rumanian Fence," *New York Times,* June 24, 1989, A17.

81. *New York Times,* November 30, 1989, A20.

82. For example, see Nestor Ratesh, *Romania: The Entangled Revolution* (New York: Praeger, 1991), esp. chap. 4. Andrei Codrescu, *The Hole in the Flag* (New York: William Morrow and Co., 1991), raises questions about the Romanian events, in chapter 13. His final analysis finds a role not only for "plotters" inside Romania but also for plotters in both Soviet and American intelligence agencies.

83. Jonathan Eyal, "Romania: A Revolution Hijacked or Redefined?" *World Today* 56 (March 1990): 39–40.

84. Michael Shafir, "New Revelations of the Military's Role in Ceausescu's Ouster," *Report on Eastern Europe* 1, no. 19 (May 11, 1990): 26.

85. Eyal, "Romania," 40.

Bibliography

Abrams, Eliott. "Keeping Pressure on the Sandinistas." *New York Times*, January 13, 1986, A15.

Africa Watch. *Liberia: A Human Rights Disaster*. New York: Watch Committees, 1990.

———. *Liberia: Flight from Terror*. New York: Watch Committees, 1990.

Agee, Philip, and Wolf, Louis, eds. *Dirty Work: The CIA in Western Europe*. Secaucus, N.J.: Lyle Stuart, 1978.

Ambrosius, Lloyd. *Woodrow Wilson and the American Diplomatic Tradition: The Treaty Fight in Perspective*. New York: Cambridge University Press, 1987.

Ameringer, Charles D. *U.S. Foreign Intelligence: The Secret Side of American History*. Lexington, Mass.: Lexington Books, 1990.

Amin, Saikal. *The Rise and Fall of the Shah*. Princeton, N.J.: Princeton University Press, 1980.

Amnesty International. *Romania: Human Rights in the Eighties*. London: Amnesty International, 1987.

———. *Sri Lanka: Extrajudicial Executions, "Disappearances" and Torture, 1987 to 1990*. New York: Amnesty International U.S.A., 1990.

Arat, Zehra F. *Democracy and Human Rights in Developing Countries*. Boulder, Colo.: Lynne Rienner, 1991.

Azimi, Fakhreddin. *Iran: The Crises of Democracy, 1941–1953*. London: I. B. Tauris and Co., 1989.

Behr, Edward. *Kiss the Hand You Cannot Bite: The Rise and Fall of the Ceausescus*. New York: Villard Books, 1991.

Bienen, Henry. "Populist Military Regimes in West Africa." *Armed Forces and Society* 11, no. 3 (Spring 1985): 357–77.

Bill, James A. "U.S. Foreign Policy and Iran: A System of Reinforced Failure." In David P. Forsythe, ed., *American Foreign Policy in an Uncertain World*. Lincoln: University of Nebraska Press, 1984.

Birnberg, Joanne E. "The Sun Sets on Tamuz 1: The Israeli Raid on Iraq's Nuclear Reactor." *California Western International Law Journal* 13 (Winter 1983): 86–115.

Blainey, Geoffrey. *The Causes of War*. 3d rev. ed. New York: Free Press, 1988.

Blaiser, Cole. *The Hovering Giant: U.S. Responses to Revolutionary Change in Latin America, 1910–1985*. Rev. ed. Pittsburgh: University of Pittsburgh Press, 1985.

Blum, William. *The CIA: A Forgotten History*. London: Zed Books, 1986.

Brierly, J. L. *The Law of Nations: An Introduction to the International Law of Peace*. Oxford: Oxford University Press, 1963.

Brinton, Crane. *The Anatomy of Revolution*. New York: Vintage, 1938, 1965.

Brogan, Patrick. *World Conflicts*. London: Bloomsbury Reference, 1989.

Brown, Seyom. *The Causes and Prevention of War*. New York: St. Martin's Press, 1987.

Bull, Hedley. *The Anarchical Society: A Study of Order and World Politics*. New York: Columbia University Press, 1977.

Burkhalter, Holly, and Omaar, Rakiya, "Failures of State," *Africa Report* 35 (November/December 1990): 27–29.

Cehelsky, Marta, and Wells, Henry. *Guatemala Election Factbook*. Washington, D.C.: Institute for the Comparative Study of Political Systems, 1966.

Chan, Steve. *International Relations in Perspective*. New York: Macmillan, 1984.

Chaplin, Ari. "The 'Popular War' Doctrine in Romanian Defense Policy." *East European Quarterly* 17 (September 1983): 267–81.

Codrescu, Andrei. *The Hole in the Flag*. New York: William Morrow and Co., 1991.

"Cold Comfort." *Economist* 297 (October 21, 1985): 5–12.

Conroy, Michael E., ed. *Nicaragua: Profiles of the Revolutionary Public Sector*. Boulder, Colo.: Westview Press, 1987.

Coplin, William D. "The World Court in the International Bargaining Process." In Robert Gregg and Michael Barkun, eds., *The United Nations and Its Functions*. Princeton, N.J.: Van Nostrand, 1968.

Cotterell, Robert. "Legality and Political Legitimacy in the Sociology of Max Weber." In David Sugarman, ed., *Legality, Ideology, and the State*. London: Academic Press, 1983.

Cronje, Suzanne. "Doe's a Dear . . . a Reagan Dear." *New Statesman* 110 (December 6, 1985): 17–18.

Darnton, Robert. "Did East Germany Have a Revolution?" *New York Times*, December 3, 1990, A13.

Dawisha, Karen. *Eastern Europe, Gorbachev, and Reform*. Cambridge: Cambridge University Press, 1988.

De Silva, Chandra Richard. *Sri Lanka: A History*. New Delhi: Vikas Publishing House, 1977.

De Silva, K. M. *Managing Ethnic Tensions in Multi-Ethnic Societies: Sri Lanka, 1880–1985*. Lanham, Md.: University Press of America, 1986.

Dillon, Sam. *The Commandos: The CIA and Nicaragua's Contra Rebels*. New York: Henry Hold, 1991.

Dix, Robert H. "Varieties of Revolution." *Comparative Politics* 15, no. 2 (April 1983): 281–94.

Dorman, William A., and Farhand, Mansour. *The U.S. Press and Iran*. Berkeley: University of California Press, 1987.

Dougherty, James E., and Pfaltzgraff, Robert L., Jr. *Contending Theories of International Relations: A Comprehensive Survey*. 2d ed. New York: Harper and Row, 1981.

Doyle, Michael W. "Kant, Liberal Legacies, and Foreign Affairs." *Philosophy and Public Affairs* 12, no. 4 (1983): 226–29.

———. "Liberalism and World Politics." *American Political Science Review* 80, no. 4 (December 1986): 1151–69.

Dunn, D. Elwood, and Tarr, S. Byron. *Liberia: A National Polity in Transition*. Metuchen, N.J.: Scarecrow Press, 1988.

Ebenstein, William. *Today's Isms*. 7th ed. Englewood Cliffs, N.J.: Prentice-Hall, 1973.

Eyal, Jonathan. "Romania: A Revolution Hijacked or Redefined?" *World Today* 56 (March 1990): 39–40.

Falcoff, Mark. *Modern Chile, 1970–1989: A Critical History*. New Brunswick, N.J.: Transaction Pubs., 1989.

Farhi, Farideh. "State Disintegration and Urban-Based Revolutionary Crisis." *Comparative Political Studies* 21, no. 1 (April 1988): 231–56.

Fauriol, Georges A., and Loser, Eva. *Guatemala's Political Puzzle*. New Brunswick, N.J.: Transaction Books, 1988.

Feith, Herbert. *The Decline of Constitutional Democracy in Indonesia*. Ithaca, N.Y.: Cornell University Press, 1962.

Fischer, Mary Ellen. *Nicholae Ceausescu: A Study of Political Leadership*. Boulder, Colo.: Lynne Rienner Publishers, 1989.

Fisher, Glen. *Mindsets*. Yarmouth, Maine: Intercultural Press, 1988.

Forsythe, David P. *The Internationalization of Human Rights*. Lexington, Mass.: Lexington Books for D.C. Heath, 1991.

————. *The Politics of International Law: U.S. Foreign Policy Reconsidered.* Boulder, Colo.: Lynne Rienner, 1990.

Franck, Thomas M. *Judging the World Court.* New York: Priority Press, 1986.

Friedman, Thomas L. *From Beirut to Jerusalem.* New York: Anchor Books, 1989.

Funderburk, David B. *Pinstripes and Reds: An American Ambassador Caught between the State Departmant and the Romanian Communists.* Raleigh, N.C.: Edwards and Broughton Co., 1988.

Gafton, Paul. "Romania Renounces MFN Trade Status with the USA." *Radio Free Europe Research,* Romanian SR/4 (March 1988): 3–5.

Galiullin, Rustem. *The CIA in Asia: Covert Operations against India and Afghanistan.* Moscow: Progress Publishers, 1988.

Galtung, Johan. "Nonterritorial Actors and the Problem of Peace." In Saul Mendlovitz, ed., *The Creation of a Just World Order.* New York: Free Press, 1975.

Galy, Michel. "La guerre civile, loin de Monrovia." *Le Monde Diplomatique,* July 1990, 3.

Gasiorowski, Mark J. "The 1953 Coup d'etat in Iran." *International Journal of Middle East Studies* 19, no. 3 (August 1987): 261–86.

Gati, Charles. "East-Central Europe: The Morning After." *Foreign Affairs* 69, no. 5 (Winter 1990/91): 129–45.

Gershoni, Yekutiel. *Black Colonialism: The Americo-Liberian Scramble for the Hinterland.* Boulder, Colo.: Westview Press, 1985.

Ghoshal, Baladas. *Indonesian Politics, 1955–59: The Emergence of Guided Democracy.* Calcutta: K. P. Bagchi and Co., 1982.

Gilberg, Trond. *Nationalism and Communism in Romania: The Rise and Fall of Ceausescu's Personal Dictatorship.* Boulder, Colo.: Westview Press, 1990.

Gilbert, Dennis. *Sandinistas: The Party and the Revolution.* New York: Basil Blackwell, 1988.

Gill, Frederico G. *The Political System of Chile.* Boston: Houghton Mifflin Co., 1966.

Gilpin, Robert. *War and Change in World Politics.* Cambridge: Cambridge University Press, 1981.

Gleditsch, Nils Petter. "Democracy and Peace." *Journal of Peace Research* 29, no. 4 (November 1992): 369–76.

Gleijeses, Piero. *Shattered Hope: The Guatemalan Revolution and the United States, 1944–1954.* Princeton, N.J.: Princeton University Press, 1991.

Goldstone, Jack A., ed. *Revolutions: Theoretical, Comparative, and Historical Studies.* New York: Harcourt, Brace, Jovanovich, 1986.

Goldstone, Jack, et al., eds. *Revolutions of the Late Twentieth Century.* Boulder, Colo.: Westview Press, 1991.

Greene, Thomas H. *Comparative Revolutionary Movements: Search for Theory and Justice*. Englewood Cliffs, N.J.: Prentice-Hall, 1990.

Greenhouse, Steven. "Soviets, at Rights Parley, Assail Rumanian Fence." *New York Times*, June 24, 1989, A17.

Gross, Lawrence M. "The Legal Implications of Israel's 1982 Invasion into Lebanon." *California Western International Law Journal* 13 (Summer 1983): 548–92.

Gurr, Ted Robert. "War, Revolution, and the Growth of the Coercive State." *Comparative Political Studies* 21, no. 1 (April 1988): 45–65.

———. *Why Men Rebel*. Princeton, N.J.: Princeton University Press, 1970.

Haas, Ernst. *When Knowledge Is Power: Three Models of Change in International Organizations*. Berkeley: University of California Press, 1990.

Harrington, Joseph F., and Courtney, Bruce J. *Tweaking the Nose of the Russians: Fifty Years of American-Romanian Relations*. Boulder, Colo.: East European Monographs, 1991.

Harsch, Ernest. "Amos Sawyer: Fighting for Rights." *Africa Report* 32 (July/August 1989): 27–30.

Hawes, Gary. "Theories of Peasant Revolution: A Critique and Contribution from the Philippines." *World Politics* 42, no. 2 (January 1990): 261–98.

Henkin, Louis, et al. *International Law: Cases and Materials*. St. Paul, Minn.: West, 1980.

Hennayake, Shantha K. "The Peace Accord and the Tamils in Sri Lanka." *Asian Survey* 24, no. 4 (April 1989): 401–15.

Hlophe, Stephen S. *Class, Ethnicity and Politics in Liberia*. Washington, D.C.: University Press of America, 1979.

Holloway, Joseph E. *Liberian Democracy in Africa: A Study of Inter-African Relations*. Lanham, Md.: University Press of America, 1981.

"Honesty Watch." *Economist* 305 (November 28, 1987): 46.

Howe, Marvine. "Rumania Determined to Avoid Poland's Plight." *New York Times*, November 1, 1981, A21.

Hunt, Michael H. *Ideology and U.S. Foreign Policy*. New Haven, Conn.: Yale University Press, 1987.

Huntington, Samuel P. *Political Order in Changing Societies*. New Haven, Conn.: Yale University Press, 1968.

Immerman, Richard H. "Guatemala as Cold War History." *Political Science Quarterly* 95, no. 4 (Winter 1980–81): 629–54.

International Committee of the Red Cross. *Protocols Additional to the Geneva Conventions of 12 August 1949*. Geneva: ICRC, 1977.

Ionescu, Dan. "An A to Z of Personality in Romania." *Radio Free Europe Research*, Romanian SR/11 (February 1989): 9–17.

———. "Romania's Diminishing International Standing." *Radio Free Europe Research*, Romanian SR/3 (March 1989): 31–36.

Jones, Howard Palfrey. *Indonesia: The Possible Dream*. New York: Harcourt, Brace, Jovanovich, 1971.

Jones, Walter S. *The Logic of International Relations*. 6th rev. ed. Glenview, Ill.: Scott, Foresman, 1988.

Jowett, Benjamin. *Thucydides, Book V*. London: Oxford University Press, 1900.

Kamm, Henry. "Gorbachev Speaks to Rumanians on 'Openness' to a Cool Response." *New York Times*, May 27, 1987, A1.

———. "In Rumania, Gorbachev Is Gone and So Is Food." *New York Times*, May 31, 1987, A5.

Kapfered, Bruce. *Legends of People, Myths of State*. Washington, D.C.: Smithsonian Institution Press, 1988.

Kaplan, Neil J. "The Attack on Osirak: Delimitation of Self-Defense under International Law." *New York Law School Journal of International and Comparative Law* 4 (1982): 131–56.

Keohane, Robert O., ed. *Neorealism and Its Critics*. New York: Columbia University Press, 1986.

Kifner, John. "In Rumania, All Hail the Chief and Dracula, Too." *New York Times*, December 24, 1983, A2.

Kirkpatrick, Jeane J., and Allan Gerson. "The Reagan Doctrine, Human Rights, and International Law." In Louis Henkin et al., *Right v. Might: International Law and the Use of Force*. New York: Council on Foreign Relations, 1991.

Kissinger, Henry A. *Years of Upheaval*. Boston: Little, Brown and Co., 1982.

Kromarek, Pascale, ed. *Environnement et droits de l'homme*. Paris: UNESCO, 1988.

Lacy, William. "Liberia: The Road to Recovery." *Current Policy*, no. 343 (October 28, 1981).

Lawyers Committee for Human Rights. *Liberia: A Promise Betrayed*. Washington, D.C.: Lawyers Committee, 1986.

———. *The Reagan Administration's Record on Human Rights*. Washington, D.C.: Lawyers Committee, 1987.

Leary, Virginia. *Ethnic Conflict and Violence in Sri Lanka*. Geneva: International Commission of Jurists, 1981.

Levy, Jack. "Historical Trends in Great Power War, 1495–1975." *International Studies Quarterly* 26 (June 1982): 278–300.

Lichback, Mark Irving. "An Evaluation of 'Does Economic Equality Breed Political Conflict' Studies." *World Politics* 41, no. 4 (July 1989): 431–70.

Liebenow, Gus. "The Libyan Coup in Perspective." *Current History* 80, no. 464 (March 1981): 101–5.

Londregan, John B., and Poole, Keith T. "Poverty, the Coup Trap, and the Seizure of Executive Power." *World Politics* 42 (January 1990): 151–83.

Lowenkopf, Martin. *Politics in Liberia: The Conservative Road to Development.* Palo Alto, Calif.: Hoover Institution Press, 1976.

McGehee, Ralph. *Deadly Deceits: My Twenty-five Years in the CIA.* New York: Sheridan Square Pubs., 1983.

Manor, James, ed. *Sri Lanka in Change and Crisis.* London: Croom Helm, 1984.

Maoz, Zeev, and Russett, Bruce. "Normative and Structural Modes of the Democratic Peace." Paper presented at the annual meeting of the American Political Science Association, Chicago, September 3–6, 1992.

Marx, Karl, and Engles, Friedrich. *Manifesto of the Communist Party.* New York: International Publishers, 1932.

Mason, T. David. "Indigenous Factors." In Barry M. Schutz and Robert O. Slater, eds., *Revolution and Political Change in the Third World.* Boulder, Colo.: Lynne Rienner, 1990.

Mayers, David. *George Kennan and the Dilemmas of U.S. Foreign Policy.* New York: Oxford University Press, 1988.

Miller, Susan M., ed. *Max Weber: Selections from His Work.* New York: Thomas Y. Crowell, 1963.

Modelski, George. "Is World Politics Evolutionary Learning?" *International Organization* 44, no. 1 (Winter 1990): 1–25.

Moore, Mick. "Economic Liberalism versus Political Pluralism in Sri Lanka?" *Modern Asian Studies* 24, no. 2 (1990): 341–83.

Morris, Roger. *Uncertain Greatness: Henry Kissinger and American Foreign Policy.* New York: Harper and Row, 1977.

Mueller, John. *Retreat from Doomsday.* New York: Basic Books, 1989.

Neier, Aryeh. "Flimflam on Central America." *New York Times,* December 14, 1985, 15.

Nelson, Daniel, ed. *Romania in the 1980's.* Boulder, Colo.: Westview Press, 1981.

"Nicaragua v. The United States." *International Legal Materials* 25 (1986): 1023.

Nirumand, Bahman. *Iran: The New Imperialism in Action.* New York: Monthly Review Press, 1969.

Noble, Kenneth B. "Doe Leads the Good Life as Liberia Grows Poorer and Its People, Fractious." *New York Times,* March 26, 1990, A4.

Nydell, Matt S. "Note: Tensions between International Law and Strategic Security." *Virginia Journal of International Law* 24 (Winter 1984): 459–92.

Oakes, John B. "Ceausescu on Rumania, the West and East." *New York Times,* August 4, 1982, A23.

O'Brien, William V. *Law and Morality in Israel's War with the* PLO. New York: Routledge, 1991.

Okolo, Julius Emeka. "Liberia: the Military Coup." *The World Today* 37 (April 1981): 149–57.

Ponnambalam, Satchi. *Sri Lanka: The National Question and the Tamil Liberation Struggle.* London: Zed Books, 1983.

Posner, Michael H. "Shultz's Liberia—and President Doe's." *New York Times,* January 25, 1987, A25.

Powers, Thomas. *The Man Who Kept the Secrets: Richard Helms and the* CIA. New York: Washington Square Press, Pocket Books, 1979.

Prados, John. *Presidents' Secret Wars:* CIA *and Pentagon Covert Operations since World War II.* New York: William Morrow and Co., 1986.

Pye, Lucian W. *Aspects of Political Development.* Boston: Little, Brown, 1966.

Ram, Mohan. *Sri Lanka: The Fractured Island.* London: Penguin, 1989.

Ranelagh, John. *The Agency: The Rise and Decline of the* CIA. London: Weidenfeld and Nicolson, 1986.

Ratesh, Nestor. *Romania: The Entangled Revolution.* New York: Praeger, 1991.

Reinhard, Jon. *Foreign Policy and National Integration: The Case of Indonesia.* New Haven, Conn.: Yale University Press, 1971.

Reisman, W. Michael. "Sovereignty and Human Rights in Contemporary International Law." *American Journal of International Law* 84, no. 4 (October 1990): 866–77.

Riding, Alan. "In Rumania, the Old Order Won't Budge." *New York Times,* November 25, 1989, A7.

Rodney, Carlisle. "The American Century Implanted: Stettinius and the Liberian Flag of Convenience." *Business History Review* 54 (Summer 1980): 175–91.

Rogers, Momo K. "The Liberian Press: An Analysis." *Journalism Quarterly* 63 (Summer 1986): 275–81.

Rogowski, Ronald. *Rational Legitimacy.* Princeton, N.J.: Princeton University Press, 1974.

"Romanian Expectations Concerning Domestic Developments." *Radio Free Europe/Radio Liberty,* East European Area Audience and Opinion Research, December 1984, 1–10.

Ronnas, Per. "Turning the Romanian Peasant into a New Socialist Man: An Assessment of Rural Development Policy in Romania." *Soviet Studies* 41 (October 1989): 443–558.

Roosevelt, Kermit. *Countercoup: The Struggle for the Control of Iran.* New York: McGraw-Hill, 1979.

Ross, Russell R., and Savada, Andrea Matles, eds. *Sri Lanka: A Country Study.* Washington, D.C.: GPO, 1990.

Rule, James B. *Theories of Civil Violence*. Berkeley: University of California Press, 1988.

"Safeguarding Human Rights." *Current Policy*, no. 775 (December 10, 1985).

Schlesinger, Stephen, and Kinzer, Stephen. *Bitter Fruit: The Untold Story of the American Coup in Guatemala*. New York: Doubleday, 1982.

Schutz, Barry M., and Slater, Robert O., eds. *Revolution and Political Change in the Third World*. Boulder, Colo.: Lynne Rienner, 1990.

Sesay, Amadu. "The OAU and Regime Recognition: Politics of Discord and Collaboration in Africa." *Scandinavian Journal of Development Alternatives* 4 (March 1985): 25–41.

Shafir, Michael. "Former Senior RCP Officials Protest Ceausescu's Policies." *Radio Free Europe Research*, Romanian SR/3 (March 29, 1989): 3–13.

———. "The Mazilu Riddle: Romanian Official Fails to Appear before UN Body." *Radio Free Europe Research*, Romanian SR/10 (August 1988): 23–26.

———. "New Revelations of the Military's Role in Ceausescu's Ouster." *Report on Eastern Europe* 1, no. 19 (May 11, 1990): 26.

———. "Political Culture, Intellectual Dissent, and Intellectual Consent: The Case of Romania." *Orbis* 27 (Summer 1983): 403–20.

———. *Romanian Politics, Economics, and Society: Political Stagnation and Simulated Change*. London: Frances Pinter, 1985.

———. "The UN Publishes Mazilu's Report on Human Rights and Young People." *Radio Free Europe Research*, Romanian SR/7 (September 1989): 15–21.

Shipler, David K. "Shultz Is under Fire for Asserting Liberia Has Made Gains on Rights." *New York Times*, January 16, 1987, A1.

Shugart, Matthew Soberg. "Patterns of Revolution." *Theory and Society* 18, no. 1 (January 1989): 249–71.

Siegart, Paul. *Sri Lanka: A Mounting Tragedy of Errors*. Geneva: International Commission of Jurists, 1984.

Simon, Jeffrey D. *Revolutions without Guerrillas*. Santa Monica, Calif.: Rand, 1989.

Simon, Roger. *Gramsci's Political Thought*. London: Lawrence and Wishart, 1982.

Singer, J. David, ed. *The Correlates of War: Vols. I and II*. New York: Free Press, 1979, 1980.

Singer, J. David, and Small, Melvin. *Resort to Arms: International and Civil Wars, 1850–1980*. Beverly Hills, Calif.: Sage, 1982.

Singer, Marshall R. "New Realities in Sri Lanka Politics." *Asian Studies* 30, no. 4 (April 1990): 409–25.

———. "Sri Lanka in 1990: The Ethnic Strife Continues." *Asian Survey* 31, no. 2 (February 1991): 140–46.

Sisay, Hassan B. *Big Powers and Small Nations: A Case Study of United States–Liberian Relations.* Lanham, Md.: University Press of America, 1985.

Skocpol, Theda. *States and Social Revolutions.* Cambridge: Cambridge University Press, 1979.

Small, Melvin. *Was War Necessary: National Security and U.S. Entry into War, 1812–1950.* Beverly Hills, Calif.: Sage, 1980.

Small, Melvin, and Singer, J. David, eds. *International War: An Anthology and Study Guide.* Homewood, Ill.: Dorsey Press, 1985.

Smith, Lewis. "Liberia: Muzzling the Media." *Africa Report* 32 (March/April 1987): 11.

Socor, Vladimir. "Romania Rejects Final Document Adopted by CSCE." *Radio Free Europe Research,* Romanian SR/1 (February 1989): 20.

———. "Social Protests Continue." *Radio Free Europe Research,* Romanian SR/1 (January 1988): 21–23.

Southwood, Julie, and Flanagan, Patrick. *Indonesia: Law, Propaganda, and Terror.* London: Zed Press, 1983.

Spinrad, William. "Charisma: A Blighted Concept and an Alternative Formula." *Political Science Quarterly* 106, no. 2 (Summer 1991): 295–312.

Stefanescu, Crisula. "Human Rights Activist Doina Cornea Complains about the Position of the Romanian Intellectual." *Radio Free Europe Research,* Romanian SR/8 (November 1989): 13–15.

Stoessinger, John G. *Nations in Darkness: China, Russia, and America.* 5th rev. ed. New York: McGraw-Hill, 1990.

Tambiah, S. J. *Sri Lanka: Ethnic Fratricide and the Dismantling of Democracy.* Chicago: University of Chicago Press, 1986.

Thomasson, Gordon C. "Liberian Disaster: Made in the U.S.A." *New York Times,* July 14, 1990, A15.

Thompson, Michael, et al. *Cultural Theory.* Boulder, Colo.: Westview Press, 1990.

Tilly, Charles. *From Mobilization to Revolution.* Reading, Mass.: Addison-Wesley, 1978.

Tismaneanu, Vladimir. "Personal Power and Political Crisis in Romania." *Government and Opposition* 24, no. 2 (Spring 1989): 184–95.

Tomasevski, Katrina. "The Right to Peace." *Current Research on Peace and Violence* 5, no. 1 (1982): 42–69.

United Nations. *The Realization of the Right to Development.* New York: United Nations, 1991.

United Nations, Security Council. *Resolution 487.* June 19, 1981.

———. *Resolution 501.* February 25, 1982.

United States Institute of Peace. *Journal* 3 (June 1990): 4.

U.S. Congress. House. Committee on Foreign Affairs. *Foreign Assistance Legislation for Fiscal Years 1990–91: Hearings and Markup before the Subcommittee on Africa,* 101st Cong., 1st sess., March 8, 9, April 25, 1989, 207–12, 244–50.

———. *The Human Rights Implications of the Sinhalese-Tamil Conflict in Sri Lanka: Hearings before the Subcommittees on Human Rights and International Organizations and on Asian and Pacific Affairs,* 98th Cong., 2d sess., August 2, 1984, 6–24.

———. *The Indo–Sri Lankan Agreement: Hearings before the Subcommittee on Asian and Pacific Affairs,* 100th Cong., 1st sess., August 6, 1987.

———. *Liberia: Recent Developments and United States Foreign Policy: Hearings and Markup before the Subcommittees on Africa and on Human Rights,* 99th Cong., 2d sess., January 23, 28, 29, 1986.

U.S. Congress. Senate. Committee on Foreign Relations. *Emergency Situations in Sudan and Liberia: Hearings before the Subcommittee on African Affairs,* 101st Cong., 2d sess., November 27, 1990, 78–79.

———. *Liberia and Ghana—Policy Changes in West Africa,* 97th Cong., 2d sess., June 1982.

———. *Liberia and United States Policy: Hearings before the Subcommittee on African Affairs,* 99th Cong. 1st sess., December 10, 1985.

U.S. Department of State. *Country Reports on Human Rights Practices.* Washington, D.C. GPO, annual.

———. *Terrorist Bombings.* Washington, D.C.: GPO, 1983.

Valenzuela, Arturo. *The Breakdown of Democratic Regimes: Chile.* Baltimore: Johns Hopkins University Press, 1982.

Van Dyke, Vernon. *Human Rights, the United States, and International Community.* New York: Oxford University Press, 1970.

Van Evera, Steven. "The Case against Intervention." *Atlantic Monthly,* July 1990, 72.

Walker, Thomas W. "Nicaraguan-U.S. Friction: The First Four Years, 1979–1983." In Kenneth M. Coleman and George C. Herring, eds., *The Central American Crisis: Sources of Conflict and the Failure of U.S. Policy.* Wilmington, Del.: Scholarly Resources, 1985.

Waltz, Kenneth N. *Man, the State, and War: A Theoretical Analysis.* New York: Columbia University Press, 1959.

Wijesinha, Rajiva. *Current Crisis in Sri Lanka.* New Delhi: Navrang, 1986.

Wilson, A. J. *The Breakup of Sri Lanka: The Sinhalese-Tamil Conflict.* London: C. Hurst and Co., 1988.

Winchester, N. Brian. "United States Policy toward Africa." *Current History* 87, no. 529 (May 1988): 194.

Wiseman, John A. *Democracy in Black Africa.* New York: Paragon, 1990.

World Bank. *World Development Report.* New York: Oxford University Press, 1990.

Zacher, Mark W., and Mathew, Richard A., "Liberal International Theory: Common Threads, Divergent Strands." Paper presented to the annual meeting of the American Political Science Association, Chicago, September 3–6, 1992.

Zariski, Raphael. "Ethnic Extremism among Ethnoterritorial Minorities in Western Europe." *Comparative Politics* 21 (April 1989): 253–72.

Index